D1528885

Caught in the Mix

CAUGHT IN THE MIX

An Oral Portrait of Homelessness

PHILIP MICHAEL BULMAN

AUBURN HOUSE
Westport, Connecticut • London

Library of Congress Cataloging-in-Publication Data

Bulman, Philip Michael.
    Caught in the mix : an oral portrait of homelessness / Philip
Michael Bulman.
       p.   cm.
    Includes index.
    ISBN 0–86569–229–7 (alk. paper)
    1. Homeless persons—United States—Interviews. 2. Homelessness—
United States. I. Title.
HV4505.B85   1993
305.5′69—dc20   92–43385

British Library Cataloguing in Publication Data is available.

Library of Congress Catalog Card Number: 92–43385
ISBN: 0–86569–229–7

First published in 1993

Auburn House, 88 Post Road West, Westport, CT 06881
An imprint of Greenwood Publishing Group, Inc.

Printed in the United States of America

The paper used in this book complies with the
Permanent Paper Standard issued by the National
Information Standards Organization (Z39.48–1984).

10 9 8 7 6 5 4 3 2 1

To my wife, Jodi Schneider

Contents

Acknowledgments

First, I would like to thank all of the homeless people who granted me interviews, including some whose accounts, through no fault of their own, do not appear in this book.

I am grateful to many people who provided background information and helped me to arrange interviews. In the Central Florida area, I received assistance from Jean Sisler, Marvin Jones and Tom King of the Coalition for the Homeless of Orlando; Dr. Patrick J. Powers, Rev. James. T. Blount, Beverly Spangler and Rev. Vincent Holmes of the Christian Service Center for Central Florida; Don Moody of the Orlando Union Rescue Mission; Mike Robinson of Great Oaks Village; Lew Petzold of the Human Crisis Council; Mother Blanche Bell Weaver of the Rescue Outreach Mission of Sanford; Herb Aguirresaenz of Anthony House; Mavis K. Starke of the Cross Roads Mission; and Emily Peck of the Human Services Council.

In the Tampa Bay area, I received help from Jim Rapp of the Praying Hands Mission, Carol Simmons of the ACTS Homeless Day Center, and Steve R. Wolf of the Virginia H. Lazarra Emergency Shelter.

In North Florida, I received assistance from Danny Heaberlin of the Haven of Rest Rescue Mission, Vera Willinger of the Trinity Rescue Mission, and Rev. Kaleel Ellison of the City Rescue Mission.

In South Florida, I received help from Cammy Gibson of the Salvation Army, Shelly Dreer of Camillus House, Dr. Frank Jacobs of the Miami Rescue Mission, Evelyn Perry of the Miami Women's & Children's Center, Jackie Groendyk of The Lord's Place, and Paula Tibbets of Covenant House.

A number of people provided information about homelessness and how it is related to other social problems. I would especially like to thank Fred Karnas of the National Coalition for the Homeless, Deborah White of the National Coalition Against Domestic Violence, Rita DeYoung of the Florida Coalition Against Domestic Violence and Dr. Linda Saltzman of the National Center for Health Statistics.

To these friends I am grateful for providing hospitality and that most precious of commodities, temporary shelter, during my travels: John and Lynda Barry, Marcia Gelman and Shari Spires.

A special thanks to Howard Hess and Cindy Schreuder. Were it not for them, I would still be attempting to print out pages of my manuscript on my ancient daisy wheel printer.

Finally, I would like to thank my wife, Jodi Schneider, for her support, encouragement and suggestions.

Introduction

At least 600,000 Americans are homeless on any given night. They sleep in shelters, cars, abandoned buildings, tents, parks, under bridges, in doorways, cardboard boxes or just out in the open with nothing but a jacket or discarded newspaper to cover them. Some manage to get off the streets quickly, but they are replaced by others who have lost their housing; between 1.3 million and 2 million people experience homelessness in the course of a year. A still larger number of people, perhaps as many as 3 million, live on the edge of homelessness. This group includes many who were once homeless and now live in substandard housing as well as others who live in precarious economic circumstances; many of them live "doubled up" with friends or relatives.

Homelessness is a direct result of poverty. Tens of millions of Americans live below the poverty line, and members of this group are more likely than others to lose their housing. Additionally, many middle-class people become homeless after one or more family members loses a job.

The economic recessions of the 1980s and 1990s have pushed millions of people into the streets. At the same time, the "safety net" that once helped people who were faced with a financial crisis has been torn by relentless cuts in housing and social welfare programs. Additionally, many government programs designed to help low-income people have failed to keep pace with inflation. These programs are no longer sufficient to deter hunger or homelessness. For example, a record 23.6 million Americans received food stamps in August of 1991, yet many food stamp recipients report that it is impossible to feed their families for an entire month on food stamps alone; they turn to soup kitchens and food pantries run by charitable organizations in order to avoid hunger. At times, some homeless people simply steal food.

Housing programs also suffered grievously during the 1980s; federal housing programs were slashed by as much as 80 percent. As a result, the housing crisis worsened just as an unstable economy and cuts in social welfare programs contributed to a growing homeless population. Many homeless people hold full-time jobs, but minimum wage workers and other low-income people often find it difficult to find housing that they can afford.

In some cases people become homeless as a result of medical problems. Those with no health insurance may be forced to spend everything they have on medical expenses if illness strikes. Addicts often face long waiting lists if they try to enroll in publicly funded recovery programs. Mentally ill people, many of whom have no health insurance, may find it impossible to obtain treatment. While the deinstitutionalization of mentally ill people once helped to fuel a growing homeless population, many of the mentally ill people on the streets today have never been in institutions.

The disintegration of traditional family structures is also an important factor in the rise of homelessness. Battered women often become homeless when they decide to flee from their attackers. Some teenagers lose their housing when they run away from home or are forced out of their homes by parents who do not want them.

Homelessness remains a largely hidden problem in most cities. The network of emergency shelters and day centers that has sprung up in response to the housing crisis allows many homeless people to spend the night in shelters where they have access to showers, laundry facilities and clean clothing donated by charitable organizations. Consequently, many homeless people are well groomed; they do not *look* like street people. For every disheveled man who is panhandling on the street or every noticeably deranged "bag lady" who openly digs through garbage cans, there may be dozens of other people who appear perfectly fine but are actually homeless. As a result, people in many cities are unaware of the enormity of the problem.

In addition to a grueling day-to-day fight for sheer survival, the homeless face enormous challenges in their struggle to obtain permanent housing. Unemployed homeless people who have children find it difficult to obtain the day care that would make it possible for them to apply for jobs. Employers often discriminate against the homeless, refusing to hire them. Employed homeless people who work during the day cannot visit the social service agencies that could provide crucial assistance, and employed and jobless individuals alike often encounter skepticism or even open hostility when they do visit government social service agencies. And open hostility is common on the streets as well; the homeless report that some people scream at them and hurl rocks, eggs, insults and an occasional bullet their way. Police sometimes help homeless people find shelter, but in some cities the police have been instructed to arrest the homeless on charges such as vagrancy; it is now illegal to be desperately poor in some localities. In cities from New York to Miami the police have conducted sweeps of parks and other areas where large numbers of homeless people live, arresting those who refuse to move and confiscating their meager possessions. Ironically, some homeless people regard these arrests as a blessing. An arrest can result in at least one night with a place to sleep and at least one hot meal.

One suspects that the experiences of homeless people throughout America are similar in most respects. Perhaps the most haunting of these experiences is a sense of exclusion from the social and economic mainstream so profound that the homeless sometimes feel prompted to remind a journalist that, "We're human," as if the press, or perhaps all of American society, had somehow forgotten that.

The phenomenal growth in the number of homeless people in America during the past 15 years was once viewed as a social and economic disaster as well as a national embarrassment. In recent years, however, some people have come to regard it as normal. Concern has given way to indifference and "compassion fatigue" as the efforts of homeless coalitions, religious and other charitable organizations and concerned individuals have failed to solve the problem. Government agencies, by and large, have done little to help. Candidates for public office rarely mention homelessness, and almost never offer comprehensive plans to help homeless individuals and families escape poverty. Indeed, some politicians portray concern for the poor as an anachronism, a sentimental and unrealistic notion from a distant era.

Many Americans now live in conditions that are comparable to the shantytowns of South Africa, while others, who are a bit more fortunate, live in housing that is similar to what might be found in the impoverished coal mining regions of Russia. But while these countries are finally beginning to come to terms with their failures to provide decent housing and a modicum of social and economic justice for their citizens, the United States has yet to do so.

A NOTE ON STYLE AND THE USE OF FICTITIOUS NAMES

All of the interviews in this book were conducted in Florida in 1991, and the ages given for each person are for the day the interview took place.

A number of people requested anonymity; they offered a variety of reasons for their requests. Some were simply embarrassed about becoming homeless, while others were trying to keep their whereabouts a secret. In a few instances names were changed to protect the identities of sexual assault victims. In cases where the names of adults were changed, the names of their children were also changed. Ages and other identifying information may have been altered as well. Additionally, one homeless shelter director asked that the shelter itself remain nameless. Fictitious names are identified by an asterisk (*).

Explanatory information that was not spoken aloud appears in parentheses ( ). Other information that may be of interest to the reader, such as a burst of laughter or the use of significant gestures, appears in brackets [ ]. Most of the interviews have been edited for the sake of brevity.

Many homeless people become familiar with government agencies and programs, and quickly adopt the acronyms favored by social service agencies. The following is a list of commonly used acronyms.

AA - Alcoholics Anonymous

AFDC - Aid to Families with Dependent Children is a program that is designed to prevent families that include minors from becoming utterly impoverished. The program is commonly known as welfare.

HRS - The Florida Department of Health and Rehabilitative Services is a state agency that administers a variety of social welfare and health programs.

HUD - The U.S. Department of Housing and Urban Development

NA - Narcotics Anonymous

Section Eight - a federally subsidized housing program that pays a portion of the monthly rent for qualified low-income people

Chapter One

Flight: Women

Women who have left their husbands or male partners make up a significant proportion of the homeless population. In some cases their departure is merely the result of a soured relationship, but often these women are the victims of domestic violence. Battering is the leading cause of injury for which women seek medical attention in the United States, more common than automobile accidents, muggings and rapes combined. Domestic violence hot lines receive some 2 million telephone calls annually, and more than 175,000 women flee to the safety of battered women's shelters each year. In 1990 just over 1,300 women were murdered by their husbands or male partners.

Some battered women live with men who discourage them from pursuing their educations or otherwise gaining marketable skills. As a result, they are particularly ill prepared to make a living and support their children. More than 1,200 programs and shelters for battered women are operating nationally, but these shelters are often filled to capacity. In some urban areas they turn away seven out of every eight women who ask for help simply because they do not have room for them. Many of those who are turned away eventually go to homeless shelters. One federal survey of homeless shelters found that 21 percent of shelter residents were domestic violence victims.

In Florida alone, more than 9,000 women take refuge in shelters set aside specifically for battered women and their children each year. Thousands more are turned away because there is no space for them. Domestic violence hot lines in Florida received more than 80,000 telephone calls during a recent year.

Elizabeth Jones*, 27, is a native of Georgia. She was interviewed at the family shelter run by the Coalition for the Homeless of Orlando, where she was staying with her children: Richard, 7; Jodi, 5; and Carol, 1.

How long have you been here?
A little over a month.
Have you been in Orlando very long?
No, I've been here about a month-and-a-half.
What brought you down to Florida?
I left my husband. Actually, it was a very abusive situation. My mother lives here in Florida and she takes care of children for a living, and so she's pretty familiar with the legal systems and things concerning children. She said that Florida had excellent rules concerning children and their care, and that I wouldn't have to be afraid of anything if I was here, so I came here.
The laws are better here than in Georgia?
Yes, it's very backward there. It's very backward there.
Were you staying with your mother when you first came here?
I stayed a week with my mother, but she just has a small apartment, and she's not allowed to have more than three people live there, so her landlord gave her an eviction notice to put us out.
Where did you go after you left your mother's house?
I came here.
How has it been?
It's hard. First of all, I'm dealing with a lot of emotional problems with myself and my children because of what we've all been through, and then everybody here has come from broken homes of some sort, so it's hard getting along sometimes, and it's hard dealing with the stress of not knowing what tomorrow holds for your family. And then the hours that we have to keep here - the children are always exhausted, and they're ornery and tired; it's hard for them.
Are your children in school?
Yes, they missed the week that we were at my mother's, because I didn't know where we were gonna go or what we were gonna do, so I didn't enroll them in school until we got here. And they did make it very easy to put the children in school. All I had to do was fill out the papers, and they started that day.
What was your living situation before you came to Florida?
My husband was in the military. He just got out last June; he didn't work since. He's always been an alcoholic, and I've always put up with abuse

from him. It just so happens that this past year I have noticed the children's behavior starting to mock his, and after some pretty scary situations with my husband, I realized it was my life; I had to get out, and so I left. But materialistically, we had everything that a person could ask for, you know, a four-bedroom house in the country and new furniture, new clothes, new cars, everything.

But emotionally, I was ready to kill myself or kill him the day I left. I decided to leave instead, thank God.

Are you looking for a place to live and for a job?

Yeah, I mean my car blew up on the way down here, so I don't have transportation or anything now.

How did that happen?

I had a leak in my coolant, and I knew I had a leak, and I was stopping every hundred miles or so and filling it back up, and I got to Ocala, and my mind just went blank of what I had to do to take care of the car. I knew it was two, two-and-a-half hours to Orlando, and I was hurryin', and all of a sudden, boom, there went the engine. My step-father drove up and picked me up, and I just junked the car. I mean, the day I left, I didn't care about anything except just me and my children's lives, and that was it. So, since I've been here, I've put in applications. I'm thinking right now about going to college. That's something I've always wanted to do; my husband's never allowed me to do. I want to do that. And I've applied for HRS help, food stamps and AFDC until I can get on my feet, because I've never been on my own, and now I'm on my own with three children to support, so I had to swallow my pride. My mother talked me into going for it. She said all those years you paid taxes, now you can at least take some of it back. She helped me get all that taken care of, and now I'm waiting on an apartment from HUD, or I'm going tomorrow to check out this apartment complex in Pine Hills that lets you pay according to your income. So, it's a nice area and brand new apartments. They screen everybody that comes in, so it should be a nice place, it should be clean, and I'm going to see - if I can do that I'm going to get out of here as soon as I can.

Have you been able to get food stamps and AFDC?

Yes. I got the food stamps; the AFDC and Medicaid takes 45 days, and the 45 days is right about up this week, so I should be getting my first check and my Medicaid card this week sometime.

Have you been looking for work, too?

I've looked. I just have a high school diploma; there's really nothing more I can do than just waitressing or cashier or something like that, and I've got three kids that are gonna have to be taken to the day care center or a baby sitter, and I realize that working for four dollars and something an hour would be useless to me right now because I'd have to pay it all to the baby sitter. So I want to pursue my education. I want to go to college and get qualified in something more important that I can support my children on, and the government will help me do that too. They have Project Independence. It's just government help. They help buy you bus tickets and things to get you back and forth to school if you want to go to school. The way my mom put it is: the government doesn't want you on welfare any more than you want to be on it, so they'll provide whatever they can in order to better your lifestyle, so that you can get off of it as soon as possible. And I'm going to take advantage of everything they offer so I can get off of it as soon as possible. [laughs]

What do you do during the day?

Well, today I went to the lake with my baby, and I had some paperwork I had to turn in at the housing office, so I walked there; I walk everywhere I go because I don't have any money to buy bus tickets or anything right now, so I just put her in the stroller and walk everywhere I have to go. Tomorrow I've got to go to Legal Aid, and I'm gonna go see that apartment, and that's in Pine Hills, so it will take me about a hour to walk there, and then see what they have to say about the apartment, and then another hour to walk back, so that consumes most of my day. [laughs]

Is there a day care center here where you can leave your baby?

No. They have what they call extended day program for the school-age children, and what they do is send a teacher in from six until eight in the morning - because we have to be out of the shelter at six in the morning - and the extended day teacher keeps the school-age children from six to eight, when the regular teacher comes in. And the regular teacher leaves at three, and she comes back from three to five. So that allows the school here to keep your children from six in the morning till five in the afternoon, but any child under school-age cannot stay. There's no day care center here. I think they have a grant with one of the day care centers downtown or something; if you get a job they give you three free weeks of baby sitting or something like that, but when the three weeks is up you gotta pay yourself.

Are you getting enough food?

I have my food stamps, so we eat on that during the day. I just buy what I can at the store to feed us a lunch in the afternoon. This whole week I had to spend it on all my family, 'cause the kids were out of school for spring break, but normally, before that, it was just me and the baby, and the kids in school eat lunch there. At night the churches supply our supper, and they usually have a really good supper. And in the morning, I don't know who brings it, but it's usually just cereal and juice and coffee in the morning, sometimes fruit.

Do the people who are staying here look out for each other, take care of each other?

I don't see it, no. There's a lot of negativism; I try to stay away from it because I'm down enough. I'm trying to keep my spirits up; I don't need to be around people that are complaining all day. But that's mostly what you see here, is people just sittin' around complaining all day. Instead of trying to go out and better their situation, they complain about the situation they're in, and I just try to avoid everybody. I'm friends with one lady and her children.

We became friends real quick because we came from similar environments. Our children are going through a lot of the same problems, and we can talk and keep each other's spirits up. And if I can't get my apartment, that means I have to wait for Section Eight housing to get me one, and that means I have to stay here another month.

How about people who aren't staying at the shelter? Have you found that people are helpful or hostile?

Actually, I've come in contact with both. There are very generous people out there. When we're waiting outside to come in, sometimes - it's happened a couple of times - a car will just drive up and hand money out the window to you. Or like yesterday morning, they drove up and brought us food from Dunkin' Donuts and wanted to know if we would like to have it. So it's the strangers that are helpful. The people you know, sometimes they act like they are ashamed of where you are and what you're going through, and that's what's hard to accept. People who you think you've known for a long time turn on you, and then on the other hand there's strangers that don't even know you, want to help you.

Do you mean family members haven't been helpful?

My mother's been wonderful. But other family here - which I can understand their situation - they have their own problems, and they don't want to have to deal with this too. But I go to my mother's on the weekend. I don't want to go there every day. There's one or two girls here that go to their mother's every day and stay all day, but I don't want to be a burden to her. She's got kids all week that she baby sits. So on Saturday or Sunday, one or the other - I'll ask her what's more convenient for her and she'll let me know - and I'll go spend that day. It gives me a chance to get away and relieve myself of some of the pressures, and come back with a new attitude at the end of the week. [laughs]

What do you do if you need medical care before you get your Medicaid card?

Oh, we're all sick. I finally had to take my two little girls to the doctor the day before yesterday because they were so bad. I took 'em to the health clinic, and they billed it to me. They're gonna charge me $3 for each child per visit, and $2 for each medication they gave us, so that's not bad, and by the time the bill comes I should have my first check; I'll be able to pay it. You just have to wait a long time, but, you know, at least that's somewhere you can get medical attention. I have my approval paper from Medicaid; I could take that to the hospital, and they would just bill it, and then when my Medicaid came through, or my Medicaid card came, I would just have to take my card back to the hospital because Medicaid will pick up any hospital bills three months back, so I could use the hospital right now because I've already got my acceptance letter.

What do you do if you have your three children and you have to be outside during the day because the shelter is closed, and it's raining or cold?

We get rained on, or we search for a place where it's not raining. It's happened several times.

For a week or so there it was freezing, it was in the 30s I think. I just bundle the kids up and wrap a blanket around them and bear it. That's when we all got sick, and we all been sick ever since.

They had fevers, they got over the fever; now they just still have the cold, lingering cold like I have, it just lingers, doesn't want to go away. But they don't get enough sleep to get well because of the times, the time periods. They feed us at eight (p.m.), from eight to 9:30 we have to eat and shower - that's an hour and a half for me to feed my three children, bathe my three children, and feed and bathe myself, and at 9:30 the lights go out and they want everyone immediately silent. Well, the baby's up crying so I've got to walk her, and then these (her other children) don't want to leave my side, so they gotta walk with me.

Do you think living in the shelter is harder on women than on men?

I think it's hardest on children. At least we're grown, we can understand that there will be an end to this situation, and, you know, as an adult I can live on five or six hours of sleep every night, and walkin' miles every day to go where I have to go. I can handle that 'cause I'm an adult, but children *need* 10 or 12 hours of sleep at night, they need their rest, they need their play time, they don't need to constantly be reminded of the seriousness; they're too young. It's hard on 'em emotionally.

Have your religious beliefs had any effect on how you cope with your situation?

Yeah, well, what's had an effect on me is that I've been going to counseling. And my mother has been in counseling for the past year, in

AA, and co-dependency - I don't know if you've heard of that - and Life Works, because her husband is an alcoholic. And I'm in a twelve step program myself; I'm in a co-dependency class myself right now. I was born and raised in a Baptist church. But all my life, you go to church and try to get saved and then you fall back and drop out, and you go and stop and go and stop. I think I've just now, at this point in my life learned what the right way is to become one with God. And it's not through any church or any religion or anyone or any preacher; it's through yourself. I mean He's in here. [points to her heart] And all my life, because of the abuse I've allowed myself to put up with, I've had such a low self-esteem and thought so little of myself; when you don't like yourself there's no way that you can be close to God, and I'm gradually learning that there is happiness, and when you're one with the Lord, you know yourself. You know your feelings and you're able to express them. I still can't do that real well because the whole time I was with my husband, you know, you feel what he says feel; if he says shut up, you do, you don't express it. And it's coming out, and I'm allowing my children to do the same. For about two weeks there they were hell on wheels. Every emotion that has built up in them all their life came out at once, and I could not do a thing with them, but I didn't hit 'em. I held 'em, I let them fight me, I let 'em call me names, I let 'em just do whatever they wanted, and now they're falling back into a happy path. They've gotten it all out, and they have realized that, when I have a feeling, I can say it without being swatted away with a belt. What's going to make it all better is having our own place, where they can feel secure and safe and like something belongs to them; in this place everything that's here has to be shared with 70 other people. It will be good for all of us, even myself, to know this is mine.

How has being homeless affected the children? I know you have an infant...

Oh, she's happy anywhere she is. She's just an angel. Richard and Jodi have had a hard time; they've had ups and downs like me. They have good days and bad days; we're doin' it one day at a time.

Is it difficult to explain, or do you think they understand?

They understand. Richard, my oldest, he does understand; he understands all too well, and he also will tell me, "I would rather be here than where we were." And Jodi, she's still kind of young, she's five. She's been through a lot more of different kinds of abuse than Richard, and I'm still trying to deal with her and her counselors to get her out of her baby stage, because about a year ago she regressed, and from the five-year-old daughter I had to a two-year-old daughter. And she's still not out of that yet, but the counselors are workin' with her, and they're wonderful.

Where do you get counseling for yourself and the children?

The teacher of the school back here is wonderful. She brings in counselors from different places to work individually with the children in the school. I think it's the Orange Playhouse or somethin' where they take care of sexually abused children. She's brought them in I think. And on Thursday afternoons at four, I attend a spouse abuse support group right here at the Coalition, and on Tuesday afternoons from 6:30 to 8:30, my whole family goes to the Presbyterian church down Church Street where they have professional counselors. We divide up into our own age groups: the children have their classes, the infants have their class, the women have their class, and it's abuse counseling for the entire family. And it's done wonders. It's wonderful. I mean they even help the baby; believe it or not, abuse affects one-year-olds, and they've even helped my baby. It's good, I love it, I wouldn't miss it. That's my number one priority right now in life, is to make it to those meetings.

Will you be able to leave the shelter soon and move into an apartment?

It's going to be another month before my name comes up (for Section Eight housing) and I just don't know if we can handle it that long; this is so stressful. But I found out that the same apartment complex will allow low-income families to pay according to their income, and right now my only income is the AFDC. Of course, you know, once I get in there I can get a job close by that I can walk to, and start building up my income and gradually build up my rent until eventually I'm doing it all on my own. But I'm gonna go by there tomorrow and see if I can get an apartment there on my income. It's a subsidized housing program. I'm not sure if the government pays the remainder of the rent for you or what; I'll find out tomorrow. Hopefully, I'll be able to get in on it.

With three children, how much do you get from AFDC?

$250 a month. That's because I'm living here. They took $100 away because I don't have to pay rent, but when I move into my own place and report that I'm paying rent, they will raise it to $350 a month.

Have you found that when you give the shelter as your address, potential employers and landlords react negatively?

Never in my life have I applied for a job that I did not get. I've applied for at least 30 jobs in this city in the past month, and no one has called, and I'm sure it has a lot to do with the fact that I'm living in a shelter, and they have the idea that this will be a fly by night person who comes in and works for two weeks and quits when they get their first check, or something. I'm sure it has a lot to do with it, yeah.

Do other outsiders harass you in any way?

I don't think so. As far as I know they don't know I'm homeless. [laughs]
I just have my baby and my stroller and my purse.
I've heard that some homeless women have been harassed by men.
No, I haven't had that problem.

Pat Parks, 51 ("too old to be in this situation"), is a native of Garner, North Carolina. She was interviewed in Kissimmee at Our Daily Bread, a soup kitchen run by the Christian Service Center for Central Florida.

How long have you been in Florida?
About four-and-a-half years.
What brought you down here?
Out of a divorce situation, and basically speaking it was out of harassment, and I just about *had* to move down here.

And I knew some people down here, and I said, "Well I'll go on down to Kissimmee and, you know, try it." So I'm here, and now, if you say you don't like it, someone will say, "Well why don't you just get out?" You don't like it, and then again, I say, "Well why don't you pay me enough to get out?" That's the thing. But see, what happened, I came down - I'm originally a cosmetologist, that's my trade - but at first I was a little bit burnt out on that, and I said, "Well, I'm just not gonna worry about it." But then I got to thinking about it, I checked, and I didn't have reciprocity in Florida.

I had a couple good jobs, but I had a car accident, so I lost my car. And down here there's no transit system, so you are stuck. So you gotta find somebody, you gotta live two and three together, do anything, and work through a temporary force until you can build yourself back up to where you wanna be, that's just the way it works. And there are a lotta good people that work through the temporary forces too. I know some that aren't, I mean, that don't care, but I'm talkin' about people that have had bad luck, and get in that rut, and they gotta do that for the time being until they can do somethin' else.
Have you been able to get steady work through the labor pool?
Basically they've been picking me up pretty steady. Now most of the labor forces, they wanna use housekeepers, but I have a real bad problem 'cause I'm short, I'm little, and you know, as far as gettin' out on some jobs, but basically now they send me out more like dish washing jobs, or car washing, 'cause they found out that I'm fast and I can do it even though I might have to have help, to reach up and get something. [laughs] That's the truth, it's used against me because I'm so little, so short, to a certain

extent, but the other extent is I'm strong enough to say, "Hey, let me try that."

The thing about it is, it depends on the tourist business and all that in Florida, 'cause like I go out to Disney and work, you know, go out to the Dolphin, Swan, places like that, dish washing, and that dollar car wash right by the airport, which hopefully speaking, we can get out this afternoon to go there, or either to the Dolphin (The Dolphin and The Swan are luxury hotels at Walt Disney World). They told us to be back at three o'clock. So there we sit, and don't know how we're gonna pay our rent tonight, so that's why we're here.

There you go, you're in that rut. [laughs] Do you understand? I mean, I'm telling you the truth, and I wanted to tell just exactly like it is. There are a lot of good people that get stuck in this.

A lot of us try to get food stamps, and yes, people use it for other things, I agree with that. I'll be the first one to agree with that 'cause I've seen it - but not me.

But see my situation too, I'll say it, 'cause I think it ought to be told. I was livin' up in St. Cloud, which is not far from Kissimmee, and this guy, I got, well, anyway, I don't know how it happened, but I got tied up with him and we lived together, and he abused me very bad. And right now I'm goin' to a court situation too. I'm under protection, witness.

So they moved me over here, and I stayed in a women's shelter for four weeks until my face started clearin' up, and then thought, "Well what am I gonna do?" You know, I had to do something, so I went to Allied (a labor pool), and started tryin' to get my stuff together, where I'm goin' from here.

Have you had to live outside at all?

No, I haven't done that. I'm fortunate enough not to have done that. But he beat me so bad I was in the hospital two days, and then I went to the women's shelter straight from there, I didn't go back to him, see, and I stayed there four weeks. Actually, I have had to sleep in cars a couple times, yes. Not under a bridge, but, you know.

And then you lost your car?

Yeah.

So you couldn't do that anymore, right?

Yeah, right, I didn't have no car. If you don't have a car down here, there's no transit system, so you really just don't have much choice, you know. And Allied, if you find a place to live that's in the area - well there are three temporary forces.

But Allied is the best one, and we pretty much know, if you get in there, and they know who you are, that you will get off to work. You may not work for two days, but like the other day I worked 17 hours straight because, you know, I knew I had to when I had the opportunity to do it.

Did you stay at the women's shelter in Orlando?

In Kissimmee, and I prefer not to mention no addresses or nothing like that.

I understand.

It's confidential.

Sure. If you hadn't been able to go there...

I would have been completely homeless. But they do have a shelter in Orlando and in Kissimmee, you know, but it's basically for abused women, and the court system put me in there.

So I had to get out of that, and then this is as far as I've come so far.

When did all that happen?

The first of February. (The interview was conducted in May.)

Have you been able to get food stamps?

Yes. Well, when I was in the shelter, see you're considered homeless if you're in the shelter like that. Right now I'm reapplying, but I have to go through Allied now since I am earning some money, so I don't know if they're gonna give them back to me or not again. But when I was in the shelter I got them, you know, 'cause then you're considered homeless - well, which I was, 'cause I lost my home and everything when all this happened to me. And I was not about to go back. I'm too strong a person. But my main point that I want to make clear, really, is that there are a lot of good people that work out in these places, that have been down a lot of roads, and we all understand each other. There's the bad and there's the good, but there's a bunch of us that we are just trying to get back on our feet. And thank God it's there for the time being, you know, no matter how much sacrifice you have to do - get up 4:30 in the morning [laughs], you don't know if you're going to get out or what, but you just do what you have to do. I use the word survivor. You can call us survivors, the ones that are really trying.

How were you treated when you applied for food stamps?

Well see I had no problem because I was in the shelter, because I was considered homeless. So you just about automatically get them. But see now I'm supposed to reapply and take, you know, the Allied, what I make there, back again. So I don't know what they're gonna do then, see. They gave them to me for three months when I was living there, but now I gotta go back, my application's in now, so I don't know what they're gonna do. But basically speaking, I don't like - it's really depending - but some weeks I don't even make $90 for my own survival. Maybe I'm a stubborn person, but I consider myself a strong person. I've got two grown boys, and I know all I have to do is make a phone call, but I had a boy in Saudi Arabia, and he's been through enough. I don't want to call him and say, "Hey, send me some money." He'll be out in about a month. So what I'm trying to do is work it so I can, you know, let him know that I'm okay. He doesn't even know all this happened to me. All I'm saying, right now, for the time being, it's called survival. [laughs]

Have you always been able to get enough food?

Oh yeah. Like in St. Cloud, when I was livin' over there, there was a center like this, but then the place that we had had a kitchen in it, and you could go get free food, you know, they'd give you food. But see, living in a motel room, you don't have somewhere to cook and things. And you can't afford to eat out. [laughs] It's plain and simple. But there was a place over there which helped me out a couple times.

When you were attacked in February, did you have health insurance?

Right now they're working on - there's a thing called victim's crime compensation, and all the paperwork is in the process, and hopefully speaking, you know, they're gonna help out, pay the hospital bills, even though it hasn't been to court yet. It has taken me four months, and he's not even in arraignment yet, and he's lookin' for me too.

Anyway, they tryin' to get victim's crime compensation it's called; it's a brand new thing, it hasn't been in effect very long. And they goin' hopefully pay the hospital bills, which was close to $3,000, and then maybe give me some money to get started back up again. See all that's in the process now. All my papers and everything are, you know, they're just workin' on it.

So you didn't have any insurance to cover that?

No, no.

What do you do about health care now?

Well, when I was livin' with this guy, see, you know, if he had any money at all, he would help me out. But right now I have no idea what I'd do, 'cause I'm stuck with that hospital bill, and unless that covers it there's nothin' I can do, not a thing I can do. Either lay there and die or hope and pray they take me back or something. [laughs] I know you think I'm crazy, but I just have to laugh; it keeps you from cryin', you know. [laughs]

So you're staying at a motel with some friends?

I'm stayin' with two other people. We're splittin' the rent, $8 a night. And it's not a whole lot of fun, you know, 'cause you don't have no privacy or nothin', but that's the only way, that's called survival, just remember that word, that's a big word in our category. [laughs]

So the lack of privacy bothers you?

Oh yeah, sure it does. 'Cause I'm used to - I love to cook, I love to garden, I love to can.

But since I came to Florida, I just, you know, everything has just happened, it's pulling me down to where I am now.

If all goes well, what will happen in the next year?

Well, they've told me that they will fly me back to North Carolina, and then fly me back to be a state's witness if I want to go back. So right now, see I'm kinda just, I don't know, I'm just stuck in a rut. Do I really want to stay here and see this through, or do I just want to get lost and pretend it never happened? But I want it to go through, you know, so that's why I'm at Allied. And people will say to you when you work there, "Well why don't you go get a real job?" But they don't know. Unless you're walkin' in these shoes, you don't know.

And that's what I'm saying about the labor force people, is that, don't judge before you know, walk in them shoes. [laughs]

Some of the people who I've talked to who work at the labor pools say it's not a good deal because you don't have steady work. They say the thing to do is to try to get a permanent job...

[exasperated] That's what I just said. Everybody throws that in my face, but still they don't understand the whole thing, you know, that I'm doin' that until I can get my hairdresser's license down here, or either go back. I can't afford to go lookin' for a permanent job and all that stuff and stay down there eight hours a day waitin' to go out on a ticket; it's impossible. So that's the rut.

A lot of people say there should be more programs to aid homeless centers and women's shelters, but others say we're already doing a lot...

They're doing it, it has come a long way, I'll put it that way. But there's not nearly enough, no. You wouldn't believe - there's not nearly enough. I've *seen* people be turned down; that's one reason I left the shelter. They said you don't have to, but I said no, I said my face has cleared up, and I'm gonna make room for another. They help eight people, this one here; the one in Orlando is a little bit bigger. But no, they're having to turn people away all the time, especially women who were beat up, with nowhere to go. And I saw men coming over there.

The system here is really funny, and the funding for these type of places here is very hard, very hard. I know because, you know, well I know all these people at the shelter, we've talked about it, and they're trying to open a new shelter but they can't get the funding right now. So it is a problem.

What about the other people who were staying there? Do they have a place to go when they leave?

A few did; they have like family in another state or, you know, something like that, they had somewhere to go. But I basically didn't, but I just said, "It's time for me to get out." And they said, "Well you can come back. You call us if you can't get a place; you're welcome back, you know that." I said, "Okay, but I've been here four weeks, let me try it on my own and see what happens." If I have to call back, I will. That was my understanding.

Oh, there's children in there, poor children, it was terrible. I'm not going to sit here and say that a man sometimes doesn't get abused; I'm not gonna say that because I'm sure it happens, you know. But I'm just sayin' what I've been through, my knowledge, my experience, it's pathetic that there's not enough room for people that are homeless, period. In fact, down the motel where I stay, they've got a bunch of tents in the woods right there - I haven't been down there, but I've been told - 'cause they've got nowhere to go. It's bad, I'll just put it that way. I'm just fortunate that I still have a bed to sleep in. If I don't get out to work this evening I might not have one. [laughs]

Just use the word survival and not enough help, not enough help for people, not enough funding.

Sharon Smith*, 29, is a native of Erie, Pennsylvania. She was interviewed at the family shelter run by the Coalition for the Homeless of Orlando, where she was staying with her children: Joseph, 9; Anne, 7; and Lucy, 5.

How long have you been in Florida?
A year.
What brought you down?
I left my old man. I left my husband. We just couldn't get along anymore, and my family's down here, so I just came down here.
Where were you living before you came to the shelter?
Oh, I was staying with my mother before I came here, and, you know, it's really hard. She let the kids get away with everything, so I decided to come here. I don't really like it, but it's a place to go. It's really hard; you can't come in till 7:30 (p.m.), you eat at eight o'clock, they shut the lights off at 9:30, you get up at five o'clock, and you have to be out at six. So it's really hard, especially on the little kids, so hopefully that be changin' soon. I got my apartment - I'll be moving the 15th of this month - from Section Eight. They pulled my name, so...it's really rough; kids always sick - my daughter been sick since she got here. I've been here two months, and she had an ear infection since; she can't get rid of it. It's just really

hard; I don't like to complain, so usually I don't say nothin'. But it's hard, it's really hard, especially when there's a lot of kids here; there been a lot of kids, but some of them leavin' now. Like this one woman, she had six kids, this other woman had five kids. I mean it's really hard because they about the same age, and they fight constantly. Other than that, it's alright, I guess. The teachers are nice, the volunteers are nice; Mr. Jones (the shelter director), he's really excellent, I really love him, he's really good.

They all really good people. I had a few problems with my caseworker, but...

Were you able to come right here after you left your mother's house?

Yeah, I got really lucky.

[The interview was interrupted briefly when a child walked into the room.]

This is my seven-year-old. This the one had an ear infection.

How's her ear?

She had a temperature of 102 last time I took it, but she feel like she cooling down some. I just get headaches every time she cry, you know, but I know what it is. She cry in the middle of the night. We don't have to worry much longer, thank God. There's one woman here since December (the interview was conducted in April); she didn't get pulled yet, and it's rough on her, she really get upset. Now, she only have one kid, so I guess it's not really bad, you know. It could be worse; she could be on the streets. I thank God there's shelters like this to come to.

Have you been out trying to find a place to live during the day and then coming back here at night?

Well they've (her children) been out all week; they started back to school today 'cause it was spring break, and I don't put 'em in day care. My little girl was in day care when I was lookin' for a job, but she got really sick in day care with a 105 temperature, and they never called to let me know she was really sick. I just took her out, you know, 'cause, well she could have gone into convulsions. I just took her out. I'll just wait till I move, and I'll let my sister baby sit her.

Have you had any luck looking for work?

I used to work at Ponderosa (a restaurant) and I quit. I'm gonna go back, you know, as soon as I move, 'cause it's really hard goin' to work and comin' back here; you can't really sleep at night, sleepin' on a floor is not really comfortable. And with the lights on, they keep them lights on, so - they (her children) go to sleep about 10:30 every night. She went to sleep one night at one o'clock and got up at five o'clock.

The lights are on all night?

Yeah, so they can monitor people, ya know - so many people in here. And you can't trust nobody. You never know what they gonna try to do.

Don't people look out for each other?

Some people; some people in here are really snobbish. You know, they act like they better than you, which - I think - everyone in here are the same, 'cause they don't have a place to go. But I know quite a few people in here, and they look out, and I look out for them. Now, some people I can't stand in here, especially the ones that don't have kids - they complain about the kids - they make too much noise. They shouldn't be in the shelter then, especially a family shelter, 'cause kids will be kids no matter what. I mean you can't beat 'em; they won't let you spank 'em in here. And they know it, especially my little five-year-old. She says, "You can't hit me. I'll tell Mister Jones." They know you can't hit 'em, but it won't last forever. You will get apartment eventually, and then you can control 'em better. All the kids in here are good; they just get wound up around 7:30 'cause they get tired. And the school back here is really good, really good.

What do you do during the day?

Walk around or go sit in the park. And then if it's rainin' or cold, they won't let you in till six o'clock. So you got, you know, 12 hours just to do whatever. It been cold down here; probably the middle of February it was really cold. They didn't care; they laughed. And rainin' - they don't care. I mean I know they just volunteers, but they could get more people in. Hopefully I never have to come back to a shelter, hopefully; I know what it's like. And I would tell everyone that need to come, this is the best place to come, I think.

Did you ever have to stay anyplace other than here or your mother's house?

I stayed two days at the Salvation Army, but she was really strict, you know. I mean you couldn't bring food in or nothin'. Like here you can bring soda in if you want it, snacks you can bring in, but at the Salvation Army you couldn't bring nothin' in. You have to eat what they give you.

What do you do for medical care? Is there a doctor here?

No, there's no doctor.

What do you do?

Go to the emergency room. Everyone take their kids to the emergency room or to the health department the next day. I took her - my other daughter - to the health department one day and I sat six hours. I said, "Never again." The health department is really busy; everyone go there.

They should have a visitor nurse or a doctor come in like once a month or every other week to check on the kids; there's so many kids. There's probably maybe 20, or even more.

Do you get enough food?

They feed you good here. There's a lot of sweets; they give you a lot of sweets, like cupcakes, at night, which, they complain 'cause the kids don't go to sleep. How can they go to sleep if they eatin' sweets? But the food is good here sometimes.

Where do you get food during the day?

Sometimes they give you like lunches. Or, you know, like I got money; I just buy sandwiches and stuff. There's the Daily Bread, it's a shelter that they feed you at. There's a lot of shelters here that feed you, but I won't go. I can't; I couldn't bring myself to go to a place like that. There's too many bums. [laughs] And, you know, I consider myself homeless, not a bum. There's people that are yukky, bummy-looking, winos, they go there, and I can't bring myself to go to a place like that. You don't never know if it's good food, or what they do to it. They could drop it on the floor, and I'm funny, I'm funny what I eat, so I won't go. Some people go, but now me and my friend, we won't go there; we'll go to 7-Eleven, or just get an extra plate at night and keep it by us and take it with us in the morning. I went there once. I think the second day I got here, I went. I said, "Never again." I took my kids. They give you rice and soup, I mean cheap food, which, some people are starvin', so they should be thankful, but not me. I think a lot of people feel like that. Which, I'm not better than nobody, but I just can't take my kids to a place like that where they see all these bummy people, which, if they can afford alcohol, they can afford food or a place to live instead of livin' out on the street. That's the way I feel about it. Or drugs, if they can afford that, they can afford a place to stay instead of bein' in the shelter or on the streets.

How do people outside the shelter treat you?

If you're sittin' outside, if they know you're homeless, they'll drive by and they'll give you money, or bags of lunches, you know, they're really good about that. Usually we sit out front in the morning till it get light out. People drive by and they give you money. One day me and my friend was sittin' out there and we got $40, just sittin' there. Because there's no place to go, especially on the weekend, everything closed until so late. We just sit there, especially with six kids, we got six of them on the weekends; it's really hard.

What do you do?

Well, we take 'em to the park, to Lake Eola (a city park in downtown Orlando), or to the library. They get tired in the library, they get restless, so we take 'em to Church Street (Church Street Station, a popular tourist attraction in downtown Orlando, includes a complex of retail stores and night clubs).

What if it's raining?

[laughs] If that's a problem we stay, you know, under a roof until it stop rainin', or we'll make rain coats for the kids out of garbage bags. I thought I would never live in the shelter. It happened; it happens to the best of people.

Do you have enough clothing?

They give you clothes. You know, they furnish shampoo, everything. The only thing is, if you don't have money, you have to worry: oh, how I gonna wash the clothes? 'Cause they don't wash the clothes here. I guess, so many people, how could they tell which clothes are which?

So what do you do?

A lot of people wash them out in the sink and hang them, you know, over the stalls in the bathroom. [laughs] I take mine to my mother's and wash them, or my sister's.

The kids are good in here, but if you want your kids to go to sleep, how can they sleep when other kids are runnin' around?

I've heard that some people here have a hard time finding jobs because if you give the shelter as your home address, some employers don't want you. Is that true?

Yeah, it is. They like, discriminate against you, 'cause, really, you're stayin' in a shelter, you know. Then other times they hire you right away. It depends on who it is. I guess they figure if you're homeless, how you gonna keep a job?

Were you working before, when you were staying at your mother's house?

Yeah, at Ponderosa.

And then you had to leave the job when you came here?

Yeah, well my daughter was sexually assaulted, and she got really, I mean - that happened last summer - and she starting to get really nasty at times, so I just quit. She'd cry when I went to work, so I couldn't handle it. So I'll go once I get my own apartment; when she's in school, I'll work. I mean, it's impossible now since I'm in a shelter. She need my time now. You know, it didn't help me leavin' their father. They go, "You left Daddy; you might leave us." You know how some kids are.

She doesn't like to be alone because she's afraid?

Yeah, she's afraid, she's really insecure. She's a smart child but she's basically insecure. He (her son) is too, at times; you know, he always want to be by me. He try to tell me what to do. [laughs]

Do you think there's anything you could have done differently to avoid becoming homeless?

I don't think so. Well, my mom is remarried, and her husband is a alcoholic. I can't really say nothin'. It's her house and everything. My father, he died three years ago.

A lot of people in here, you know, they just left 'cause their husbands or boyfriends abused them. Mostly everyone in here left 'cause of that.

Do you think being homeless is harder for women than for men?

I think so. They should have more shelters for women and children.

Will you be able to stay in your new apartment indefinitely?

Yeah, until my income switch, you know, change. I mean, if I hit the lottery I won't be living there, because they go by your income, whatever your income is. I'll be paying $32 a month, so that's nothing.

I have a terrible headache I can't get rid of.

Chapter Two

Flight: Teenagers

About 1 million minors run away from home every year in the United States. The vast majority of them return home after a few days or weeks, but some never do. As many as 300,000 unaccompanied minors become homeless in the course of a year. These "throwaways" often leave home with the consent of their parents; indeed, many are ejected from their homes by their parents. Most homeless shelters turn away minors who are not accompanied by a parent or legal guardian; children and teenagers are referred to runaway shelters. Ironically, many runaway shelters will not provide shelter to anyone who is 18 or older. A homeless 17-year-old is viewed by social service agencies as a runaway on Monday, but is transformed into a homeless person on Tuesday if it happens to be his or her 18th birthday. One exception to this is Covenant House, an organization that provides shelter to young people up to 21 years old. A number of other shelters and agencies that help runaways also try to provide transitional housing programs, but in some cases the best they can do for someone who has just turned 18 is to refer them to a homeless shelter.

Florida alone has some 36,000 runaway teenagers and children in the course of a year. While most runaways stay very close to home, some migrate to other states, and certain regions, ranging from the coastal cities and towns of California to the Miami and Fort Lauderdale areas, tend to be magnets for interstate runaways. About 14 percent of the runaways in Florida are from out of state.

Honey Pauley, 19, is a native of West Virginia. She was interviewed in Fort Lauderdale at Covenant House, a shelter for runaway children and teenagers.

Are you new to Florida?
No, I've been here about two years.
What brought you down here?
My mother lives down here; it's like that's the only place I had to go, so I came down here.
How did you come to stay here at Covenant House?
I was livin' on the streets in West Virginia, on drugs and everything like that, so...hitchhiked down here, and they told me about this place, so I came here the night I got to Florida.
You were on the streets in West Virginia for awhile?
Uh-huh.
For how long?
Since I was 11 till 16. It's not all it's cracked up to be, I can tell you that. Everybody wants to be on their own; they get out there and it ain't worth it.
Did you leave your father's home? Or what was your situation?
No, I was on drugs when I was livin' with my mother in West Virginia, and I got kicked out because the drugs drove me to where I got a little bit out of it and I tried to kill my mother. So I went to stay with my aunt, and then she threw me out when I was 11. And I just went on the streets from there, and I hitchhiked from there to Florida, and I just popped up.
What kinds of drugs were you using?
Crack, marijuana, snortin' coke, acid, you name it, just about everything but heroin I was doin'.
You weren't going to school then?
No, I wasn't. I had no place to stay so I wouldn't want to go to school lookin' like a - a street person, I guess. [laughs] I didn't want people knowin'.
So how did you get by?
I begged. That's how I got by. I begged everybody that I would see for help. And it's like, once they found out why I was on the streets, they'd turn their back on me - 'cause of the drugs. I slept in parks, alleys, you name it, any place I could find. Garbage dumpsters, I'd sleep behind them. You name it, that's where I was at.
What did you do for food?
[laughs] Put it this way, you see in the movies people diggin' through garbage dumpsters; that's what I was doin'. It's not just in the movies; it's

reality, it's what you do. And it's not fun, somethin' that somebody else ate, they throw half of it away and then you've gotta eat after them - after it's already been in the garbage. That's pretty sick, but that's what I had to do.

Did you ever have to steal food?

Oh yeah, I'd do whatever I had to, I'd steal or whatever and have somebody pawn whatever I stole to get the money for me. But I had 'em pawn it and I got the money and I went out and did drugs instead of buyin' food or whatever I needed.

Didn't you run into problems with the law?

Not until I moved down here. [laughs] Not until I got to Florida; I did not have problems with the law. They arrested me because I had drugs on me. They pulled me over at four o'clock in the morning, I was walkin' down the street and I had a bunch of drugs on me: cocaine and marijuana, and I had a couple rocks (crack cocaine) on me. And I was with my boyfriend, and they arrested him because they found out his name, he had a warrant out for rape, so they tried to arrest me for accessory to it, which I didn't even know it had gone on, so I got off of that, and then they threw the drug charge on me, kept me in jail for three months. And then I got arrested again for not payin' my court fine for the drugs, so the law don't like me down here, put it that way. [laughs] They just don't agree with me. There's a bunch of cops in Fort Lauderdale, Miramar and Miami; they see me, they will make up a charge to bust me, no matter what. I could be sittin' there waitin' on a bus, they'll swear up and down that I'm prostitutin'. That's how bad they hate me.

When you were out on the streets, what did you do to raise money for drugs?

Oh, I'd go to somebody I knew. I'd go to my mother or friends that I knew and say I need to borrow money so I can get this; I'd tell them I was gettin' food or somethin'. It wouldn't be for food; I'd be usin' it for drugs. And they'd give it to me. Once they found out what I was really doin', they all turn their back on me. So it didn't work out too good.

Did you sell drugs to make money?

Yeah, I sold drugs for some people. And I'd get like 10 percent of what it was sold for. If they didn't give me the money - usually instead of gettin' the money I'd have 'em give me drugs in place of it, and that's all. It's a lot easier that way; I didn't have to go around searchin' for somebody else to get the drugs from. I'd just get it from the guy I dealt for.

What did you do about medical care?

To see a doctor I went to the emergency room. Sometimes I'd give 'em a fake name, sometimes I'd give 'em my real name. And there's somebody in this world, there's somebody in Miramar I should say, who's got mail goin' to their house for somebody they don't even know [laughs] 'cause of fake addresses and all that, so they don't know who I am or where I live, and the hospital bills were just building up. I mean, I couldn't afford to pay it, so somebody's bein' sued out there somewhere and it's not me. [laughs] Which I call messed up, and I know now I shouldn't have done that, but I was always on drugs when I did it. I mean, I just had a baby, not even two months ago. And I was clean the time I was pregnant with her because I started thinkin' about that baby in me; I can't mess her life up. I was clean for almost 11 months. And it's like, right after I had her, last week, I went out and relapsed, and smoked a rock. And I shouldn't have done it, 'cause now, I got a check cashed today that was for me. It's like, I had somebody go with me 'cause I knew if I'd of went by myself and got it cashed, I wouldn't have come back, 'cause I'd have been right out in Miramar gettin' drugs again, no matter what, 'cause I didn't have the baby inside of me to worry about. 'Cause now she's livin' with my mother and she's doin' alright. To where I wish I was livin' with my mother and doin' alright. [laughs] But I'm not doin' that.

Do you have any other children?

No, I'm only 19. I'm not old enough to have more than one child. [laughs] Not me, oh no, I'll never have any more either, not me, I ain't crazy.

How long have you been at Covenant House?

About a month-and-a-half.

When did you get busted and go to jail?

I got busted in November, and I was in all the way till the end of January. And that's while I was pregnant, which I wasn't doin' the drugs at the time; I was just dealin'. I wasn't doin' anything; there's no way. But then I went to a place, and I was planin' on givin' my daughter up for adoption. And I didn't do it. They kicked me out of there for sayin' "Oh my God," for takin' God's name in vain. So they kicked me out of there and I came here that same day, which I got lucky to be able to get back in here, cause they kicked me out last year for drugs, so nothin' was goin' too well.

But now things are startin' to pick up, my daughter's with my mother, once I get on my feet I'll have her back, I'll have an apartment, everything will be fine, which I'm glad. I'm glad I didn't, 'cause when I looked at her that day, I said, "There ain't no way I'm givin' her up for adoption." When I looked at her, I said, "Uh-uh."

You said from the time you were 11 until you were about 16 you were living on the streets. What happened when you were 16?

I ran into my cousin. He let me stay with him for awhile, then he kicked me out when I was 17, and he kicked me out for drug abuse just like my aunt did, and when I left there I hitchhiked down here - 'cause they told me that my mother was here - and nobody would ever tell me where my mother was at. So I came down here, ran into her, and she's the one that told me about Covenant House, 'cause she found out, 'cause, I don't know, a friend of her's daughter, they weren't gettin' along, and she could come to Covenant house, so she found out about it and had me sent here. I thank God for this place to tell you the truth, 'cause there's no way I'd wanna be back out on the street. I mean, I never prayed in my life until I came to Covenant House, because if it weren't for this place I'd be out on the streets usin' again. I pray every morning now, and every night before I go to bed, that I've got a roof over my head and a bed to sleep in. And I never prayed in my life. This place is here [laughs] and I'm glad, 'cause I don't know what I'd be doin'. Well I do know what I'd be doin'; I'd be out on the streets with the drugs again, and I don't need that, I really don't, 'cause I can't handle it no more. [laughs] I can't take it.

Did you ever feel that you were in danger when you were out on the streets, or does it depend on where you are?

Yeah, it does, it does depend on where you're at. It all depends 'cause some people, when you're on drugs, some people get this kind of feeling to where you gotta look over your shoulder every 10 minutes 'cause somebody might be after you, but I was the type of person that when I was on the drugs, I didn't care. I did not care. I would fight anything that walked in front of me. I did not feel no danger to myself. When I got into a fight, I didn't even know I was hurt until I came down off the drugs, and then I took my rear end to the emergency room. That's about the only time I'd go to the hospital or to the doctor or anything. You know, I just didn't care. I was on the drugs, so there was no danger to put me through. I was it, you know?

How old were you when you first started taking drugs?

I was nine years old.

I've got a daughter now to raise. So I mean, I went to an NA convention last week that they were havin' at one of the hotels, and then I went to another NA meeting last night that they had here in-house, and I'm gonna just keep going until it helps me out. That's all I can do. Hey, it makes me happy, clears my heart up, takes a load off of me.

When you were on the street, did you find that other people would help you?

People wanted to help me, but I was out there, and as soon as they found out why I was out there, they just turned around and walked away. I guess because they were totally against drugs, for one, they didn't care, for two, and you're out here, it's because of what you did, for three. They said, "You did it, you gotta pay for it." It's like, you did a crime, you may as well be able to do the time, 'cause if you don't, you ain't gonna be able to get nowhere in life. And they just turned their backs on me, and once they started turnin' their backs on me, it makes you see nobody's gonna care about you till you care about yourself. So I had to, I just said hell with it, I've gotta get off of it, and I came back here then. That's the only thing I can do. You gotta reach out for help before somebody will even offer to help.

Were you always able to get enough clothing?

When I was on the streets, no. You don't get anything. You just wear what you've got on your back, and if you're lucky enough to find someplace to be able to shower, then you better do it, 'cause all I had was the clothes on my back. I mean I went without a shower for two years. I finally was able to take a shower after two years when I was in West Virginia. It's like I didn't take a shower from the time I was 11 until I was 13 years old. And it really stunk. I tell you what: [laughs] it's not a pleasant smell. It makes you wanna puke yourself, just to see yourself even on the streets, 'cause you ain't got nothin'. There's nothin' on the streets for nobody; they think there is, but there ain't nothin' there. I mean, yeah, you got your freedom. I'll tell you what; freedom's not all it's cracked up to be.

Do you think you could have done anything differently to avoid all these problems?

Drugs is what put me on the streets.

I could have tried to been one of those kids that said, "Hey, I don't know what it is, but I'm not gonna try it." But I just wasn't, 'cause all kids are curious; they're gonna do somethin' no matter what. I mean I don't care if you're a preacher's child, you're gonna do somethin', no matter what it is.

Were you pretty much alone, or were there other people your age out there too?

Oh, there are always people out there your age, but a lot of times, you're out on the streets, you're by yourself anyway, whether you got people around you or not, you're still on your own, 'cause you could have 15 other people with you, right there on the streets, but you're still by yourself 'cause you ain't got the love that your family could give you. You ain't got the ability to be able to do what you have to because they're bringin' you down right along with bringin' yourself down. I mean you don't have anything that you could have if you're with your family. Like me, I don't have a job right now - which I'm trying to work on getting. You don't have anything; you don't have a job, you don't have family, you don't have clothes, you don't have love, you don't have anything. I don't care how many people you're with; there's nothing there for you. That's about it; you don't have anything.

Did you find that the people who were out on the streets would look out for each other?

Oh yeah, they'd look out for each other, but it didn't always work, 'cause there'd always be somebody to kick their ass too. Excuse me, but that's what it would be. You're always, I guess you could say a family in one way; you look out for each other but that's the only way that you were there for each other. I mean, you see food, you're gonna get that for yourself, say the hell with everybody else. About the only way you were a family that stuck together was when somebody was after you or somebody had gotten hurt, you know, no other way than having somebody else after you.

Before you came to Covenant House did you ever go to a church or a social service agency to try to get some help?

Yeah, when I was on the streets in West Virginia I went to my home church, and I asked them for help. They even found out why I was on the streets. They kicked me *out* of my church 'cause I was usin' drugs. But I guarantee ya, churches, no matter what, down here, I guarantee ya, will help you out. 'Cause I have went down here, to churches, told them my story, and they've given me everything I needed. They do help you out no matter what.

My home church...they weren't Christians, so-called Christians anyway. They were just there tryin' to act like, "Oh, we're better than you; we do this, you do that."

They do help you out. It doesn't matter what you've done wrong, if they're honest to God true Christians they will help you out.

What about government agencies? Have you ever tried to get food stamps or anything like that?

Oh yeah, I gave 'em my mother's address, which she let me do. I've gotten food stamps, I've gotten Medicaid, I've gotten checks from the government to where it helps me out. As a matter of fact, I got a check from 'em today. And it helps me out a lot, it helps out. You get your food and what you need.

How do they treat you when you go to apply?

To be honest with you, they treat you like shit while you're there. But once you leave it's like you're God's gift to the world 'cause you're not in their face now, you're not there begging, you've already gotten what you need. But while you're there they treat you like shit. They don't care. They give you what you need just to try and show they care, but they don't. But they still give you what you need.

How long do you think you'll be here at Covenant House?

I wish I could stay until I get my feet firmly planted on the ground, but probably about another two to three weeks, 'cause it's only a short-term crisis shelter, so you can't really expect that much. But I've been, like I said, all together I'll probably be here almost three months. They help you out as much as they can.

Are you planning to go back to school?

Oh yeah, I want to go back to school for either working to become a veterinarian or something to do with children. I'm definitely gonna go back to school as soon as I can get the money saved up.

How old were you when you stopped going to school?

When I got kicked out of my aunt's house I was 11 years old.

So you need to get a GED first?

Right, which I'm workin' on that here, 'cause they have a GED class here.

Some people in other shelters have told me that it's harder to find a job when you give a shelter as your address. Have you run into that?

Oh yeah, when I was here last year I went out on a job search. I got a job. Then they found out I was livin' here at Covenant House and they fired me. They don't want people in crisis shelters. They want people they know that they can count on. Then again there's places like AT&T; they will accept you no matter where you're at. They don't care if you don't have an address to give 'em, but give 'em some address. But they don't care if you're on the streets or not; they will hire you if you're qualified for the job.

What kind of place was it that fired you?

It was just a fast food restaurant. And I'll guarantee you, other than AT&T, you go to bigger companies, and fast food restaurants gonna fire you there too, livin' in a crisis shelter. There's a lot of people out there that just don't care; they don't care what you need. They're not gonna let you work for 'em.

What was the worst part of being on the streets?

The worst part? Almost bein' killed. Because I've been shot at bein' on the streets - just for bein' on the streets. There's people that ride by in cars that will just shoot at you because you live on the streets, you're homeless, you're a drug addict, and they're gonna try to hurt you in some form or another. That's about the worst experience I had, was almost dyin'. It's not a pretty sight; you see your life flash before your eyes. That's it; it's just all over. The streets ain't a place for nobody.

Hey, I just tell it like it is. The streets ain't a place; better get off while you can.

Joseph Kelly*, 13, is a native of Orlando. He was interviewed in Orlando at Great Oaks Village, a shelter for abused and runaway minors that is run by the Orange County government. He had recently been arrested for drug possession.

How long have you been staying here at Great Oaks?
Last time I was here about three months, but this time I've been here about three or four days.
When were you here last?
About six months ago.
How did you come here?
I had a warrant out for my arrest and I got busted for a dope charge. They put me in Laurel Oaks.
Is that a hospital?
Yeah.
How long were you there?
About a week. No, about two days.
Do you know why they put you there?
Dope.
Is that a psychiatric hospital?
No, it's for people that smoke dope. And for people that sell it. And for people that's bad and hyper.
Is it mostly teenagers there?
Yeah.
How long do you think you'll be here?
I'm leaving Friday.
How long ago did you run away from your house?
Four months ago.
Where have you been staying since then?
My buddy's, selling dope.
An older friend?
Yeah. I had an apartment, had a house, had a car.
Were you going to school?
Yeah.
What kinds of drugs were you selling?
Rock.
Crack?
Yeah.

And you got busted?
Yeah, they stopped the car and found dope in it.
Was that the first time you were ever arrested?
No, I've been arrested a few times along the way.
How many times?
Three.
Who did you live with up until a few months ago? Both your parents?
Just my father.
Where is your mother?
I don't know.
Does she live in Orlando?
Yeah. I see her sometimes.
Did you leave home because you didn't get along with your father?
He got into dope.
He did?
Yeah, he did. Started smoking that dope, stealing my stuff.
What happened?
He started selling my rings and stuff that I had, my jewelry and stuff.
Why?
He sell my gold, my rings, all this.
Why?
Dope.
He needed money for dope?
Yeah.
What kind of dope was he using?
Rock - crack cocaine.
Was he abusing you?
Yeah.
How?
With a rubber hose. He used a rubber hose.
He hit you?
Yeah.
Did you always have a place to stay after you left your father's house and before you came here?
I had an apartment with my friend.
So you always had a place to sleep?
Yeah, we had food, had clothes, had a car, had everything.
How much money were you making?
About $300.
A week?
No, a day.

You must have been selling a lot of rock.
Yeah, a lot. My buddy's here too.
So, you were making enough money so that you didn't have any problems getting food or clothes?
Yeah.
How do you like it here?
It's okay.
Would you rather stay here or go home?
I would rather stay here. I ain't goin' home.
Do you have any brothers or sisters?
Yeah.
Are they staying with your father or somewhere else?
My sisters stay with my grandma and my brothers stay with their mom. My other two brothers, they stay with their auntie.
Would you rather be staying with your father than staying here?
He smokes dope.
He's smoking crack?
Yeah.
Is your grandma in this area? In Orlando?
Yeah.
Do you think there's any chance you might be able to go stay there?
Yeah, if they let me.
Did you have to stay in jail for awhile when you got busted?
I had to stay in jail for a little while.
Did you go to trial yet?
Yeah.
What happened?
I got released.
Were you convicted of any charges?
No.
What grade are you in in school?
Seven.
What do you think you'll do when you finish school?
I don't know.
When you were selling product, were the police bothering you at all?
No.
Because you're so young?
I don't know.
Where were you selling? Out on the street or somewhere else?
On the street.

Chapter Three

Crime Victims

High crime rates have become a staple of modern life in many areas, and Florida is no exception. Some 53,928 robberies were reported in 1990; a robbery occurred every 10 minutes. During the same period, 280,832 burglaries took place, giving the sunshine state a rate of about 32 burglaries every hour. Most victims of economic crime are able to resume their normal lives, but for a handful the incident is enough to propel them into the abyss of homelessness.

Ruth McGlothin, 39, is a native of Milwaukee, Wisconsin. She was interviewed in Tampa at the ACTS Homeless Day Center.

How long have you been in Florida?
Since July 7th. (The interview was conducted on July 29.)
Did you come from Milwaukee?
Yes.
What brought you down here?
Everybody told us there was so much work, and they lied. [laughs]
You're not here alone then. You're with...
My husband.
Do you have children?
No.
What kind of work were you looking for?
Any kind, waitress, cleaning, maid, anything.
What were you doing when you lived in Milwaukee?

I was a mail sorter.
For the post office?
Yes, making good money [laughs], not livin' on the streets.
What about your husband? What kind of work did he do?
He was unemployed right then, but he was a cement layer.
Did you drive down?
[Angrily] We came with a friend, and he dumped us down here. He took off with everything we owned.
Tell me about that.
Well, he was livin' with us in Milwaukee, in my home, and, you know, we were supporting him, and we all decided to come down to Florida. And when we got down here, we got a room; me and my husband went out for a walk, we came back, and we didn't have nothin', our car, everything.
Your car was stolen?
[Intensely angry, almost in a rage] Yeah, everything, my money, my purse, everything, we didn't have nothing left. And we've been on the streets since, 'cause without money, you can't live. And yes, I am very hostile. If I find the guy, he's dead. And everywhere we've gone, it's the same story. Unless you have kids, you don't get help. They do not help married couples. You're either better off bein' single, or better off havin' kids, 'cause ya don't get help.
So, when you came down you had savings, money to keep you going for awhile?
Yeah, we could have got a place for probably about four months. At the prices down here, I could have definitely got a place for four months. And as it is...
And your clothes, did he take them, too?
Most of 'em. What we got on. [laughs] And what we've gotten, people givin' us stuff. But other than that, yeah, he took everything.
How long had you known him?
About three years. Like I said, he lived with us. This guy better never show up. He better not show up in Wisconsin, and he better not show up down here. And everywhere I've gone so far, it seems like, forget it, like I said, you gotta either be single or you gotta have kids, 'cause otherwise they don't help you.
Where are you staying at night?
We finally got a place today; it's called the Good Samaritan Inn. We finally got a place today after walkin' about thirty-some miles to get help, and that was clear out of Tampa. Do you know where Plant City is?
Yeah.

Past there. That's why I said...[laughs] I have the cramps in my legs. But we finally got a place. So they gave us a month, and by then I should have this job and we should be on our feet.

Where had you been staying before?

Bushes, the woods, in between abandoned buildings, you know, that's where. Under bridges, under freeway bridges when it rains so you can get out of the rain. You can't sleep where there's a building, an old abandoned building, because the cops will come and take you away. You can't crawl inside a house because of all the coke addicts and the hookers down here because you'll get shot. We walked into one abandoned house and a guy came after us with a gun. And all we told him was, "Hey, we're homeless, too. We want a place to sleep," And he says, "Not here." A girl cannot walk down these streets, 'cause you get harassed - they think you're a hooker. I cannot walk down the streets. You know, there's millions of people that are homeless, but unless you're on drugs or an alcoholic, you don't get help. They're tellin' you to go out and be on drugs or be an alcoholic...I found that out. I found it out the hard way, 'cause we got dumped. And the cops don't help you. The cops said it might be four years down the road before they find my car, even though I told 'em probably where the guy went back - the guy probably went back to Wisconsin. It took four days for them to file a report, which the guy could be, you know, California. It's hard tellin' where he is.

How long had you been down here when you got ripped off?

Two days...and we're one of the lucky ones, but there's a lot of homeless people don't care. I'll tell you that right now. Three-fourths of the homeless don't wanna work, and three-fourths of the ones here don't wanna work. But then there's the section that do wanna work, and they're the ones that can't find it.

Have you been applying for jobs?

[laughs] That isn't the word for it. I probably have in over 500 applications since I came down here. Every place, every restaurant, every motel, anywhere that we see a sign that says Help Wanted, we're there, we stop in. A lot of them say, "Well, we're just taking applications." They might have had that sign up for 10 years, and probably have 8,000 applications. You run across a lot of places down here like that. And then when you're homeless, it's a little hard givin' an address and a phone number, which, right there's a strike against you, until we found this place, and they allow us, you know, to use their address and their phone number. You can't walk into a place lookin' like a bum, they look at you 'cause you're all eat up from fire ants and that. You can't live that way. People look at you like, "What have you got, lady?"

You've got a lot of marks on your arms. Are they all bites from fire ants?

Yep, and mosquitoes, and whatever else bugs are out there [laughs], giant grasshoppers, cockroaches, you know. I guarantee ya, in the last two weeks I've lost over 15 pounds, since I came down here [laughs] 'cause you don't know where your next meal's comin' from.

Have you found that potential employers aren't interested in you once they find out you don't have a permanent address?

You don't tell them you don't have a permanent address. You cannot tell them that, 'cause they can call here, and this is our address. And they'll answer the phone. I haven't had any problems. I don't tell 'em I'm homeless. I don't tell 'em, "Hey buddy, I live on the street," 'cause if I did I wouldn't have a job, I'd never get a job, I guarantee it.

Have you been able to get enough food?

No, there's days I've gone hungry. I've gone hungry for four or five days. Today's the first day I ate in three days, and that's because, you know, they give doughnuts. I've gone out and begged for money, I've panhandled, my husband stands on the freeway ramps askin' for money and food. You know, that's how you get your food, 'cause if you go to food pantries, they give you canned goods, but how can you open up the can? You ain't got a can opener. How can you? You can't. And that's what they give you, is canned goods. It's no good; it don't help the homeless. It don't help people that don't have a place to cook. Why give it to them? It's stupid. Give 'em a sandwich, give 'em a carton of milk, give 'em something they don't have to cook. But you can't get that kind of stuff - it perishes - and the food pantries don't have it, they have canned goods. And I go out there every day and I panhandle, and so does my husband, so we can eat, but there's days you don't get a cent.

Where do you go?

Mainly freeway ramps, the exits, stand there with a sign.

Are people friendly, hostile, or do they ignore you?

Oh, you get some very nasty remarks. But every once in awhile somebody will come up and give you a business card, and you call, and hopefully they have work for you. They might have one day work. Like this one place my husband went to - he met this guy at a motel - and the guy says, "Sure, I've got work for ya." So my husband went and did all the work, and the guy left him there. He was cleaning up the job, he just left him, never paid him, nothing, after workin' nine, 10 hours of back breakin' work. And then you're screwed again, 'cause that would have been money for us, that would have been money for food. There's a lot of people out there like that, that take advantage of you. I've met more nicer people here than I have out on the street. There's more homeless people that'll give you the shirt off their back. The homeless help the homeless. And the other ones that got the money don't seem to give a shit. That's the way I feel.

So people that are out on the streets are pretty good about helping each other?

Oh yeah, they help each other. Oh yeah, I guarantee it. And they don't have nothin' in the first place. But like if one person gets their food stamps before the other person, then you help that person out. Or if somehow you got some money to buy some lunch meat, you help, you give, I guarantee it. That's the only way you survive; that's the only way.

But you haven't had very good experiences with other people who aren't homeless?

Some, yeah, but like the people that are supposed to be helpin' the homeless, I think they're a bunch of malarkey. I think they're all malarkey. And I could name a lot of them, 'cause I've been to every one of them that's supposed to help ya, and they don't. They don't give a damn, and that's the way I feel about it.

What do you mean? The social service agencies?

Right, this is the only one that's actually helped. This one helps more than the ones that are supposed to help you get off the streets. They don't. And don't be a couple and go out there, because you're screwed, you're *screwed.* They're tellin' ya either be single or have kids. Now, I'm one of those people that can't have kids. So don't condemn me because I can't. I mean, I've worked all 39 years of my life; I've worked every damn day. I lived on a farm for 18 years and worked. Because I'm down now, they condemn me. They look at ya like you're trash, and we're not, we're human beings, we just had bad luck, all of us. Everybody that's here had bad luck. But it's gonna get better. It's definitely gonna get better. None of us can get any lower; we're at the lowest point that we're ever gonna go. Everything's gotta go up. You should go out there and live it. Just get a sleeping bag and go out there and live it. Take a video camera, whatever you want, but live it, 'cause no one can tell you, there is not one person, not even one homeless person, that can tell you exactly what it's like until you live it. That's the honest to God truth.

Did you try to go to the Salvation Army or any other shelters?

Oh yeah, you can go to the Salvation Army, but they split you up, and I will not be split from my husband. I mean, we're in this together. Why should we be split? Because we're married? I have legal paper that says I'm married. But they want my husband to stay here, and me to stay here. For two nights? What's two nights? You're back out on the street. You can stay there for $8 a night. Where the hell are you supposed to get this $8 a night until you find work? And you can't find work lookin' like a slob. We can come here during the week, take a shower, wash our clothes, but Saturday and Sunday, and here comes Monday morning, you stink. [laughs] And people look at ya like that. It's not because you want to. But you walk into a gas station and you're in there too long, they're gonna call the cops because you're loitering. It's real fun.

Have you tried to get food stamps?

I get food stamps.

How were you treated when you applied?

They just asked me how a woman could live on the streets by herself, you know. I said, "It's easy. It's just as easy for a woman to live out there as a man." You just don't take nothin'. A woman is harder. I mean, it makes you harder. I think more people are more leery of a woman on the streets, 'cause a woman will kill. I'd kill. I'd kill tomorrow. I would, if I had too. I would. If it came down to it, I actually would. That's the way I feel.

Do you think women are in more danger on the streets?

Oh yeah, definitely. This one guy that's homeless, I don't know if he was tellin' the truth, but he said that his wife went to meet him at work, and because she wasn't a hooker, they blew her away. They shot her because she wasn't a hooker. I mean, you got guys comin' up, pullin' up to you constantly. I don't care how you dress, I don't care what you look like, they pull up and say, "Come on. How much?" And it's constantly, constantly. I can walk out there and I guarantee ya I'd have 15 cars pull up to me within five minutes because they think I'm a hooker. And I could have slacks on, I could have a uniform on, they don't give a shit, that's all those guys think you are, that's all. Between that and coke, the cokeheads, you can walk five feet and somebody comes up to you and asks you if you want coke. All this town is is coke, coke and hookers. It is, I swear to God. And for the women that are straight, it's hell, it is actually hell.

Have you tried dealing with any of the other social service agencies other than food stamps?

Every one. [laughs]

And?

Nothing, 'cause I'm a couple [laughs], 'cause I don't have kids, I'm not single, I'm not on drugs, I'm not an alcoholic.

What about the police? Have they been helpful?

[laughs] No. I don't wanna say what they are. To me they're a bunch of j-offs. They don't care. They haven't helped me. They haven't even found my car, they haven't found my stuff, and it's been almost three weeks. They'll never find it, I know damn well they'll never find it; I don't even think they've been out lookin' for it. All they're out there is to harass you.

Instead of catchin' the people that are doin' the crimes, they're harassin' the homeless. They're sayin', "You can't sleep here, you can't do this, you can't do that, get off the streets, quit panhandling." It's bullshit. Leave the poor people alone. Get after the people that really deserve it, not us poor people. You know, we're not hurtin' nobody. We might need some place to sleep, but we're not hurtin' nobody. We're not goin' out there and robbin' you. I doubt if there's one homeless person out there that would rob you. They'll come up and ask. They might ask you, "Hey buddy, you got a dime? You got a quarter?" But they're not gonna rob you. There might be one percent that would - out of a hundred percent - that would rob you. But otherwise, some of the homeless would probably give you the shirt off their back if you asked for it; that's the way they are, 'cause they know, they know what it feels like to be hurt, to be hungry. They're not gonna rob you; there's no way. There's no way. And the cops should know that, but they don't; they harass you.

Have you had to try to get medical care for anything since you've been here?

Just for my ankle, from walkin' on it so much, I sprained it - and blisters.

Did you go to a doctor?

Yeah, they sent us to a free health clinic downtown for the homeless. It's just for the homeless. You go in there, and they help you.

How was that?

Really nice, very nice. They're the ones that told us where to go to get help. There's a counselor there, and he's the one that more or less got us our place. If it wasn't for him, we'd still be out on the streets. He was really nice.

And you can stay at this place you're going for a month?

Yeah.

It's not a shelter, though, is it?

No, it's like a boarding house, a motel boarding house. You've got a room that you sleep in and you share a bathroom, stuff like that.

You're going there tonight?

Uh-huh. The place is nothing but roaches, but it's better than outside, definitely.

Constance and John Crimley were interviewed in West Palm Beach at The Lord's Place, a family shelter, where they were living with their children, Kamilah, 3, April, 2, and Dakota, four months old. Constance, 30, is a native of Green Cove Springs, Florida. John, also 30, is a native of New Haven, Connecticut. The interview opens with Constance alone; John joins in when he arrives home from work.

What brought you down to Palm Beach County?

Well, me and my husband come down, but he come down looking for work.

When did you come down here?

We left about the third of June. (The interview was conducted in July.) We left Jacksonville about the third of June.

What kind of work was your husband looking for?

He works on golf courses. He was lookin' for like irrigation or landscaping on golf courses. That's what he was mainly lookin' for.

I see. So there wasn't anything in Jacksonville for him?

No, he wasn't makin' enough money to support the family, so he figured he'd come down here and see if there might be a little more money and everything, so he just decided to come down here.

Did you come down together?

Yes, we all came down together.

So then what happened?

After we got here we stayed right down here at the motel, stayed there for about a week, and then we went out to breakfast one morning and someone broke in our room, took our money, so we didn't have no more rent to pay for the motel stay, so my husband ended up calling a lot of different places, eventually he called Traveler's Aid, they give us a place to stay for about a week - at a hotel. We stayed there about a week and everything, then after that we went down there again and got another voucher to stay there again another two weeks. Then after that we were kinda here and there. After we left the hotel we was tryin' to get in the Salvation Army shelter, we tried to get in there, but since I didn't have a ID, I had to go to the police station, I thought they could give me a ID, but they couldn't give me one.

You couldn't get into the Salvation Army?

No, because I didn't have an identification card at the time. And we went to the police station, the lady in the office, she kinda helped us out, she talked to some people, talked to a reverend, he got us a place to stay for the night. After that we came here, but my husband didn't have a job, he was just doin' day labor at the time. The guy told us, the only thing, they couldn't put us in there unless my husband had a job, so after that we just left, we went back to the police station, told them what happened again, so they helped us out again, and another pastor from another church helped us out, he put us up at a motel and gave us food and everything, for the next three days, and after that the church gave us some money for the week, to live off of for the week. Then we came back down this way to the motel and stayed there for about a few days, and at the time, I had a little money, that's when I went up to the driver's license place and I got me an identification card, and after that, that next day, we went to the shelter, and we stayed there for about a week.

Which one?

Salvation Army, since I had a ID, we just went there and stayed there for about a week.

What kind of work is your husband doing now?

He's working on an estate right now, he's doin' paintin', keepin' up the grounds, irrigation on the estate and everything, a little bit of everything.

You were living in an apartment when you lived near Jacksonville?

Yeah, we stayed there about nine months.

So it wasn't till you got down here that you started having all these problems.

Yeah. Well, we didn't have a place to stay anyway because my husband, he had just started this other job, so I just stayed with my mother for about two months, till June, and he found he wasn't makin' enough, couldn't save enough, so he decided just to leave up that job and come down here, he figured it would probably be better down this way than up north, so we just packed up and we just left.

When your money was stolen, did they take your clothes too?

No, they didn't take our clothes, just the money that we had. All the money we had, that we had saved up to come down here. [laughs]

Did you ever have to sleep outside?

We had come close a few times to stayin' outside, but no...

[At this point John Crimley arrived home from work and joined the conversation.]

So you found that some of the churches were able to give you a hand?

Constance: Well yeah, a couple of Baptist churches helped us out. They really helped us out when we needed it. Otherwise we would have really been out in the street. If somebody hadn't helped us out at the police station, we would have really been out in the street.

So you didn't wind up living outside at all?

Constance: No, it worked out okay.

John: Unfortunately, what happened to us, basically I came down to get a job. You know, 'cause you always hear Palm Beach is rich with jobs and the cost of livin' is high and the wages are high in the jobs - better than north. That's one of the reasons why we're here. Where we're at right now, we can't help it, you know, we can't help it, 'cause we got the kids with us. And it's hell - h-e-l-l, tryin' to feed them, me, her, tryin' to make ends meet, man, it's hell. Because the opportunity is not really there because -

I really think because it's not a lack of education, it's not that - I think it's because of the color of the skin. And the population, so many on one side, this side of town, that side of town, then you got the rich side of town over there, and you have middle class, you got middle class mix here. It's basically like, you gotta hump, I mean you really gotta hump here to make it. Like last night, me and my wife was in here, and some chick came up to the window, and she looked average, she was a black lady, she looked like she was on drugs, but then again you can't say, she might have some kind of sickness about herself. She said she had a four-month-old baby, and her baby needed food, and she lived in a rooming house, she needed $5 because the lady was gonna let her stay there for $5 if she brings her food there. So we gave her what we had, baby food, you know. And I felt kind of bad.

Constance: Yeah, I did too.

John: You know, 'cause we doin' bad, but fortunately I'm workin'. She's doin' worse than we are. Looking at that, that really made me feel, wow. I said, "There's somebody really here who's doin' worse than I am."

Constance: That really tore me up when I saw that; it did.

John: And that really hurts, it hurt, it really hurt. God, what can I do? I can't give her the money because the money we have is for us to survive off of. If I give her our last that we've got, we won't have. I felt like that - to give it to her - but I thought about my kids first. This came first in my mind, my kids. I said, no, we'd be better off giving her some food, baby food, and that's it. She walked on down the street. I couldn't give her no money 'cause she'd probably use it for drugs; I thought about that more than anything else. It was a heartbreaking situation at the time. I felt for her. I really felt for her. I really did. You know, what you see here, man, is unbelievable, honest. It's like this hotel over here, you see this hotel over here? I'll show you. [indicates a small hotel across the street]

Constance: I thought I'd seen everything. [laughs]

John: You oughta see something. You see this hotel over here, now this hotel is vacant, it's what you call squatters. It was vacant, somebody bought it out. People went in there on their own and lived there, they're squatters. And I'm wondering, are you allowed to do that? And you are allowed to do that, you are allowed to go in a vacant building and live.

But it's not legal, is it?

John: I don't know if it's legal or not, but the police can't do nothing about it.

Constance: I've always wondered why the police haven't done nothing about it.

John: They can't do nothing about it but call it vagrancy or trespassing. That's it. What can you do? You can't arrest a person 'cause he ain't got no place to stay. The only thing you can do is help. But you know somethin', in our case, we had a lot of help, we had a lot of help, by us bein' here, we got a lot of help, by me talkin', seekin' and findin', not beggin', helpin' yourself to get out of this one situation and get in one situation to get out of that one. You try to get on your feet. It's like crawlin' before you walk, it's like that, that's how we got here. You know what I'm sayin'? And it ain't easy, man, 'cause the kids go hungry, the old lady, she's yappin' all the time because she want it better, and you can't help it because of the situation that you're in. You know, you're out there every day workin' for the labor pool, and you're makin' *peanuts,* you're actually makin' peanuts, you're makin' twenty-somethin' dollars a day, let alone your kids gotta eat. You gotta eat, your wife's gotta eat, gotta have a roof over your head. You put all that together, it cause frustration. Sometimes with a lot of other people it cause crime. "Man, I'll break in this house and see what I can find and go steal it." It causes that, it causes anything. But I guess if your head is level, you gotta take it every day, and just pray to God that you can find work every day, and do your best to try to use the system as much as possible as you can to get by. Because there's so many systems that people don't even know about, that they don't even use to help theirselves.

Constance: You might have to have a job...

John: Some people don't know that, honey. It comes from the federal government anyway, but they don't know it. They'd rather help another country than help us, 'cause they helpin' Russia now, and we need help, *we* need help. We're hungry, we need help. They helpin' them over there. So we got poverty over here, man. Look at this thing here, you gotta *look* at it, you gotta *look* at it.

'Cause after last night, man, that was it.

Constance: That really hit us hard, didn't it?

John: Yeah, it got me too, but I wouldn't let you know about it.

Constance: It got me though. It really did.

John: But then again, the drugs can be avoided, that can be avoided. That can be avoided. That's their fault. I won't feel sorry for them 'cause they doin' it to themselves. They got a choice: do it or don't do it. And they chose that, so I don't feel sorry for 'em. I feel sorry for the ones that don't have, and tryin' to get somethin' for themselves, and every time they try so hard, the deeper they go under. The deeper they go under, believe me, they goin' deeper and they fall right on their face, and they try so hard. I know a guy now, he's my friend, he's livin' in his car. He says it's cheaper.

He'll buy a can of sardines or he'll buy a can of tuna fish, buy some mayonnaise and eat out of a can. That's it. He's content. He's drivin' around, buy a little gas, and he's gone. He works days, he's content. But why? I don't understand. I mean having a roof over your head, and family, and a good job - what happened to the old good U-S of A, the good old American style of living?

Constance: It went.

John: Is it so populated that we can't help each other? With everybody at each other's throats, or racism? What for? Why? I can see the answer now. When I looked out that window, saw that girl last night, I saw the answer to everything, right there. That just got me. This is it, huh? A lot of people don't like each other. A lot of people don't like each other 'cause a lot of people got money, don't wanna give to - it's like the people I work for. They got so much money, they could spend $3 million and don't know it. Three million dollars, that ain't nothin', that's pocket change, pocket change. I don't understand that. And all these poor folks. I asked the boss, "Did you give to charity?" "Charity? What charity? We're the charity." You're gonna die and leave it behind. Somebody else'll get it; they gonna die and leave it behind.

You mentioned earlier that you thought it was hard to get jobs down here because of racism...

John: Most likely there's some racism, plus if you're qualified for a job you're overqualified because they don't wanna pay you what you ask for. Basically, they'll pay you $4.50, up to $5. That will take care of a teenager goin' to high school, but that cannot take care of family or single person at all. And I think racism is all around, it's here, but it's here - it's bad here.

Here in Palm Beach County?

John: It's here, bad, very bad.

Do you think it's worse here than up north?

John: Boston, like Boston, I've been to Boston. It's worse, it's worse. Connecticut is not that bad at all. Connecticut's a good place to live. Or New York is okay. Pennsylvania's okay, Ohio's fine. Virginia is okay. North Carolina, you got a few rednecks in there, but you can get along with those. But you go down to Georgia, uh-uh, that's where it starts - and Tennessee. Georgia and Florida, if you're black you stay back, all the way back. If you got education, you're the last one to be hired and the first one to be fired. Or that's the way I feel about it; I just see it. But I ain't gonna blame it on bein' black or bein' white, it's just the way of the world, how the world works right now 'cause, man, this is poverty. I used to watch some programs - Walter Cronkite - where people used to stand in soup lines, with loaves of bread, and the war was about to go on, but this is modern time now, this is similar to it.

They talk about go to school and get a education. You still got a problem then. See, I know people that got a good education - master's degrees - they're out there on the streets. I went to 7-Eleven around the corner to get a cup of coffee, I seen a girl gettin' up off the ground [imitates someone yawning and stretching]. I said, "I can't believe this." Yeah, she was gettin' up off the ground, combin' her hair, yawnin', and the mattress is right there, and you could see where she's sleepin' at. Right around the corner, at 7-Eleven. I said, "Jesus, what's wrong here?" Right in the alley way, and you can see, she's got her clothes there, and she's got her comb. And she was dressed decent. She was dressed decent; I freaked out on that, buddy. She was about 30 years old. And she had clean clothes on. She's a human being, outside, sleepin' outside. It's good to sleep outside, but in a tent, it's fun. But outside in the open like that, where somebody can come and do what they wanna do to you...she had nowhere to go, no help. Whose gonna help her? These people out here in the streets ain't gonna help her unless she's got five bucks to do drugs, take her to bed, you know what I'm sayin'?

Were you able to get help from any social service agencies when you started having trouble?

John: Yes, Traveler's Aid helped us out a great deal. Traveler's Aid only will help you at least for two weeks. They give you time enough - at least fortunately, they gave us time 'cause I have a family here. If I was single, they wouldn't have gave me time of day. Tell me go to the Salvation Army and stay one night in the Salvation Army, and you ain't got nowhere else to go. Either you go to a mission somewhere, you go into all these missions, all these places, you're in a circle. I guess what a human being is tryin' to do is tryin' to seek shelter and go to work, most of them are. The Salvation Army, no. The Lord's Place is about the best place I know, and I'd like to know who's runnin' it. If it's Catholic (The Lord's Place is run by Catholic lay people), they're doin' a good job. I think they're doin' a good job about it. You get some churches, don't give a hoot about you because the way you are, because they treat you like trash, and you're human. You got a lot of people out here go to these churches in need, and then they treat you like dogs, then they treat you like dogs. There's no reason for that, but that's the way it is. And other agencies we went to - the Salvation Army, we went to Traveler's Aid.

Constance: We went to the police station, they helped us out.

John: They helped us more because of the churches, because of the religious thing, they helped us out, they really helped us out, and that was it.

Constance: We were looking for emergency housing, but they didn't have any available.

John: If you know the feelin', you know the feelin'. I can't describe the feelin'. I can't describe it, but it's scary. If you're gonna die or somethin', but you know you're gonna die, but you gotta go ahead and die, it's like that, you get that gut feelin', butterflies, because you know you gotta worry about the next day, and that hurts, 'cause you can't get where you're goin' the next day. It's scary, man, it is scary. That's why I feel sorry for a lot of people in a worse position than I am, 'cause I know what they goin' through, 'cause I felt that same fear. Some of 'em can be helped; some of 'em can't. Some of 'em can help themselves. The ones that can't help theirself, they need to seek help, they really need to seek help. You got black and white together, on the same road, and they're both not gettin' ahead. Palm Beach got it bad, with the transient mess, just up and down the street all night long, 'cause they ain't got nowhere to go. They got nowhere to go. You can go to jail. That's a good place to go. You do some crime or hit somebody up side the head, even go rob somebody. Boy, you get free meals, whoa, you get free meals, you get to get your fingers printed, and you might stay two weeks, you know? That's how they play it.

There should be more places here to help these people, stop these transients from coming through Florida, stop the population. I know they can't do nothin' to stop the population. There's gotta be a place to help these people. Okay, remember the refugees comin' from Baghdad, went over to Kuwait? Remember that? Hundreds of thousands of people - that's similar to what's goin' on here in Florida. And you know what they're doin'? They're turnin' these people away. Absolutely, they're turnin' these people away. Oh, yes, they are, look at 'em out there. Some of them turned us away too, like Salvation Army, they turned us away.

Why?

John: Because of my family. Well, the Salvation Army got rules and regulations, but their rules and regulations stinks, and it stinks where their noses don't belong, I mean it really *stinks*.

You mean they wouldn't let you in because you didn't have ID?

John: We got IDs, I'm just not allowed to see my family. But boy you're full of it when you tell me I can't see my family. But I can understand their rules, but you can't tell me I can't hold my baby in my arms. You're full of it; you ready to get hurt then. And they don't like me for that, and I don't like them, and I don't like their organization, period. That's their business, but I would never recommend nobody to go there, not that Salvation Army.

They wanted to split you up?

John: I guess because of the sex thing, because they have to split people up, the transients and the transient ladies, and could you imagine, if they put together, there'd be all kind of mess there? But families, you can't split a family up no matter how hard you try. You cannot split a family up. You cannot. You cannot do it. I mean you cannot discipline a grown man from his family. You cannot do it. And they wrong for that.

A lot of people think we should have more programs to help homeless people and others think we're already doing enough. What do you think about all that?

Constance: They're not doing enough.

John: They're not doin' enough. The reason why they're not doin' enough is because we've got too many homeless people. It shows for itself.

Constance: I think they're makin' it hard for certain ones to get in there. There's so many rules and stipulations, they're makin' it hard for certain ones to get in there.

John: You're talkin' about the federal government. The federal government, they open the door for people, low-income people, whatever they want to call it, to help themselves, like trainin' programs. I remember when they had trainin' programs, like, you remember CETA? But they cut all that. They cut that. It got so bad, now it's gonna be all over. Pretty soon, there's gonna be so many people over there on Palm Beach sleepin' on the rich people's front doorstep, beggin' for bread. It's gonna get that way unless the federal government helps these people, feed 'em, give em a house, give 'em somewhere to live.

Constance: They need to change some of their rules and regulations, too. They need to change.

John: I can understand it, but give these people somewhere to live, give 'em some hope, some kind of somethin'. Give them somethin'. This is old sweet America. What happened?

Eleanor Collier, 39, is a native of Egg Harbor, New Jersey. She was interviewed at the family shelter run by the Orlando Union Rescue Mission, where she was staying with her children: Ebony NaCole, 12, and Ivan NaThaniel, 8.

What brought you down to Florida?

Well, my husband died, and I wanted to relocate, start brand new with the kids; I have two kids by him. So I flew down last month, and I looked around. I'm a union member - construction - so I found out I could transfer my union book, come down here and work. And living is pretty cheap, so I decided to go back home, and go back and wait for my kids. So we caught a train down the third of April. We had situated, we had some place to go, 'cause I did that when I first flew down. But by the train bein' late getting here, it made us late getting to the apartment, so it was closed, so we ended up in a hotel on Colonial Drive - Days Inn. So, kids didn't get to school that day, so next day I told them they could stay home for the day, they could swim in the pool and everything - they wanted to swim.

So then we went out shopping to K Mart and we was robbed of all our money. We got back to the hotel, all I had was two gold chains of my husband's; he had two gold chains with a medallion on it. So, the chambermaid, I asked her, if she knew how to get in touch with the police, report what had happened, 'cause all I wanted to do at that point was just go back home. So I called the police, and they told me to call the Salvation Army, and they said wasn't anything they could do. And so then the chambermaids kept working with me to call different people, and I called here. Well I didn't have any money to get here. I kept explaining that to them. I was about, maybe six miles from here - I guess, about that, that's what the girl said. So they told me that I was welcome to come here - the two kids - but I explained to them I couldn't get here because we had our suitcases, stuff that we had brought down with us, everything else would have been here in like three days, and we had mailed that, you know, because I knew I had the apartment. So my daughter went to the store, found a pawn shop, she came back and she told me. So I ended up pawnin' my chains, my husband's chains, calling a cab and we got here. The cab wouldn't even take the fare once he found out what happened to us. So that's what brought us here. And we were allowed to stay. Durin' the course of tryin' to get the apartment, with no money now, I ran into problems, so there was different type agencies that wanted to help me. The one agency, HRS, the guy gave me the run around; he wanted this, that and the other from the landlord, and I brought it to him, he wasn't satisfied with her wording. So he wanted a lease; I explained to him I couldn't have a lease when I haven't paid any rent, but told him he was welcome to call her, but he still gave me the run around, one thing led to another, where she decided she wouldn't rent to me because she didn't want the headache. So that, really, we have to stay here until I get out of here, so we're really here now. I'm looking for work. The only thing I have goin' in my favor right now is bein' here, and my husband's Social Security for my two kids. So we're looking forward to that so we can try to make an adjustment. I mean, it's okay here, you know, three square meals, someplace to lay your head, a room and everything, but I'm very independent, used to having my own, providing for my children. So that's why I'm uptight.

How long have you been here?

Since the Sixth of April. (The interview was conducted on April 30.)
Have your children been with you the whole time?
Uh-huh. That's why it was so hard because, had I been by myself, I would have hitchhiked back home, seriously, seriously. The best part about Florida I guess, to be honest, is like, all I thought I could get was just some type of assistance maybe to go back home. I had no idea they had places like this place here. In Jersey I know they have a rescue mission where you go to eat and leave, I know that for sure because I've worked there in Atlantic City. But I never expected all this, you know, a roof over our head, a room, three good meals a day, clothing if you need it - but we have our own - but still if you want it it's there for you. All weekend they usually do things with the kids; counselors take them to the beach or something. Some of the counselors will drive around helping you look for jobs, taking you to jobs or doctors or hospitals or wherever you have to go. So they help you here a lot; they really do. I never expected this; all I thought I'd get help with was maybe staying a few days and trying to get a way back home and that was it. It surprised me; I can't believe it.
You gave up your house or apartment up north?
Yes, I sold everything because we knew we were gonna relocate. I was married to the man 15 years, and it was time for a change. We had a hard time adjusting to his death; he's only been dead nine months. We still have a hard time adjusting to his death, and I just felt like we had to get away. The kids went through a change in school, I went through a change, we're still going through a change. And we don't want to forget him, but we want to be left alone. And every time we felt like, great, this week is really a good week, somebody would bring him up or, you know, we wanted to just leave him rest, and we couldn't do it there because 15 years of our life was right there. So we just felt like we had to get away.
Had you lived all your life in Egg Harbor?
Oh, New Jersey, within the area, those small towns, uh-huh.
What kind of work do you do?
Construction labor, 11 years, labor local 415, Atlantic City, New Jersey.
How did you get robbed when you came down?
Well, we were at a K Mart, and my zipper of my pocketbook, it's like, it's messed up. And we were tryin' on things because everything is so different down here, and it's cheaper. And we was just into what we were doing; I laid my pocketbook down, and we thought about it, we went back, pocketbook's gone. Not my whole pocketbook, my wallet. Because see, it's like, inside my pocketbook I have like, identification here [demonstrates], I have this part for this, that and the other; the thing that was taken had all our money in there.

So were you able to come right here or did you have to stay in another shelter or outside first?

No, I thought I was at first. I didn't want to part with my husband's chains; I pawned them, I'm gonna get 'em back. But I ended up pawning them just to get here. They said they would have had, that particular evening, I think there was one counselor, and they said if there had been a second counselor somebody could have came and picked me up. But there was only the one and they couldn't leave the place unattended.

How are your children coping with being here?

Oh, they're adjusting, it's just that, my children and myself, we're not used to being confined. It's not so much being confined, it's like [sighs] we do things differently, you know, but here we have to abide by the rules and regulations, okay, so, you know, kids. [laughs] My kids have to go to bed at a certain time, where maybe I'd leave them up a little bit later, or, you know, just different things, or, they've made friends from school but their friends can't stay here because it's a mission, but they're coping with it, they're coping.

How about you?

Oh, adjusting to it I guess, that would be the word. Since I was 18 I've been out on my own, very independent, I've always had. I call this rock bottom; I've never been this low down before, really down, where, you know, I'm a homeless person. I've never been out there like that. I've worked two jobs sometimes; I've never been like this.

How is your job hunting going?

Well, construction, that's what I'm in. They have a $10 million contract at Disney World, but when the war went on and everything it put us in recession. So my business agent was told that was happening; he said I have to wait sort of until we're out of recession. But there is a $10 million contract, expansion at Disney World; once that start I'll be able to work. The only thing I don't like about that, there's a big difference in pay. In Jersey I'd make $15 an hour; down here it's $9.97. In Jersey my overtime was double time, which is $30 an hour; here it's time-and-a-half. But I can work with it.

So your union has a local down here?

We're international, uh-huh. But for right now, like I know there's a freeze on everything, so I can go on out looking for just anything to do just to have something to do while the kids are in school. I'm supposed to go back to Ramada Inn Friday - housekeeping - that's a big drop in pay. I also have a hotel license with the casinos. In Atlantic City they start you off at $7.55 an hour, and their top pay down here is $4.55 an hour, so I'm taking a *big* drop in pay. But the kids are - even though we're confined, like here, we don't have our freedom, like in our own apartment or own house, you know what I'm saying - they're a little happier here. There's nobody to remind them of, "Well your dad this, your dad that." And nobody really knows unless they tell them. So they're adjusting better by being here. We just got a little sick because of the heat. [laughs] We have to get used to the heat, but other than that we're okay.

Do you still have family up north?

Uh-huh. I come from a family of 10, my mother's 69, my dad's 79, everybody's still living.

Do you have any family down here?

No...I love my family, but I wanted to just like make a new start for me and the kids. We'll go back to visit, but not to live again; I wouldn't go back, there's so many memories. It's a lot of good memories, but we just wanted to get away.

What is the worst part of being thrown into this situation?

Well, children don't always get along, okay, and I'm protective of my children, so if I was in my own place, Ivan would have more freedom, but here it's like you try to prevent a problem, if you see something starting to happen you try to stop it. So I'm more protective of Ebony and Ivan, the answer is always no, you can't place your kids here with me 'cause I don't feel like going through no changes, no headaches with other parents or with counselors, just sit here, you know, because Ivan's hyperactive, he like to run, he's just really an active child. That's about it, you know, coping.

Are the other people here good about looking out for each other, taking care of each other?

I think so because when I came here I didn't know anything about anything, and everybody's, "Well, do this, do that, go here, go there, we'll show you." So I think so, uh-huh, I really think so.

What would have happened if you hadn't been able to come here?

Oooh. [laughs] I definitely wouldn't have stayed at the Salvation Army because they told me that we could stay there, but we'd have to be there like four in the afternoon I think, and be out like six o'clock in the morning; okay, so I'm thinking ahead, I'm like, my kids have to go to school, how am I gonna do that? Plus I had like a couple suitcases and a box with me; couldn't put it in storage, I didn't have any money. So I probably would have ended up - I brought a leather coat, which was on sale at $300 - probably ended up selling that, tryin' to pay some money to carry me back to New Jersey. I definitely wouldn't have stayed there. The only problem, I got my Social Security check to follow when we came back here because I knew we didn't want to live in Jersey, and here, the kids liked it better, just being warm, because when we left, our winter coats, we got down here off the train [laughs] you know it was like, "Mom, it's hot." So I would have came back. But I would have had to get out of here fast because their dad was always strict about education, get that education, and they had been out of school, you know, and they had to get back in, and I knew that. So we definitely would have got out of here some kind of way.

Have you had to deal with any other social service agencies? You mentioned you talked to HRS. How did they treat you?

Well, the food stamp part, that went fine. She just had to verify everything that I was saying about I did live in Jersey, different things like that, she found out I wasn't lying, and the only income I had was Social Security. She was okay. It was just that I didn't like the other guy, what do you call him? Going in for financial aid, trying to get some type of assistance, I didn't like where he was coming from. He just about said to me that he thought I was lyin', and he didn't say it like that, but that's what he was saying, and I said to him, "All you have to do is just pick up the phone; everything I'm saying can be verified, just pick up the phone."

He was very negative toward me, you know, *very* negative, really, and I felt bad about him running me back and forth because I'm very independent and he made me feel like I was begging him, and I felt bad because I never had to beg for anything before. I felt like I was his equal. I'm a high school graduate, a year of college; I mean I was his equal. First of all, I felt bad even bein' there, you know, and he just treat me like, he's like, "Well, you know, we have people coming here every day saying this, that and the other." I'm like, "Look, I'm me, I can't speak for everybody, all you have to do is pick up the phone, verify everything I'm saying, I have no reason to lie to you, I hate even being here, I'm forced here, I have no choice but to be here." But I didn't like his attitude toward me, because really he was callin' me a liar. So to be honest I don't think I really would have gotten help from him, you know, really, if the landlord would have done everything, I don't think. He'd have found another reason not to give me the moneys. The money wouldn't have came to me, it would have gone directly to the apartment manager, but I don't think he would have did it. He was a black guy, like me. Sometimes black people get ahead in life, forget where they come from. They uppity, and you see a lot of that here, you do, you see a lot of it here, and it turns me off, because no matter what I never forget where I come from.

You say you see a lot of it here. Do you mean in Florida?

In Florida, black people in a position where, it's like, they look down, you understand? It's like the guy was lookin' down on me like he had that authority, "Well I could give her this if I want to; I can turn her down. Well, let me turn her down, she doesn't sound right." He was judgin' me by what somebody else had did, and I felt like he didn't know me. All he had to do was pick up the phone, call, see if I'm on Social Security, see if I came down a month before that, flew down, you know, but he wouldn't even do that. I told him he could even pick up the phone, call the landlord, the one that was gonna rent to me. He told me that was my job, so he was, you know, really...

So you didn't get any assistance from HRS?

No. But like I said, I have another apartment in mind.

I'm gonna try to get that, but I'm gonna need some assistance to get in because I have to get furniture and everything. With the first apartment, I took a one-bedroom, it would have been a one-bedroom, because I could have had it furnished, and I could have like worked my way into doin' everything else, you know? Savin', then getting furniture. So this one here, it's like no furniture, so I'm gonna go back to them, try to get assistance again, and if he starts that same negative attitude, then I'm educated enough, what I'm going to do is ask to speak to his supervisor, keep going higher and higher and higher and higher, because, you know, he can't judge me 'cause of what somebody else did, he don't even know me, and all he had to do was pick up the phone to verify everything I said to see if I was lying. He wouldn't even do that.

Keith Lewis, 58, is a native of Jackson, Michigan. He was interviewed in Jacksonville at the Trinity Rescue Mission.

How long have you been in Florida?

I've been in Florida for about two months.

What brought you down?

Well, I went to see my brother, and now I'm on my way back. I'm just down to visit him, and I broke down; now I'm heading back.

Oh, your car broke down?

Yeah, that's why I'm here. [laughs]

How long have you been here in Jacksonville?

I've been here just about two days. Tomorrow will be my third. I'm tryin' to leave.

How are you getting back? Are you going back to Michigan?

Yeah, I'm going by thumb; that's the only way I can go. That's the only way to go. Now, how long it's gonna take me, I don't know. I'll be lucky if I can make it in three days.

Your car just died on you?

Yeah.

What kind of work do you do?

Construction.

Do you have a place to stay in Michigan?

Yeah.

What have you been doing since you wound up here in Jacksonville?

I haven't done a thing. I checked out a couple of jobs, but I'm leaving tomorrow.

Do you have a house or an apartment in Michigan?

I have a house.

I don't have any money. I got rolled.

When did that happen?

It happened yesterday.

How much money did you lose?

About a hundred and eighty bucks.

Oh, that would have been enough to get you back up there.

Oh yeah, that would have been enough to get me back up there. There was nothin' I could do about it. There was two guys. There was nothin' I could do about it.

Were you robbed out on the street somewhere?

Yeah, two against one. What am I going to do?

Chapter Four

Economic Catastrophe: Caught in the Mix

The descent into homelessness is, as many homeless people point out, simply a matter of dollars and cents. In a society where steady employment is increasingly difficult to find and traditional family structures are unraveling, the loss of employment is often enough to precipitate a financial disaster that quickly leads to homelessness. Additionally, the lack of affordable housing in many areas makes it difficult for minimum wage workers and other low-income people to find adequate shelter even when they are working.

A.B. McCullum, 45, is a native of Heidelberg, Mississippi. He was interviewed at the men's shelter run by the Coalition for the Homeless of Orlando. He lived in Titusville, Florida, for many years before moving to Orlando.

How long have you been here at the shelter?
Two months.
How long have you been in Orlando?
A little over a year.
How did you wind up in Orlando? Did you come here for a job?
Well, I working at Martin Marietta...
I got stopped, gave me a ticket for drivin' without a driver's license, so I got a problem with the law, put me on probation a couple times, I don't know, I wind up in jail at 33rd (Street) for six months. My wife and I were separated, so I decided to stay over here, restart my life all over again.

You can't get your job back now?

No, not the one I lost, no, I don't think I can, and I haven't had a steady job since then. Well I had one...I didn't have any transportation, and I had to walk five or six miles every night - midnight shift...work, eight, ten, maybe twelve hours; it just didn't work out, so I haven't had a full-time job since then.

Before you lost your job, where were you living, and what was your living situation?

Well, I was livin' in Titusville. I've got a home over there. I built the house in 1970, and, my wife and I, we raised five daughters. And over the years, you know, our marriage just didn't work out, so I'm over here trying to regain my life. She over there.

We're supposed to be goin' through a divorce, whatever; I wish she make up her mind and do what she want to do. That's the reason why I've been homeless; I'm over here. The work force is, I don't know, I guess it might pick up, but it been kind of bad. Then you have a lot of people from up north working coming down here; that don't help none either, working down the labor pool or whatever. I noticed that a lot of people - either they're goin' back up north or wherever they come from - some people are doin' more camping out - but I can see the difference in here; it's not full up like it used to be, because they used to have to turn a lot of people down when it real cold. They don't have to do that anymore. So I can see it everywhere that it's been slacking off. About the work, I don't know, it might pick up. I'm trying to get a full-time job. I'm expecting to get one; I've been interviewed. I go back tomorrow to find out definitely - I guess I'll find out definitely - I'm supposed to be getting a job downtown.

Where were you living before you came here?

Oh, I was livin' with a guy out on West Church Street.

I was in a room there, just a room. And I paying some - he went up to $70 a week - just a room.

So you didn't just get out of jail recently?

I got out on October the ninth of last year.

After you left the other place, did you start staying here right away?

Yeah, I started staying here.

Have you ever had to stay outside?

Well, I don't know if it's appropriate for me to say - a couple of nights I did stay in the park. [laughs] Well, as I was working out at the labor pool too, a couple of nights I did sleep in the car because they have a labor pool car they take people out with who are working for them; you come in late at night, I sleep in the car. But it's not too good and everything, there's people come around and steal stuff from you; I lost a watch and a jacket behind me. That's when I made up my mind to have to find something - a shelter. In the end, sometimes you come in the shelter, you're still missing clothes and stuff. I just thank the Lord that he saved my life, nothing serious happened to me, you know.

Have you always been able to get enough food?

Oh yes, you go around to different places. I ain't had no problem as far as food, you know. You might have to walk here and walk there, but it's worth it.

What about clothes?

Well, clothing has been pretty fair. You might not be able to get exactly what you wanted, but they keep you clean, you can keep clean. A lot of people be giving stuff - clothes - you can keep clean. They let you take a shower, whatever. A lot of people go down to the Salvation Army and take a shower.

But in here, you got to live in here to take a shower - I think - I'm pretty sure. So, it works out, you've got to get up and do something for yourself. Nobody going to tell you to wash; ain't nobody going to bathe you. You know what I'm saying? You know where food at, and they giving it away, and you've got to walk and get it. If you're that lazy, then you don't need to eat. Some days you might not feel like walking. That's up to you. You either eat, or walk, or what. This is the first time I've ever been in - whatever some people say - soup line or homeless people 'cause I always had a decent job and had my own home, a car, my family. This is the first time I've ever experienced this, and it's been kind of hard on me.

I think a lot of other people should come by and experience this - people who have had it so well all their life. We've got a lot of very intelligent people out here in the street. Everybody out here ain't no bum. Everybody out here ain't high on drugs. This is people just got caught in the mix. Very, some really intelligent, educated people out here. I was surprised at the amount of people that are real educated and real smart, very intelligent people out here. It really, man, has helped me survive, knowin' that I'm not the only one out here that used to live decent. You know what I'm saying? Because, you know, if I had been the only one out here that lived pretty decent, and then turn around and lose everything and be out here, and I hadn't run across nobody else, but when you run across other people that had more than you had, and they out here with you, got more education than you have, and *they* out here with you, so that has kind of helped to build your morale up.

Have you been applying for jobs regularly?

I had an interview last week, and they keep telling me to come back, come back, you know. They haven't had a chance to go through and check out my application, I suppose - down here on Church Street, down here at Church Station downtown.

Have you found that some employers lose interest when you give a shelter as your address?

Right, I don't know whether it's true or not. I couldn't really say, but a lot of people do feel that way. They really do. They put down the shelter, "Oh, no, we ain't going to hire you." Yeah, I've heard a lot of guys say that. Now, whether it's true, I don't know. I don't know, it could be a factor. I think somebody should check into it, really, I really do. Because it seems to mean that only jobs shelter people can get is the old labor pool; you work today, you might not work for two weeks. You know what I'm saying? Unless you find a time when you're kissing behind, you might get two or three days. Some people don't know how to get out.

If you're all right with the man - the dispatcher - you can go out just about every day. If you're not - if he don't like the way you look - you might not go out. That's the way it is. Yeah, the labor pool is screwed up man, *bad*. 'Cause I'll tell you this, me and another friend of mine, we went up there for a whole week straight, we didn't miss a day, every morning, 5:30, we there. This guy, he had plenty of work that morning, and he had some guys come in there - just comin' off the street, filling out applications, and he turned around and put them to work, and we've been, I have worked for him before. My application has been in. We stayed after noon, and he sent them out to work around nine o'clock that morning. He see guys just dragging in: "Hey man, come here. What, you don't want to work for me?" And we beggin' to work. He wouldn't send us out, man. I can't believe this. So I asked the man, I said, "What's the problem?" "Well, see, I know we got him and so and so and so and so and so on; I know they going to do me a good job."

Shit, they should get rid of them labor pools.

The minimum wage went up - $4.25 - and what the labor pools did now, was see, they used to charge $1.50 for transportation, so they doubled the transportation since they have to pay you $4.25. What kind of wage are you bringing back, man? It ain't no good. Poor man just can't *make* it out here like that. You can't get nowhere with those wages, so I'm going to get me a full-time job so I can get away from it. I can't hack it.

How much do you get when you work for the labor pool?

Before April the first the highest they was paying was $4 an hour, and they were taking out withholding tax, they were taking out Social Security, and they were taking out transportation, and I worked for one company, they took out workman's comp. Workman's comp, can you imagine that? Workman's comp, working at a labor pool? I mean I worked twelve hour one day down in Kissimmee; I made $48, I go home with $37, out of $48. That's highway robbery, man. I can't make it. You can't get no decent apartment on that.

Have you ever had any health problems and had to get medical care since you've been homeless?

Well so far I haven't run across that yet. I pray to the Lord that I don't.

With the situation I'm in now, I hope I don't get sick. I *hope* not. I don't want it. That's why I say, I really want to get me a decent job where I can have some kind of insurance benefits, you know, so if I happen to get sick, then I have some insurance to take care of it. I don't want to be sick out here, I hope not.

The shelter is only open at night. What do you do during the day?

Well, we normally just go from labor pool to labor pool. You got about seven or eight right up there on Orange Blossom Trail. You make a routine route every day - go out - we might go out a couple days a week, we might not, you know, whatever. If we don't get a chance to go out, we go to the park, sit around and read, play cards, pass the time away. And you go from churches to churches.

Do the people who are staying here look out for each other?

Well, some people do. You know how it is.

You've got to expect the bad with the good wherever you are. I've lived long enough to know that, in this dirty world, everybody ain't going to be good, so don't even look for it. Everybody ain't going to act right. They ain't gonna talk right.

How do outsiders - people who aren't staying in the shelter - treat you?

Yeah, well, sometimes, like I say, we be out in the park and some of the guys might make a remark to some of the ladies walking through the park, and they make a remark, "Get a job, stop hanging around the park," something like that. Some people think you're just a bum, you ain't trying to work. It's not that. A lot of people try to work, but some days you don't work, sometimes you can't get no work. So what if you can't go? You can't come back here and lay around; you can't come back in until 8:30. So why shouldn't you go sit in the park? It's a park, you know.

It's the only place you've got to go.

Do you go over to Lake Eola?

Sometimes we go to Lake Eola. I go to the library, I go down there sometimes. And then, you know, you catch the bus, walk around sometimes, look for jobs, fill in applications. It's just a regular routine, day by day. People say, "I've got to check on this, I've got to check on this, I've got to check on that."

What about if it's cold or raining?

See that's when it really hurts. A lot of times it rains, you got bad weather, you ain't got nowhere to go. You get up under the shed under the park. You can't come inside here until 8:30.

You've got to sit out there in the fucking bad weather. Or most of the time we try to get in the labor pool. But sometimes on Saturday and Sunday, they close up. Like we have been put out in the rain, I mean it was raining, "Well, brother, we're closing up, no more business today." And they close up, put us *out* in the rain. So that goes to show you how much they care for you. They wait until it's stormin' and rainin' to put us out. So that's right there giving me something to look for. I've got to get away from these labor pools, man. Got to get back on my feet, get me a real job.

If you don't get out before the rain starts, they just put you out. That shows you how much they care for you. You see, really, I think when they really started labor pools I think they did it for mostly for drug addicts, people just really a bum, don't want to do nothing but just make a couple of dollars, get them a pack of cigarettes and a bottle of wine or whatever. I think that's what they started this off with. But a lot of other people got caught up in this, so I think we get treated like the same way. It's really not for no family man at all, to be working in the labor pool; you really just can't make it.

They have to be made up of people just, they know they ain't going to do nothing but just get high every day or buy drugs or buy a bottle of wine or liquor, a couple packs of cigarettes, stuff like that. You see, on the street, that's what a labor pool is for. It ain't for no family man, or nobody that want to have something. It can't be. They taking the money you make, and pay them. If they give you $4 an hour, they making $8 off of you. It's just that simple. And they turn around and charge you for transportation, tax, and all of this - out of *your* part, not out they part, not out of they $4, they take it out of your $4. Shit, how can you make it, man? Oh man, it's a racket.

Do you think it's harder for black guys that are out on the street than for white guys?

I can't answer that because I've seen some white guys out here in bad shape. At least it *looks* like they're in bad shape, I don't know how bad shape they are. Some people, you know, they do that to get by. I can't answer that, not really. Well, I know a lot of black guys, they get pissed off at the labor pool down there, thinking maybe there's partiality, they feel like the man be sending more white guys out than black guys. I don't know, man, you just can't satisfy everybody. If a white man would say, like, there's more blacks goin' out than whites it goin' to be controversial and, you know what I'm saying, man, you just can't satisfy everybody.

But this is what I was talking about, the day that man did us, it wasn't just race. He just plain overlooked us, period. He didn't give a damn who come in there. I don't know, sometimes people just look at you and they don't like you. It's a hard situation to say. I can't really answer that question. There's a lot of white folks out here. If they ain't in bad shape they be sure enough looking like it. A man will have his wife and kids, homeless. I'm glad I don't have to do that.

It's bad enough on a man, but when you have your wife and kids, it's terrible. It's tough on everybody, I would say. It's tough on everybody. You always gonna have somebody get a better break than others, I don't care what race you are. Somebody will always get a better break. But sometimes people just take a liking to you, give you break; some people don't get no breaks. That's life.

Do the police ever bother you?

To be honest with you, the cops haven't really hassled me. I've heard a lot of people say that the cops really hassle a lot of people around here. I don't know.

Sometimes at the park some of the guys will be drinking beer and stuff, and of course you're not allowed to drink beer in the park. So a dude will have to pour out his beer. I've seen them pour out a whole quart of beer that wasn't even open. And that's the law, so, but you know, you get pissed off a lot of times. But what really going on, that concert they've got going on down there, man, they doing everything in the book down there.

Where?

That concert they got down there.

Oh, that concert or whatever it is?

Yeah, concert. What they name? Great Me Dead, or whatever it is?

Grateful Dead?

Yeah, yeah they doin' everything in the book down there. [laughs] You know. They've been taking quite a few downtown lately though.

Have you been able to get food stamps?

I just started. I just got 'em back this morning.

They took me through a lot of changes too.

Was it hard to apply?

Well I ain't had it too bad since I been in here. I ain't had it too bad. I used to get it once before, and I just stopped gettin' them because it was taking too much hassle. But since I've been back here I decided to try again, so I got them to sign the paper here and everything, and it went through pretty good, but they want to call here, they called here but wasn't nobody here, nobody here to answer the phone. Somebody got to verify that I'm homeless.

It's a hassle.

Has being homeless influenced your religious beliefs in any way?

Well, I'll put it to you like this here. I raised in a church, and I've been religious all my life. And I have been out of church sometimes, you know, back in church, or whatever. But I believe in Christ, and always have and always will, see? Some people read the Bible more, but when you have more time you just pick the chance what you want to go for. I read more since I have more time; I read the Bible more. When I was in jail I read the Bible more. I guess it make you think sometime, when your life really falls down, when you're used to living at a certain amount of level, and all of a sudden the road will slip up on you, I guess it give you something to think about.

Some people, they kill themselves. I think the people that do that never really had Christ in their heart from the beginning. And I thank God for my mamma and daddy, they brought me up the right way. It doesn't matter how hard the road gets, but you don't forget about Jesus Christ. He will lift you up. It makes a difference. When somebody take a 45 and blow his brains out, he didn't have Christ, no way.

I never thought I'd be down like this, but I had to really search myself, you know.

Well, if you don't have no more questions, I'm going to have to run. I've got a few things I want to do before they snatch us back in here. I enjoyed talking to you.

Patricia Servo, 41, is a native of Long Island, N.Y. She was interviewed in Pompano Beach at The Lord's Place, a family shelter, where she was staying with her daughter, Gina, 4.

How long have you been in Florida?

About 15 years.

What brought you down to Florida?

Just to strike out on my own, become independent, get away from the parents.

How long have you been here at The Lord's Place?

A little over two months.

Where were you living before that?

Well, right before this we were in an apartment for one month. We were living in an apartment, and my relatives had helped to set us up in an apartment, but I couldn't afford to support us there. Before that we had a house up in Deerfield (Deerfield Beach); I was married, and that's where we lived for a year, in Deerfield.

You're not married?

I'm still married. [laughs] But the marriage did break up, yes, we're separated.

How did you lose having a regular place to live?

Well, it happened really quite fast, had a large mortgage payment, car payment [laughs], you name it, and I only was working part-time, and I couldn't pay the bills by myself, and I wasn't getting any help from anyone to help pay them. Some people did try to chip in. When they turned my water off, a fellow paid my water bill for me, a friend, but, you know, it just got to the point where we just had to get out of there and leave the house and try to get to an apartment, find something that I could support the two of us. But it was impossible to do on the salary that I make, and times aren't too good right now, it's hard to find full-time work. Even if you do, if you're not trained in anything, you know, a professional job, you really don't make a lot of money to be able to afford rent and so forth.

Had you been working part-time for a long time?

Yes, for years, I've always worked actually, only took one year off when my daughter was born, and then worked in the restaurant business. And it's hard when you have a child to work the hours that they demand in the restaurant business, you know. I was in restaurant management at one time. Right now that's difficult for me to do; you have to work nights, weekends, swing shift, and end up paying more in child care [laughs] or, you know, almost as much in child care as you make. So you just don't ever seem to be able to come out ahead. It's very difficult. I wanted to go to school. I can go to school; I can get a grant to go to school, but I have the same problem, you know, child care.

Was the fact that you and your husband were no longer living together a factor, going from two incomes to one?

Right, well his was the major income, of course, uh-huh. I had had some money of my own but I used everything that I had to pay our bills and to help...[sighs]

At one time I was self-reliant, and I did have money of my own, but through the marriage that disappeared, and my part of helping out, and it was gone. And when it was gone, he was gone [laughs] with it, no more money, no more marriage. And that's where we ended up.

Did you lose your house or were you able to sell it?

Finally it was sold; the bank settled, made a settlement on it, just so I didn't go through foreclosure, so it was sold. But I didn't make any money on it. I lost everything. The $25,000 that I put down to buy the house, I lost that money 'cause it was sold for a lot less than what I paid for it. I paid like $102,000 for it and they sold it for like $85,000. And they settled on that, the bank made a settlement.

Is that typical of Deerfield Beach? Are real estate prices declining here?

I believe everywhere, yes. With the war broke out, it was just - there weren't even people comin' to look at the house, you know.

And you had to sell it in a hurry?

Well, it was either sell it or the bank would foreclose on it, and if the bank foreclosed, of course, that goes on your credit record, and not only that, but if they sell it in an auction then they can come after you for the rest of the money; they'll place a judgment against you for the balance. So this way I won't have anybody there coming after me. I still have a lot of other bills to be cleared up, a lot.

So you had to leave the house and then you went somewhere else temporarily?

Yes, I rented an apartment in Pompano Beach, not too far from here.

But you weren't able to keep that going?

I wasn't able to make the first month's rent that I was there. I was there one month, gave her the money, moved in and - my relatives gave me some money to move in - and by the time the next month's rent was due I was on the phone again trying to borrow money from people, and I couldn't come up with all the money, and I couldn't keep having people - they can't support me. I mean I can't depend on my relatives to support me, I can't; they're not gonna do it, you know, who can blame them? They've got their own problems.

Did you have to live outside or in your car at all?

No, I didn't. I heard about this place through a friend and I came here, and I moved from the apartment to here, the same day that I came here.

Did you have a job when you came here?

Yes, part-time, I still have part-time.

Are you looking to switch to full-time?

If I can find something, yes. Right now what I get paid as a part-time employee probably averages out to be about as much as if I took a full-time job. I've been working for the Olive Garden (a restaurant chain) for quite a few years, for over three years, and I make a good hourly wage. And I try to do baby sitting and house cleaning and whatever else I can pick up, odds and ends.

Have you tried to get any assistance through social service agencies, food stamps or anything like that?

Oh yes, my daughter gets Medicaid, she's covered by Medicaid, so her doctor bills and her prescriptions, all her medical needs...

And I make too much money to receive food stamps or any kind of, AFDC, which is welfare; you have to be, I guess, very, very, very, very broke [laughs] in order to get any of those benefits. If I've got to go into a hospital Medicaid will pay over $300, will pay the bill.

For you?

For me, that's it, no doctor's bills or anything; they won't pay for me. I make too much money.

Did you apply for Medicaid recently?

I started in January, and she just received it last month, got approved last month. (The interview was conducted in June.)

How did they treat you there?

[sighs] They're okay. The first time I went in the man was very sympathetic. He said, "I'm sorry, I'm sorry, I'm sorry. But if you go out into the lobby you'll see there's people really poor." I said, "Okay." [laughs] I wasn't poor enough. And he said, "You can call churches or whatever, and maybe you can get one of the churches or something to help you out." Less expensive child care possibly, which is what I get through here, through The Lord's Place. They work with a nursery, and I pay a little bit less in child care.

A lot of people say there should be more programs to help homeless people, while others say we're already doing enough. What do you think about all that?

I think that a lot more could be done. You know, I think that people stereotype homeless people just like they stereotype people with diseases - like alcoholism and such, they tend to think that it's their fault: they should be able to *do* something about it, you know, be self-supporting. And it's not that way. I mean it can happen to anybody. One day you're okay, you know, you're supporting yourself, and then like, this situation, I never dreamed in a million years that I'd be homeless, not being able to support my daughter and myself. And I think a lot more could be done, absolutely. I think they do a lot for other countries, and I think that that's wonderful, but I think they should take a lot more focus and put it on here, you know.

Has this been difficult for Gina?

I'm sure it is. Children are pretty resilient, but the whole thing has been difficult for her. She has adapted to it wonderfully, you know. There are certain rules that we have to abide by, and I understand that, I don't have any problem with it, but she can't play outside, and that's hard for her at times I know; she doesn't understand. She doesn't understand; it's hard for her. She's only four years old. How could she really understand? But the whole break up of the marriage, and to be living - she knows we live in a shelter, and she knows mom doesn't have very much money, and she knows mom doesn't make very much money. But I try to tell her I do the best I can do for us, and that we're very fortunate to have a place to stay. But she does very well with it.

Is there any one part of this experience that has been particularly difficult for you?

Not really, it's just the fear of not being able to be self-supporting. Even when we do leave here, you know, it's scary; you go out there on your own and you try to make enough money to support us: pay for an apartment, the rent, the food, the electric. It doesn't help your self-esteem either, for me. [laughs] My self-esteem and my self-worth, I try not to beat up on myself too much, realize that I am a victim. I didn't ask - I've done all that I can and I certainly will always do all that I can to make sure that Gina and I have a home and a roof over our heads. I mean, that's all that's important to me. A lot of the things that I used to have don't seem to be as important anymore, and I can't believe today how much importance I placed on other things, like cars, and, I mean, just going to the store and not worrying about what you're gonna spend, you know. And today I go and I add up [laughs] every little penny on a piece of paper to see how much I have, how much I should spend to be able to get through the week. So it's been quite a learning experience for me also. But I think we've done very well.

Has anything good come out of it yet?

There's knowin' that other people do care about you. [A long pause ensues as her eyes fill with tears.] That you're not totally alone, and that other people do care, and that we'll make it, we'll be okay, just knowin' that we'll be okay. As down as I get sometimes, I know that somehow we'll make it.

Are the other people here good about looking out for each other, or do people stay pretty much to themselves?

We stay pretty much to ourselves; that's the way it's supposed to be, I mean that's one of the rules. You know, we don't visit each other. I mean, you say hello to someone who passes. But the lady that lived next to me with a little girl for quite awhile, we'd meet each other at the shopping center and talk. It's nice to be able to talk with someone and share with someone when they're goin' through the same thing that you are, because when you talk to someone who isn't goin' through what you are they can't fully understand, but someone who is really understands, you know? It's also, just to see that there are other people who go through what you go through, and that they're gonna be okay, and to see them move out and find a place to live, that things do work out.

How long do you think you'll be staying here?

Well, probably another few weeks anyway, maybe a month; I've already started looking through the paper to see what's available that I can afford.

Is there a problem with finding affordable housing in this area?

Yeah, it is for me. [laughs] You know, most places are at least $400 - at least - and up for a one-bedroom apartment. That's a one-bedroom, and I don't mind the two of us sharin', we can share a bedroom, there's no problem with that, but I only take home $150 a week, so it's a big part of my salary for rent, so I'd like to try to find something a little bit lower than that. And I think the area though, the efficiencies that are available, a lot of people are not renting as seasonal anymore; they're starting to rent a little bit more yearly. And it's also a problem when you have a child, we had a pet, I had a pet, I had a cat, I had to give her away 'cause they don't take pets. I decided to keep the child. [laughs] A lot of places don't want to rent to children; it's against the law not to but they can get around it very easy. So we just have to hope that we can find somethin' that they'll rent to.

Are people requiring large deposits if you're going to rent a place, or requiring more than a month's deposit?

They usually require first month, last month and a month's deposit, so it can cost you as much as $1,200 to $1,800 to move into a place. So that's what this is all about; it helps us, gives us time to be able to save that money, and when we move out we'll be able to have the money to put down on a place.

You mentioned earlier that you weren't able to get Medicaid coverage for yourself. Have you or Gina had any health problems?

I have; my doctor didn't charge me last time I went, and I can't always pay for all my medication, daily. It's gotten quite expensive, and I don't always have the money to pay for that, but I have friends who try to help out.

Have you ever had to skip taking medication because you can't pay for it?

Yes, at times; it's hard to ask people for help, especially when it's a repeated thing - you're always asking your friends to help you out with this and that, and it really gets hard, you know. I don't wanna have to do that; I hate to have to do that. One of my friends, she lets me clean her apartment every other week, and that helps, make a few dollars doing that rather than just takin' money. If I feel I can do something in return for it I feel a whole lot better.

How about Gina? Has she been sick at all?

Just the normal childhood illnesses, she's very fortunate that her doctor will accept the Medicaid; they don't normally, but she's been goin' there since she was born, and he said that they would take the Medicaid even though it's very difficult for them to get their money, but I've always paid my bills whenever she went. They never had a problem with me, and they understand that it's been a hardship, and that they're willing to work with me on that.

If all goes well, what will happen in the next year? What would you like to do?

Well, I'd still like to go to school and get some sort of professional training for something, and hopefully in the next year I'll be able to do that - if it works out that I can find someone to take care of Gina and afford to go to work and go to school at the same time. But I hope to do it.

Do you think there's anything you could have done differently to avoid these problems, or was it pretty much unavoidable?

Yeah, probably not have gotten married. [laughs] Just kidding. I don't know, really. What can I say? Have not trusted my husband, and kept more of an eye on him, and have not given my money over to him as freely as I did? Maybe. Or, gosh, I don't know, if I had taken some sort of training years ago, schooling, to be able to be more self-sufficient, get a better paying job, I'm sure I wouldn't be in the position I'm in, hopefully, if that had happened. But I know that this happens to a lot of women. And I always thought that I would be pretty secure because I always worked in the restaurant business, and I had always worked, and I always figured, well, I shouldn't really have any problem. But you never think that, well, you'll have children, and then you'll, you know, have to worry about that end of it. So other than that, I don't really know what else I could have done. Everything happens for a reason, and I'm going through this for a reason. I don't know what it is yet, but there's going to be some answer. I know I've grown stronger through this. And I know I have a different set of values, like we talked about before.

Aaron Williams, 43, is a native of Fernandina Beach, Florida. He was interviewed in Jacksonville at the Trinity Rescue Mission.

How long have you been in Jacksonville?
Since '88.
What kind of work do you do?
Construction. I'm a bridge carpenter, and I work ship yards, stuff like that too. I've been, you know, things in Florida have been doing pretty well up until the last month or so.

What happened?

The job, we got so far ahead they had to lay some of the carpenters off, okay, so I was among the few that got laid off. It's supposedly only being for about five or six weeks, which is, this is the fifth week. So I'm lookin' forward to goin' back to work this week or next week. But still, unfortunately, I had to resort to a means of sleepin' and eatin', you know, until I'm able to go back to work.

So you had to give up your...

My apartment, I just gave it up Monday.

Have you been able to get enough food since you got laid off?

Well, I had a little money saved up, and that carried me through the last month that I wasn't working. I was able to buy groceries and take care of my rent up until this point. I really feel I haven't had it that bad up until right now. After I left my apartment, then naturally all my conveniences for cookin' and storin' food, I don't have any way to do that now. Even if I had food I wouldn't have anywhere to cook it.

Did you stay here last night, too?

Last night was my first night.

So you haven't had to find a place to sleep outside or anything like that?

No, no, no, I haven't had to resort to that yet.

Do you think it will be another week or so before you go back to work?

Hopefully, hopefully another week or so. I've got three days here, so once these three days are up I'll have to try to get in one of the other missions, three days and then, two more, you know, that I can rotate until, hopefully, I'll get back to work.

You got people that are more experienced than me, you got people that this is more or less their lifestyle. Like transients, they go through this lifestyle, you know, all year round, from town to town. They'll be more versed in what people actually go through, things of that nature.

You never know what's gonna happen to ya. I'm just fortunate enough that I happened to have a living place all the time.

Have you ever been in this situation before?

No, not like this. I managed to keep working, keep saving, since I moved here.

Were you able to get unemployment compensation?

No, I didn't apply for unemployment 'cause it takes three or four weeks to even get that started, and I feel like I can find somethin' to do, rather than sittin' around waitin' on somebody to send me a check. [laughs] But if I was gonna be off long enough, say for instance if I was to find out that I couldn't get no work for maybe the next three or four weeks, then I'd go ahead and apply for unemployment. Right now I'm anticipatin' on goin' back to another job or goin' to work for somebody. The check, it takes about a month or so for you to get your first check when you apply for unemployment. That's the way I feel about it. A lot of people go ahead and apply for it, then sit around until they use up what they've got in there.

Have you tried to get food stamps or anything else from social service agencies?

No, I haven't applied. A lot of people do apply. Like I say, I haven't been out here long enough. I'm hopin' I won't have to go through all that. But it's just there if I, you know, need it. I could go apply for food stamps and probably get 'em. And I'm a veteran; I could go to the Veterans Administration, and maybe they could work somethin' out for me to stay somewhere. There's an avenue of things I'll probably do. If push came to shove, there's avenues I could take that I don't really wanna take at this point. If I can go back to work, that's my main concern, goin' back on my job. If I go back on my job, I can make it. [laughs]

How is the construction industry doing around here?

Only downtown, there's things they've got going on here, like right over here on the causeway. They had, at one time, plenty of work down here, you know, when they were building the Barnett Tower and all that, but they've finished all that. It may be worth goin' in other areas, you know, by maybe some malls, shopping centers, stuff like that, but I'm not really sure. This job here will be here for awhile, that's why I wanna get back on it; it's another couple of years, two or three years on that.

On the bridge?

Uh-huh.

The one they're building right down here?

Yeah.

What is it?

It's a causeway bridge.

Will it go all the way across the river?

All the way across the river.

Oh, I see. So it will be a huge project.

Yeah, and then they've got to tear down the old one. So it's quite a bit that they have to do there, you know, before it's completed. Then they're gonna run this monorail thing around alongside the bridge.

So, with any luck, you might be able to spend a couple nights here, go somewhere else, and then get back to work.

Yeah, get back to work. I've got a friend who told me I could stay with him, but I didn't wanna move in on him, you know. I wanna try to get to be workin' before I have to move in with him. I'd rather be goin' back to work. But he had offered me that.

Sandra Hansen, 45, is a native of Cleveland, Ohio. She was inter-viewed in Tampa at the ACTS Homeless Day Center.

How long have you been in Florida?
About two-and-a-half months.
Did you come from Ohio?
No, Pennsylvania, from Johnstown.
Oh, you lived there for awhile?
Yeah, I lived there almost four years.
What brought you down to...
Well, I lived here like eight years ago, and I liked it. So I like the climate, you know, and I thought I could get a job here. Everybody says there's a lot of work up here. There was no work in Pennsylvania 'cause it's a small town. There's no work at all up there. It's mostly coal mines and stuff like that, and there's no work at all up there, so I figured I'd come up here, it's a bigger town and everything, be able to get a job better, but [laughs] it's a lot harder, just about as hard as it was up there. So I haven't been able to come across anything yet. And I've put a lot of applications in, but I've only had one interview through the Holiday Inn, and that was it. So right now it's pretty hard.
Are you by yourself?
No, my boyfriend, he's out there with me. We're together. I think it's easier for two people, you know, to be homeless together because they have each other to count on, but when one person, it's a lot harder.
Did you come down together?
Yeah, we came together down here. We had an apartment for awhile; we had some money when we came down. We thought by the time our money ran out and the rent was due we would have a job or somethin', but no, nothin'. He hasn't been able to find one, and neither have I.
What kind of work are you looking for?
I'm looking for waitress; he's looking under janitor, custodian or security, but security up here you have to have like uniform, some of them you have to wear a gun, you've gotta be trained, pay a fee and everything, and we just don't have the money right now for him to do that. Otherwise he could get into security.
So you had some money when you came down, and you had a place for about a month or so?
Yeah.
And then what happened? Did you get evicted?
Yeah, we got evicted. We didn't have the next month's rent, and, you know, we went to a lot of places, but they don't help you, because it's only

two of us, we don't have any children or nothin', so it's hard when you don't have kids. But still, that shouldn't be a reason for people to help or not to help; they should be able to help you whether you have children or not. I could say this is the most place that's helped us since we've been up here - ACTS. If it wasn't for this, I don't know what we'd be doing.

We were on the street. Well, we still are, but we were on benches and stuff like that, and it's not very safe.

Where are you staying at night?

We're down by the river with Jim (another homeless person). We're all down there together, so we all have each other and we can all count on each other, and we do everything together, which is a lot better than being by yourself. But it's hard, but we're still looking for work and everything; hopefully it won't be too much longer.

Do you have a tent or a shelter of some sort?

No, there is a shelter thing over it, you know, it's like under a bridge. But there's no traffic or nothing, it's just around the river front, and you're allowed to stay down there, so that's where we're stayin' right now.

Are there a lot of people staying there?

No, it's just the three of us right now. There was one guy, but he moved to Orlando 'cause he got a job through Disney World, so there was four of us, now there's just three of us.

I see you have a lot of marks on your arms. Are those bites?

Yep, from mosquitoes and stuff, and ants and stuff. I gotta get some more cream to put on tomorrow.

Have you been able to get enough food?

Yeah, well we got food stamps and stuff, yeah. We're just about runnin' out now. I don't get them till the 14th of the month though. (The interview was conducted on July 29.) We're survivin' I guess you would say.

How were you treated when you applied for food stamps? Were you treated okay?

Yeah, the lady in there that took care of us, she was real nice. There's some of them that ain't, but the one that I had, she was really nice.

Do you have a car?

No, we don't have anything.

Did you come down by train or bus?

We came down by Greyhound. We've got our clothes, and brought some silverware and stuff like that that we really needed, and a few dishes and stuff like that. But a lot of it we had to leave at the apartment. We had no way to get it over here, and we didn't have nowhere to put it, really, so we had to leave it there. So when we do get on our feet and everything, we're gonna have to find a furnished place.

Do you have enough clothes?

I don't have really that many clothes. I've been tryin' to pick up some here and there, but I only got like two pairs of pants and maybe three shirts, so I still gotta get some more clothes. Now he has quite a few that he brought from Pennsylvania. He has a lot of pants and stuff. But I gotta get me some more, 'cause I had some, but they were stolen and stuff.

They were stolen from out where you were staying?

Yeah. So now we just bring everything here every day. We don't leave it out or anything, because you never know who's gonna pick it up or throw it away or what. [laughs] So we bring it back and forth every day, take enough what we need at night, and on the weekend we take a couple change of clothes and stuff like that.

Have the police helped you at all, or ever bothered you?

No, see we were staying in some park one time and they asked us to leave, but they were real nice about it, though. They told us, well we had to go somewhere else, we weren't allowed over there. That was at the University grounds. That was the only time. But they were real nice about it.

A lot of people say we should have more programs to help the homeless, but others say we're already doing...

I think there should be more programs, not just for people that's got children, but for everybody, you know, to try to get 'em off the streets so they can settle their life down and have a new fresh start. I think it would be very good for everyone, not just for certain people. I think that's what they need.

Do you think it's dangerous on the streets for women?

Yeah, I think it is, 'cause we got hit so many times, we got stuff thrown at us, and callin' us bums and everything else. We were just sittin' on the bench at night. Yeah, it is dangerous, like if you're by yourself. And some people, say they come from another state, and they really don't know what to do or where to go or how to go about doin' it, and it is hard. Because at first, when we first come here, we didn't know where to go, or where you're allowed to go or anything like that. If it wasn't for Carol (Carol Simmons, the director of the center) and them, askin' some of the people here, we wouldn't have known what to do or anything, because we never done it before. This is the first time we ever been homeless, 'cause I've always worked, he always works. If it wasn't for us not havin' money, not havin' a job, we wouldn't even be homeless right now. So that's all that it really is.

So if all goes well, what will you do next?

If I get a job and everything, or he gets one, or one of us at least gets a job, then we can, you know, work, and I would still like to come back here and volunteer on days when I'm not workin' or somethin'. I would still like to come and volunteer over here to help people get through the same thing that I went through, and help 'em out. I really would.

Joseph Richie, 29, is a native of Houston, Texas. He was interviewed in Winter Park at a shelter run by the Human Crisis Council, where he was staying with his wife, Maryanne, 27.

How long have you been in Florida?
I've been in Florida about three-and-a-half months.
What brought you here?
Well, I moved here from Pennsylvania. We were staying in Pennsylvania, and I called a company I used to work for because I needed a change of jobs in Pennsylvania because I didn't like the job I was doing: cooking at the restaurant. And I used to remove asbestos, so I called here, there's a company here that I used to work for, and I called 'em to see if they had any work goin' on, and they promised me that I'd be working 40 or 50 hours a week, ya know, they could fix me up with a place to stay and everything else. And so I packed all my stuff and got my wife and we came down here. And I didn't have much money to start with, but I came down here, and I got here and started working, and worked for about a month-and-a-half, and I wasn't makin' no money - they promised me to work 40 to 50 hours a week at $7 an hour. In the month-and-a-half that I did work, I never worked over 22 hours. And so I wasn't makin' no money; I couldn't even pay my rent. And so it caused me to have to move; I didn't have enough money to pay my rent, and so I kinda got kicked out - with no place to go, I didn't know anybody 'cause I'd only been here, you know, about a month-and-a-half, I didn't know anybody, I didn't know who to turn to. So the day before I left, I walked. I didn't have no transportation or anything else. I walked to a countless number of churches tryin' to get some help, tryin' to get somebody to refer me to somebody that would help me, the Salvation Army and all these places, but then I have my wife.

Anyway, I was not really wanting to stay at the Salvation Army or something because they split you up, you know, and I didn't really want that to happen, so I started knocking - I even knocked on people's *doors,* you know, to try to get some help, just randomly, knocked on doors. Nobody would seem to want to help me until I, finally I went to the church - I don't know the name of it, it's right there on Fairbanks and I-4, that big church - and they directed me here to the Human Crisis Council. And I came here, and I walked through that front door, and there was a secretary out there, I started tellin' her what my problem was, and before I could say too much, Lew, the director of the place here, he walked out there and called me in his office. And I explained to him what my problem was, I didn't have no money, I didn't have no place to go, I didn't have a job, and he suggested that I go get my stuff and bring my wife, and he would give us a place to stay, and hopefully I would be able to find a job, and he would help me find a job.

And so I went back home and got all my stuff, and got my wife, and got somebody to bring us over here, and he put us in the house, gave us a bed and a dresser and a room and food - he's been feeding me ever since I been here - meat, canned goods, chips, any kind of food, you know, he gives it to us. And I searched and searched and searched for a job, I've been here probably at the Human Crisis Council about two months, and I go out there and volunteer work, and my wife will go out there and volunteer work, six, seven, eight hours a day, because I couldn't find a job, and I didn't have no transportation, didn't have no money to ride the bus, so I would walk. And I'd walk so far as from here to Kissimmee, which is 30 miles, you know, it's a pretty good ways, and I still couldn't get a job. And so finally Lew, he got in his little book there, and started callin' people for me, and set me up with some interviews, and I finally did get a job. I got a real good job last Thursday. I'm working 12, 14 hours a day, making $6.50 an hour, and it's real good - thanks to Lew, I think I owe him because he pulled me in off the street and he even helped me get the job. And I've never really been homeless to the point of maybe a day or two, you know, on the street. I've never had to live on the street like some of these other guys. Of course, I'm not criticizing nobody or nothing, but a lot of them guys that live on the street, they just live from day to day to buy them a bottle of wine, you know, and that's just my own experience because I've seen it with my own eyes; they could care less about work. And there's labor pools out there they can work at. Of course, I even went to a labor pool four days in a row and set there for five or six hours and never did get out, so I don't know about that.

Anyway, thanks to Lew, I think I owe him a lot, and I don't plan on staying here too much longer because, I'm makin' good money now and I think I need my own apartment. If I was by myself it would be different, but I have a wife and I would like to get my own apartment, try to get me a car and everything, and I think I can do it. I really thank Lew for helping me, and the Human Crisis Council. I don't see how he does it; he feeds 150 to 200 people a *day* that come through here. I might exaggerate a little bit, but there's quite a few people that come through here, and if somebody comes in here that needs to take a shower, he'll send 'em right over to that house and let 'em take a shower, and give 'em a towel and soap and everything else, and give 'em food; if they don't have no way home, if they do have a home and they come to get some food, he'll give 'em 85 cents to ride the bus. Sometimes even take 'em home. He does a lot for the people; I just don't see how he does it without no help from the government. It must be rough.

How did you lose your job - the one you had when you first came down here?

Well, when I came down here I was supposed to be working 40 to 50 hours a week. I ended up workin' maybe 22, 25 hours. And since I didn't have enough to pay my rent, I had no place to live, I wasn't able to go to work, you know. I mean I couldn't live on the street and go to work and just leave; I wasn't going home from work, I was just goin', and so I had to quit because I had no way, no place to go.

Did you have a car?

Nope. No, we rode the bus.

Where were you living in Pennsylvania?

We was in Collegeville; it's about 35 miles outside of Philadelphia. We were staying at her (his wife's) mom's house.

I liked it there; I kind of wish I would have stayed. I mean I was makin' good money there workin' at the restaurant; I was making $6.50 an hour, workin' at the restaurant, trainin' to be a chef and everything, but I just, you know, I've never done that kind of work before, and I felt like I could do better somewhere else, but it didn't turn out to be that way, you know? But now I have a goal for myself and for my wife, and I'm gonna make it.

Did you get the same kind of work you were doing before?

No, I'm working in a warehouse, loadin' trucks and pullin' orders. I'm working in a warehouse.

It's a food distribution center. It's a good job; I really like it.

So what do you think of Florida?

It's hot. [laughs] It's hot. Of course, I grew up in Houston, I'd been in Houston for 19 years, so I'm kinda sorta used to the heat, but I was in Pennsylvania for almost a year, maybe a little longer than that, and I kinda got used to that good weather there. [laughs] The humidity here is something else; it really is. But I like it otherwise. It's mostly friendly people around here I guess. Personally, I think they're more friendlier up north than they are here. In Philadelphia, where we was livin' anyway, everybody you see, "Hi, hi." Unless you go to the wrong part of Philadelphia and there's nothing but a bunch of drug heads that try to rip off your car and everything else. I worked for this Stanley Steemer place down there one time cleaning carpets. We would go to Philadelphia a lot of times cleaning somebody's carpet. You know, we'd have to keep the van running because of the motor for the carpet cleaner, and somebody tried to drive off with our van one time. I was in there doing the floor and all of a sudden my hose started pulling real tight, and it jerked right out of my hand. Ran out there and caught 'em because there was a lot of traffic; they couldn't get away. Dragging my hose down the street, you know, behind me. I've seen people in downtown Philadelphia run right into a parked car and total that car out and keep on goin'. Nobody says nothin'. But I liked it down there. One of these days - one of these years, I think I might move back down there. Once I get me good savings goin' and get me a good car and everything, I might move back down there.

I would have never moved down here if they didn't promise me a good job, 40, 50, 60 hours a week. I would have never moved down here 'cause I got in a real bad jam. But now I'm doing better, like I said, thanks to Lew and the Human Crisis Council here. He's got a good thing going here. He needs a little help maybe, he needs some help to keep it goin' because there ain't very many places that homeless people can go to to get food without havin' identification, Social Security card, sign papers and everything else. You know, most of the places, they want a Social Security card, driver's license and everything else. Lew, he don't care; if somebody's hungry, they're gonna get some food. And whatever's out there they can get.

You haven't had to deal with any of the social service agencies then?

Oh no. I was just lucky because after all the doors I knocked on - and I walked all the way from Altamonte Springs - over here in Winter Park I just got on I-4 and started knockin' on churches and doors and houses and everything else, and I ended up here. And it was amazing, because out of a hundred people, one of them finally cared, you know, enough to take me and my wife both, brang us over here, give us food, clothes - when I came here I had maybe three pairs of pants and four or five shirts, and now I got so many, nice dress clothes too, so many clothes I don't know what I'm gonna do with them all. It's been nice. I like it. If the house were set up a little different over there, if maybe it had a private entrance, for your room and a few other things, I wouldn't mind staying here because it's just not bad; you can meet all kind of people out here, and listen to other people's problem's, and maybe you can help them somehow. But I have to have my own place.

Jim "Country" Cain, 35, is a native of Kathleen, Florida. He was interviewed in St. Petersburg at the Praying Hands Mission.

How long have you been in St. Pete?

About seven years.

What brought you over here?

There wasn't no work in Polk County. Come over here, there's plenty of work - out of labor pools anyway.

What kind of work do you do usually?

Actually, I'm a machinist.

Have you been able to get enough of that kind of work around here?

No, I'm workin' construction now. I've lost everything I had. I had a good job, had a beautiful '81 Grand Prix, it got repoed. Work's just slacked off. But I'm workin out of Suncoast Temps now, and I got a somewhat, sort of steady ticket.

Are you getting out every day?

Yeah. I'm savin' up money now to get me another car. If I get a car I can work every day. If this ticket, you know, peters out and I got a car, I can work every day out of one of these temps.

How long have you been staying here at the mission?

A week Friday.

Where did you stay before that?

I had my own apartment, and I lost it. I owed beaucoup back rent, and I couldn't pay it.

Here in St. Pete?

Yeah.

How long ago was that?

Two weeks ago.

Had you been there a long time?

About a year.

Did you have a machinist's job for awhile here in St. Pete?

Yeah.

What happened with that?

Couldn't get along with the boss. I was bringin' home 300 a week. It was either kill him or take a hike, so I decided to take a hike, bottom line.

How long were you there?

Two years.

Have you ever had to stay outside for awhile?

Yeah.

Where do you stay?

I hug a tree [laughs], just hug a tree. You know, if you got a sleeping bag, you go for it, no problem. It don't get that cold here, so you ain't gotta worry about that.

Have you always been able to get enough food?

Well here lately I haven't. I ain't been eatin' right. My resistance is low. I've had double pneumonia four times in the past seven, eight years.

Do you think that's from staying outside too much?

No, just, if you got the flu right now and I'm talkin' to ya, I can get it from ya. I'm just susceptible. Plus I got bronchitis.

Have you been able to keep enough clothing with you?

Oh yeah, I got all my clothes. Well, my work clothes, I got jackets, you know, flannel shirts. There's no problem with keepin' warm. The only thing I worry about is just keepin' clean.

What do you do about that if you're not staying at a mission or someplace like that?

Well, then I'll come to the mission and ask. If not, I'll go to my friend's house, I got friends. They don't have a big enough place, you know, they got like an efficiency apartment, so that they ain't got room to put me up. If they had a house or somethin', it'd be different.

Have you tried to get food stamps or other help from social service agencies?

No.

How come?

I don't figure I need it. A lot of other boys you talk to, they probably say they do. They might get 'em, I don't know; I don't figure I need 'em. See, the thing is, to get food stamps and all, you gotta take off of work, you know, and get 'em. And if I miss one day's work on this ticket that I'm on, then I ain't got the ticket. So I'm damned if I do and damned if I don't.

What are you planning to do in the long run? Will you go back to another permanent job, or will you stay with the labor pools for awhile?

Soon as I get my priorities straight, yeah. I mean like, I need a car. And I had a car lined up today, 'cause all I needed was another, you know, hundred bucks. I got a hundred bucks saved now; I needed another hundred, coulda got it, and I woulda got it, but they sold the car this morning. I'll get back on my feet. A lot of these fellahs, they get back on their feet and they forgot where they come from, if you know what I'm sayin' by that. I never have. I'll get back up, it just takes time.

How have you found it staying here?

It's alright. Well, I get up early in the morning anyway. You know, they wake us up four o'clock, 4:30 they have breakfast. Food ain't the greatest, but it fills the void, if you know what I'm sayin'.

How are the other guys who are staying here? Are people pretty good about looking out for each other?

Yeah, there's not any ass holes around here as a rule. Every now and then you get a loud mouth; just put him in his place, that's all.

Do you have any family here?

I got family over in Winter Haven, my daddy and my mamma, and I ain't got in touch with them in about two years 'cause I had no way to get over there, I lost their phone numbers somewhere along the line. But my old daddy, he knows I'm a big boy, I can take care of myself.

If all goes well, what will happen in the next year or so?

I'll be the hell out of this place. [laughs]

Yeah, I'll be alright within a month if I work every day. If I don't, see what happens, I have to go from there.

Is there anything else you'd like to add?

Yeah, I'd like to have some meat and taters in a place like this every now and then. [laughs] Soup gets old. Grits get old. But other than that it's alright.

Don Lawless, 65, is a native of Pasadena, California. He was interviewed in Orlando at Our Daily Bread, a soup kitchen run by the Christian Service Center for Central Florida.

How long have you been in Florida?

I've been here in Florida 11 years. I don't mean to come across to you as different from anybody else, but my situation is somewhat unique. I'll try to make this brief. I lived and worked in California up until I was 50 years old; I didn't get married till I was 50 years old. With my wife I came here - who was black by the way (Lawless is white) - there's no significance, but being what it is...

We came here to Florida principally because her parents lived down in Saint Croix in the Virgin Islands; it's a lot closer. I had worked something like 27 years for one company. [laughs] We came here, made immediate contact with a developer - that's the kind of work I did in California - real estate development; went to work immediately, and the next ensuing 12 years, other than having in a material sense probably a much better than average life, we had no particular problems. This job that I had was an exceptionally good job as jobs go. I got it in my pocket, it's hard to believe, I was making $500 a week the last four years on the job. [laughs] I was provided with a rent-free apartment, round-the-clock use of a company vehicle, they paid the light bill at home, in other words, we had it made. I suppose you're aware of this bullshit going on with the S&Ls. These people I worked for were right in the midst of that here in South Florida.

So in December of '89, with no prior notice to anybody, the company sold out to some people in Chicago.

I was aware, the last two or three years, that this company was operating somewhat on the fringe of legalities, you know. I wasn't concerned about that; it wasn't any of my business. But as it turned out we were all terminated with no advance notice, no severance pay, I had some bonus money coming - about $4,000. I went to the employment office, they hadn't turned in a damn thing on me or any of the other employees for about four years; Social Security the same way, I'm still fighting with the Social Security thing. I will get it. And I did start getting the unemployment: $200 a week for what, 26 weeks? This I could have handled quite easily; we had quite a little bundle saved up. When you have no living expenses except groceries you can save money on five bills a week. Although she'd never been ill in her life - my wife was 15 years younger than I - in January, the 22nd, she'd wake up complaining of severe pain, kidney pain.

Anyway, I took her to the hospital and I very naively present my Av-Med (a health maintenance organization) card. [laughs] I think although I had been terminated, the insurance was supposed to still carry us for what, a year? I was checking into the hospital, they put her in intensive care, a week later make a diagnosis of ESRD, end stage renal disease, and the mortality rate on this is something like 95 percent within several months. There's no recovery. Shortly after I was advised of that knowledge, they tell me that my god damn insurance is no good. My former company hadn't made a payment on group insurance for about seven months. Anyhow, my first hospital bill for one month and three days was $29,285. [laughs] And 75 cents for a migraine aspirin. She was in intensive care in a private room, $260 a day. It wasn't particularly my choice, the private room, but when you have what she had - this ESRD - the doctor tells me it's of undetermined etiology, you know, they don't know what's causing it, they don't what the hell you treat it. [laughs] But anyway she died on May the 14th. Only recently could I say that without... [pauses, wipes away some tears]

Well, anyway, to get to the homeless situation, took her and buried her - they ripped off all her jewelry in the hospital. This obviously was a situation of just overwhelming grief. [sighs] I had been drunk twice in my life; drinking just wasn't my thing. But after I buried her and came back to Florida from down in Saint Croix, and I had about $7,000 left - the total hospital bill you wouldn't believe. So I went back to the apartment we were living in - after I lost the job I had to rent an apartment. So I went back to where we were living, and I couldn't handle it. I packed a few clothes; I might mention that having full use of company vehicles - the

interim between the time that we left that place and she got sick was so
short, I hadn't even bought a car, you know. So anyway I just packed a
few clothes and I bought a bus ticket to Detroit. I walked in the bus station
in Fort Lauderdale, I said, "When does the next one leave? And where is
it going?" The farthest point Detroit, so I went to Detroit, and I stayed in
Detroit about a month. And I was in no shape mentally or emotionally to
think about anything, no goal-oriented behavior at all.

So I came back to Florida, I went to straighten out - this is when I learned
about the unemployment being fucked up, you know, and the Social
Security, and about 4,100 bucks in bonus money I had coming I'm not
going to get. And I went to a bar big time, you know. I had about, I don't
know, maybe a little over $5,000 left; I went to a bar - fucking jerk - with
the sole intention of getting drunk. [laughs] And I proceeded to get drunk.
And I stayed jacked up for about three weeks, and it scared the shit out of
me. I woke up in a hotel in Naples (on Florida's west coast); I had no idea
how I got there, none at all. I came back to Lauderdale, and I thought: You
must be a god damn alcoholic and didn't know it or something. [laughs]
And anyway, as you may have concluded by this time, I got ripped off one
night - good - got my teeth knocked out in front, all that shit, you know.
When I come to I'm in the hospital, they're doing a brain scan on me and
all that sort of thing, had my nose fucked up.

But to get to the point of this homeless thing, that's why I'm here. This
has been an experience. I'm glad you came here. The country generally
doesn't give a fuck about homeless people, and there's nothing I can do
about it, but this total situation - I've been in it for five months now - is
absolutely fucking incredible. This here - I'm not trying to come off like
a fucking intellectual - but this is an enabling situation here. For five
months I've observed, 90 percent of these people, in four different shelter
and feeding places, and I've been there too, you know. I have no statistics
on it, but if you would talk to 10 people - or the smart thing, young man,
is to check in one of these joints. The total conversation here, oddly enough
- it's principally males - very infrequent you ever hear sex mentioned in
here, among the age group that should be; I'm 65 years. The principle topic
of conversation here is drugs, and where to get them: crack, wine and beer,
very few mention whisky. The employment these guys secure through
these labor pools, they go out and work their ass off digging a ditch in the
hot sun, and they go right across the fucking street and buy a rock. Really.
As I see it - I don't know enough about it - but the way these agencies are
structured, no one is going to get out of these fucking places. If they do
it's not going to be with the assistance of these agencies, although
they're well-intended. I've talked to guys who've been circulating through

this place for five years. My own situation I can't comment on - I mean facetiously. When I went fucking flat broke I had $82 after they robbed my ass. [laughs] I had 82 bucks left, I had it stuck down in my coat; they missed that when I got mugged that night. But I thought, Jesus, what am I going to do? You know? I'm going to be hungry and things like that. We lived in a situation where we didn't have any neighbors for about five miles. To be quite frank, she was black, I was white, and that's still significant in this fucking society. [laughs] But anyway, we didn't have a lot of close friends, because obviously if I had close friends I could have went to them. But, I lost my train of thought...

When I hit this situation, I was unaware of a lot of things. Like this Coalition, they provide you with cold cereal - I'm not complaining - they provide you with cold cereal in the morning, you go in at seven in the evening, get up at five in the morning, you sleep on the floor, you can get a blanket, there's about 100 men in there, probably 30 of them have had a bath in the last 40 years.

And one thing that might be of interest to you: I read a study not so long ago about these kind of places. It says that most of the people who are on the staff are ex-street people themselves, and they are the most obnoxious son of a bitches ever walked. Like these avenging angels, you know? But, I hope this is of some help to you. I will make it out of this on my own efforts, I'm sure of that, I'm confident of it. And I'm not the most really empathetic guy towards people who don't give a fuck. But I was just thinking before I ever knew I was going to see you on this earth, this morning, most of the people, particularly black, born in the circumstances they are, raised in the circumstances, they've got about two-and-a-half strikes on them to start with. And then once they get into these fucking drug scenes, they're out. It's maddening; I sit down in the park and I listen to these guys, and they're reciting what they call war stories. And it's never about all the gals they took to bed, like you and I used to bullshit when we were younger - maybe you still do - it's drugs, drugs, drugs, drugs. And they're describing the behavior of a fucking idiot, self-defeating behavior, and if you point it out to them, they get very aggressive, you know, "What the fuck, how are you any fucking different?"

As I say, I'd like to provide you briefly with significant things like that. These are enablers here. Okay, now I haven't done it, but I could go up to Winter Park, where I don't feel like going, and I could get $105 worth of food stamps just by walking in the fucking place. [laughs] If I go out to California - I looked this up in a book - any homeless, indigent male in the state of California today can get $135 a month in food stamps and, hold your hat, $682 general assistance check, a homeless male. There was an article in the paper a couple days ago, did you read that? The little girl, 16 years old now, orphaned, put on the church steps at the age of six months, when she's six years old she's adopted, her stepfather rapes her, at 10 she's out on the fucking streets, at 14 she's hustling, she's 16 now and she's been through HRS, a wonderful organization. [laughs] HRS states they do not have the funds to take care of this child, she's mentally upset, they say, but they concede that, the state, it costs them $90,000 a fucking year to feed, clothe and house an abused child. And Orange County gets $243,000 a year to find foster homes, and something like $2.5 million additional. With this very small amount of money they managed to take care of 85 kids last year.

I hope you really get into this deeply though. If I was a little younger I'd do something about it; I'm too old now. I don't mean *do* something about it, but like, remember Michael Harrington, *The Other America*? If someone - I hope you possibly are the one - I don't think this society gives a fuck about it. And quite frankly, I don't think they should. [laughs] I was very active in the civil rights movement. I knew all the Black Panther leaders real good, and all that shit, you know, radical chic, writing checks, and they're doing fucking drugs with them. My own personal experience, I've taken people in off the street, and my VCR went out the fucking window, and some of my wife's clothes, and the mind set - it sounds kind of shitty of me to be saying these things - but the mind set of people here, generally, is you know, I'm in it, and as I started to say, I'm nourished. I'm not well nourished, but I've gained fucking weight on the streets. Can you imagine that? [laughs] I did; I put on 20 fucking pounds, and here I am homeless - all the starchy foods. But god damn, as I go along and I feel myself -I'm being very frank with you - at my age, statistically, I've got something like five to seven years to live. And I really don't give a fuck about living anymore. I care in a sense; I want to keep clean, things like that. There's no need to be personally offensive to other people. But as far as whether I'm alive tomorrow or not, I could care less.

My wife and I had an extremely close, very productive relationship; she was a very intelligent girl, had a good character, good personality, and she was not hard to look at either. And the thing that really threw me in that fucking drunk - I'm ashamed of that when I look back on it now; when I say ashamed, I don't know anyone close enough to feel ashamed in front of them, I don't have any relatives at all. What really threw me into that drunk - I'm not anti-religious at all - but the concept of God means about as much to me as Mickey Mouse. [laughs] I don't mean to sound immodest, but I'm obviously not an idiot. I've had a few accomplishments in my life, academic and otherwise, but this business, most of these places are structured around, you know, Christianity, etcetera, and these clients are aware and rather acute observers. See, what the fuck does Salvation Army need with a multi-million dollar high rise where the retired ones live in? I couldn't believe it; I went to Sunday morning services over there, and here we are, all homeless, obviously $5 among a hundred men, and they passed two fucking collection plates. [laughs] Here I am, I used to contribute to god damn...

The thing I want to point out, if you really get into this, let me suggest something to you, the first one of these places I ever went into, this one I'm going to tell you, what threw me into this drunk. There's a place down in Fort Lauderdale. I've seen the actual figures. I got very close to the guy running the place; that's why they threw my ass out.

These homes are occupied by ex-street people who are now staff. There isn't a degree among any of them, you know. One guy said, "Why are you grieving about your wife? I was married four times. You can get another one." This fucking guy is supposed to be my counselor.

You know they brag about not having fights around these places; the reason they don't is if you're homeless and broke, you don't want to be out walking the fucking street. They have a guy over there, he's got his problems, he's one of these staff people, and he's very abusive verbally, call you a bunch of motherfuckers and all that sort of thing, you know, and there's nothing you can do about it.

To kind of put where I'm coming from in perspective, that place down in Lauderdale, I stayed there about two weeks. I was born and raised a Catholic, but those things are meaningless to me anymore, have been for 50 years, 40 years. I went to a Catholic priest in Fort Lauderdale - I used to belong to the Saint Vincent de Paul Society, do these kind of things for people. So I walk in there, and as I was going in there, I thought, "How naive can you be at your age, you know, you've been through all this shit." So I sat down and I talked to the priest and I told him about my wife dying, and spending every fucking dime - we had quite a bit of money saved, 78,000 fucking dollars. But anyway, I told him about my wife dying. What do they call it? Catastrophic illness? [laughs] And you know, going through all the money, walking out of the house; when I left there I just walked out, never went back, all I took was a few clothes. I went to this priest before I went on a drunk, and I explained to him what happened. I said, "Look, I'm not asking you to give me any god damn thing." I just needed somebody to talk to. He says, "Would you like to know why your wife died?" And I thought, well, for her at least, if you're going to die, end stage renal disease does it. He said, "Do you attend church regularly?" [laughs] And I was not a Catholic. And I said no. And he said, "The reason

the good Lord took your wife, is that you're committing a cardinal sin by
not attending mass at Easter, Christmas, you know, holy days, and your
soul is in imminent danger of going to hell, you don't know if you're going
to take your next breath, and the Lord took your wife so that your deep
apparent grief would bring you back to the bosom of the Lord." And I said,
"You're fucking insane," and I walked out. [laughs]
    I don't see any solution to the problems of homeless people; I don't.
    What do you mean?
    A guy I talked to this morning, he went to HRS, they told him, "We'll
put you in Project Independence." He described it briefly to me. Here's
this guy's situation: he has one pair of blue jeans and a t-shirt. Okay now,
who the fuck is going to hire him? I do not see society or organizations
such as this - God bless them - taking someone off the street, the typical
person, and providing him with these things he needs; you know, the
material things might be easy, but answer some of his emotional needs and
some of the needs he has in his empty head - you can't just take the body
and put it over here. There's no infrastructure to this stuff. The guy is out
on the street, wet, dirty and hungry. Someone says you can go to Daily
Bread and eat, and you're here five years later. It would probably be a lot
less costly to directly intervene on the streets, but if you do they're going
to blow the fucking money on drugs. [laughs] Really.
    You've been on the street for about four months now?
    Yeah, going on four months.
    *Have you always been able to get enough food and a place to sleep at
night?*
    Yeah, that's what astonished me. It's been damn near 40 years since civil
rights was a big thing; back at that time I was aware there were shelters
and things like that. But I didn't know Salvation Army charges to stay
there and things like that; I didn't know any of that stuff. But yes, I truly
did; I gained 20 pounds over the past three or four months, I never had to
sleep outdoors. I was fucking humiliated. [laughs] I was stone broke. I
went to that place down in Lauderdale, I walked in, and I thought, well,
maybe my thinking is so fucked up that if I could just talk to somebody.
And I was ashamed to say, you know, I'm fucking broke and I'm homeless.
And when I began to talk about my life, I couldn't handle it. So the guy,
I guess he was sympathetic to me, he said, "Look, you need a place to
stay." And this was a controlled environment, you had to get a pass to
leave. The accommodations there, including food, is what a guy with a
lower middle class income would have. I lived there before this shit
happened. You could have your own room, the radio, private shower, and
they feed you excellently, but, you know, starchy foods.

But yes, I've always had a place to sleep, and I've had a place to eat. I have - you can stay over there 60 days, I don't intend to, and I don't intend to do this thing either. But the game here is you go to Salvation Army, you can stay there three nights free, and if you want to pay $7 you can stay there forever, but you've got to get in at five o'clock, and you've got to sit there, I guess it's like being in jail, the way these guys describe it. After three days you leave Salvation Army and you go to the mission over here, and there you're there five days, and you have this sort of prayer scene every night, you know, which most people object to, it seems. And your next shot is the Coalition; you can stay there 60 days. And if you're still around here - this is a very transient group, very nomadic, you know, they move on. Now it's harvest time, they were talking about watermelons, tomatoes, all those sort of things. But if my situation is typical, if I stay over there for the 60 days, which I don't intend to, then my next move is to go out to something called A-R-C, it's Alcohol Rehabilitation Center. And I was talking about it to a guy, I said wait a minute, I don't drink. He said, "Well go out there and tell you're a fucking rock head, and you did six rocks just to get a drink." He said, "They don't give a shit." So check in. And he described it as a clean, decent environment, and they pay you I guess the sum of seven bucks a week, you know, so you can buy cigarettes and continue your cancer trip. [laughs] A homeless person - it's a network - it's fascinating, it really is.

They know all the ins and outs. There's church groups here that - I feel sorry for the elderly ladies - you see the empathy's just pouring out of them, feeling, you know. And a guy will go, "Haven't you got anything besides fucking beans to eat around here?" [laughs] You're not dealing with the most cultured class of people in the world, believe me.

If you had had health insurance, none of this would have happened to you, right?

Yeah, the company had group insurance. If you're terminated, anything other than Chapter 11, if the company goes out of business, whatever, or 7, and it's federal legislation, the insurance remains in effect I think it's six months at the company's expense, and I think you have the option to pick it up. I gave my insurance card when we went to the hospital. And about two weeks later I went to see her - I'd see her every day when she was in the hospital - she said, "They want to see you in the business office." And I went down, and they told me, said, "You don't have any insurance." [laughs] Said, "Hey, there's no policy in effect on that." It was a group, covered about 23 people, and they hadn't made a payment for something like seven months.

But you didn't know that?

No, I thought I had it. Then we started cashing CDs. [laughs] I wouldn't
have done it, but she was in a private hospital, and they gave me 10 days
to pay that fucking bill: 29,285 bucks, or she would have to be transferred
to the county hospital. So she was there up till May the 14th. You know,
nothing prepares you for the death of someone, but man, when it happens,
it's a bitch. I visited her every day except the last day she was alive, and I
was at the Social Security office and unemployment - still trying to get
that crap straightened out. I went down the next day, and there was a wing
of rooms, four rooms, private rooms, patient, patient, patient, a hallway
leading back, there was a control desk right here [demonstrates] like a T,
and you had to sign in, put a mask on, they give you a gown. [laughs] I do
this number, I go back and she's not there and I walk back to see the nurse,
who had seen me every day for four months. "Can you tell me where my
wife is?" "Oh, she died yesterday afternoon." I said, "Jesus Christ. Why
didn't you call?" "Oh well, we thought the desk took care of that."

Anyhow, I don't mean to try to dominate this situation or anything, but
there's an old Irish saying - take it with a grain of salt - what you hear from
most people. You know, you're into a serious project, and you're gonna
hear a lot of bullshit, much of it self-serving.

*Glenda McCray, 43, is a native of Belle Glade, Florida. She was
interviewed at the Miami Women's and Children's Shelter.*

How long have you been in Miami?
All of my life - just born in Belle Glade, never lived there, never resided
there.
What brought you to the shelter?
Well, I was with my father, and he lives in a senior citizen's complex,
and I didn't wanna continue to jeopardize, you know, his livin' arrange-
ments, because relatives can come and stay a couple of days or a week, or
if you're ill, but I was lookin' for jobs and nothing was coming through,
and time was passing, and I didn't want to wear out my welcome. So that
was how I got here; I started callin' around.
He's still living there?
Yes. Oh, I've been back since then. He's 83, and I go over and cook and
clean and wash and so forth, you know, for him.
How long have you been here now?
I became a resident July fourth. (The interview was conducted in
September.) I'm in the single woman's program, and the reason I state that
is because I explained to the director that everyone that walks through
these doors, every woman that walks through these doors, is not a

prostitute, a drug addict, or a street person. Mine is unemployment, and when you're not employed, you can't pay for anything. As far as I'm concerned, you know, you use what you have saved, you use what might be in the credit union, and it just come to the point where [laughs] you use everything up. So I told her that I have credentials, I have a background, I showed her my diploma degree and resume and work history, and she asked me was I interested in the single woman's program. I told her, "Yes." I just happened to be down on my luck at the time, which can happen to anyone. One of the biggest jokes I have is that when it happens to a wealthy person, they just call it a bad business deal, but when it happens to someone that's unknown, without a name, and to those who are ignorant to certain circumstances, they always say, well, "She must have had a drug problem," or "It was a man problem." But no, it was none of those things.

What is your background as far as work...

Social work. I have a B.A. degree in child development from Spelman College in Atlanta - all girls college. I got into social work strictly by accident. After I graduated from college, I started poundin' the pavement. The first job I got was for social work tech, and I interviewed, got the job, and I fell in love with social work, but I've done other things, you know. I can sit behind a desk and push pencils and pen and paper, and I can also push a mop and a broom, too. So I've done them all because it has taken all of that to keep a roof over my head and to eat and survive.

Had you been unemployed for awhile before coming here?

Yes, the last position was in exchange for room and board, so I was still unemployed as far as I was concerned because I wasn't receivin' any pay. It was just in exchange for room and board. I've done live-in, live-outs and so forth and so on. I've baked, I've cooked. As a matter of fact, I can give you my resume before you leave. [laughs] I just updated my resume. Would you like a copy of it?

Sure.

Okay, I'll give you a copy of my resume. I have it available here; I have to go upstairs and get it. So you never know what may happen. You know, you may come across someone, or, you know, network. We had a job seminar here, three days, and we decided that the best possible way of getting a job - and it's true - is networking. I tell you, you tell somebody, that person tells somebody, the church, family, friends, and - sometimes - enemies. But 50 percent of the jobs are gotten through networking. So I will gladly give you my resume - one of them - I have three. And you never know what happens. So you can spread the word that Glenda is looking for a job. Thank you.

So you haven't been here that long?

No, I'm poundin' the pavement, putting in applications and tryin' to work the program. That was one of my questions. Is it feasible for me to work the program and pound the pavement? But so far, it's workin' okay.

I've heard from people in some other cities that sometimes potential employers suddenly lose interest when they learn that you're staying in a shelter...

That's true. You know how there's some people that can't get past the color of your skin no matter what you have up here [points to her head] or how many degree that you have or how much knowledge you have? Okay, there's some people that can't get past the color of your eyes. There's some things people just don't like. There's some people that cannot get past the fact that you presently live in or once lived in a shelter, and that includes relatives also, no matter how advanced you are, no matter how intelligent you are, no matter how many degrees that you have, and that's very true. Now there are others here and others elsewhere that are using relatives' addresses because, number one, they don't want anyone to know that they're here, they're ashamed, and they don't want any mail to come here, they want it all to go to the relatives house, and there are other reasons also, but many have said, "Oh, I just don't want anyone to know, and I don't want my friends or whatever, I don't want them to know where I am." But I made a decision. When I updated my resume, I used the shelter's address. When I send mail out, I use the shelter's address.

I'm takin' a chance, I know that, okay? But it's a chance that I've prayed about and discussed, and the Spirit has moved me to just use that address, be honest, and whatever happens happens. And that's very true, and I'm quite sure that I won't get responses because of that, not because I'm not qualified, because most of the positions that I apply for, I'm overqualified, okay? But it's the fact that they cannot get beyond that address, or the fact that I, quote unquote, am homeless and live in a shelter, and that includes family and relatives also. So it's just not the color of your skin that, people just wanna say, well racism and prejudice, no, you'd be surprised, the color of your eyes, the way your nose is shaped, you understand? The way you talk. You'd be surprised of what people cannot get beyond in order to communicate with you. So I know that I won't get responses because of that, but most people out there are just one or two paychecks from a shelter themselves, believe it or not. Economically, that's what's goin' on out there, and I know that for a fact. I have a five-page work history, so it's rough out there because I was takin' care of myself. But I know that most Americans, most of the families out there, are one or two paychecks from bein' in a shelter themselves, really, if you really did a research or a study or whatever, you would find that out.

So that's very true, whoever told you that, it's very true. I'm experiencing that now. And there's still some here that, "Oh, no, no, I can't use the center's letterhead with the logo; I'm just so ashamed." But I just decided I don't have anything to be ashamed about. And it's no one's business, this isn't somethin' I'm just broadcasting, and I'm not doin' this to prove a point, but the fact is, in order to be reached for a job, they need to call me here, not my dad's, not your house, not my sister's house, but here, where I reside, okay? I had a dynamite resume, and sometimes your address, no matter how beautiful that resume is, sometimes the address turns people off, too, believe it or not - not a shelter's address - your own personal address where you reside, because they wonder, well now how could this person livin' here in little Opa-Locka have that much smarts? The resume reads like it should be someone from Miami Lakes with the last name of Rockefeller or Kennedy. You understand what I'm sayin'?

Is there any place else you could be staying right now - with relatives or friends?

To be quite honest with you, no, and I say that because I was in my mother's home town, and I dealt with relatives. That wasn't a pleasant experience, okay? Here it wasn't pleasant, and as a part of growth, I don't want to be with anyone else right now unless it was a potential spouse, you know, or companionship or whatever, that the Lord has brought us together and we're goin' to live together or get married or whatever. But it's a part of growth because - I'm gonna be honest with you - relatives and people sometimes have hidden agendas when you move in with them. And also that person that you bring in or invite into your home may also have hidden agendas, so you're both watchin' each other. Okay, I've been mistreated by relatives, and I've been treated beautifully by people I knew very little about, total strangers, so you see the reversal? I would say no. I no longer want that, I need my own space, and I'm growing, and I've gotten stronger. I'm going back to that old Glenda, that old independent Glenda, and I don't want to be in someone else's house with the little subtleties, you understand what I'm sayin'? Not bein' discreet: "Well, the milk used to last two weeks before you got here; now it only lasts a day." "Who ate that chicken leg? I was savin' that for me or my husband." "Well now, you can eat this, but this is for us." You understand? And this includes relatives, okay? And believe it or not, some of them are sayin' they're saved, filled with the Holy Ghost, and ministers, so I've had a combination of all of it. No, the answer to that is no. Even if you ran into one right now as you walked and left this center, that said, "Oh, listen, we've been beggin' her to come," my answer is no, that's not what's in the plan for the Lord for me.

Do you have children with you here?

No, no, no, single woman, no, I don't have any children with me, which is a blessing. To drag a child through this, it would be a very traumatic experience, and I see it every day. It's a very closed environment, close quarters, it's very difficult to rear or raise a child, and for that child to follow commands and demands by the parents, so it's a blessing, really.

Have you applied for food stamps or anything like that?

I am receiving food stamps.

How were you treated when you applied?

I worked for HRS for eight years, believe it or not, the same bureaucracy that issues the food stamps. I have been treated, sorta looked down on until I let them know that I worked there for eight years. When I start pullin' out credentials and documents, then sometimes the attitude changes. But the initial, sometimes is, "Okay, come on in, little doggy. What do you want?" So I've gotten the treatment, I've gotten almost the red carpet, and I've gotten the, you know, "You're nothin' but scum. Come on, come on in, sit down, you bum." I've gotten a taste of both. And it's just like I tell the staff members here, the social workers as well as the director, I know what it is to sit behind a desk like they're doin', and I know what it is to be on the other side of that desk, also. I've tasted both of those dishes, also.

Have you gotten Medicaid or anything?

No. I don't think I'm eligible, and, you know, the food stamps, fine, but I enjoy working. I prefer to work. I don't like getting hung up on gettin' a check here. That makes a lot of people lazy, and I see that here with some of the residents. It has made some of them extremely - just sorry, just lazy people. "Well, I know that I'm gonna be able to get this check as long as I have these kids, so I'm not gonna work, I've never worked, and I have no intentions of working." And some of them have actually stated that, and some of them have actually lived that. No, I don't want to become dependent on anything like that. As long as I have strength and my health, I prefer working, okay? And there're not many benefits out there for single women anyway. The food stamps, that's a blessing, but you don't find that many benefits for someone in my category.

You have an interesting perspective on things because, for one thing, you're older than the average resident, and for another thing, you've been on the other side of the desk as a social worker. What have you learned or observed here?

What I see, first of all, I'm older, and there is a generation gap because some of them are young enough to be my children, you know, if I had given birth to them.

But, you see, I'm from that era of the Doctor Martin Luther King Junior, where you live the dream, where the doors were open, and we attended college. There was no such thing as today, well, "I'm not gonna finish high school." That was unheard of in my family, because my grandparents and my mother - my mother was a nurse, my father had his own business - building - and there was no way I could sit there in that family and do nothing. But what I see here are women, *young* women, that have no goals, probably don't know what a goal is, and will never have any, and that's sad. I see my black sisters, in 1991, still having children out of wedlock, with state-of-the-art birth control. I see my black sisters still not bein' able to read and write in 1991, with state-of-the-art educational information. You understand what I'm sayin'? That's sad to me because I'm from that era where you grabbed the gusto, and you grabbed the opportunity, and you lived the dream. So I'm sad a lot, and first of all, you can't tell them anything because they know more than you, you understand? And that's par for all of them, black and white, green or yellow. But the reason I said that is because I was from that era, Spelman College is located in Atlanta, Doctor Martin Luther King attended Morehouse, which is right across the street - all boys. So I was in that arena, and I cannot relate to this continuing to have children out of wedlock, and not bein' able to read and write, in 1991. To me, I just cannot relate to that. Then some of them not wanting to go on and continue with their education, I can't relate to that either. And, I call them family curses and generational curses that we need to try to pray about, and to just rid our souls of once and for all, okay? I talk about black because that's what color I've been all my life, so I can easily talk about them, but it happens in other nationalities also. But I always like to start from home base.

So I'm saddened by many things because it's rough out there, it's rough *with* the education and the degrees and the work history and the knowledge to go behind it. It's rough *with* all of that, so you can imagine what it's gonna be without that. And if I was born out of wedlock, and I've had a child out of wedlock, nine times out of 10, that child is gonna have children out of wedlock. You see that family curse, that generational curse? I've seen it so many times, so it saddens me that I don't hear parents here talking - maybe one, one or two - that, "I want the best for my child. I want my child to finish college, and I want my child to live the dream." I heard about two talk in those respects. The others, they don't know anything about that. It's just a struggle for them getting through the day, and that saddens me because I know the struggle that Doctor King and others, and Rosa Parks, and black and white, and other nationalities, bitten by dogs, cursed, beat up and killed. You understand? And I ask myself, "Did they go through all of that for you to just sit here and not do anything?" That puzzles me, and it bothers me also. So I don't know. It's up to the staff members, the social workers, to try to edge in that gap and really bring them around. See, it's not time to look down on them, it's time to try to lift them up, because they've been told, "You're not gonna be anything, you're a slut, you're this." And some of them have very low self images, inferiority complexes, so forth and so on. There's a lot that could be done, but see, I'm not staff. Any way I can help, I do, but I don't try to double as a social worker or whatever. I'm a resident, and that's the way I deal every day.

If you're going to be out on the street or in a shelter, do you think it's more difficult for a black person than a white person to get by?

I would say yes and no. And I have sat out there on that corner. I was an overnighter before I became a resident, which meant that each morning at seven, you had to get out, and come back in at 4:30. So I've sat down there on that corner, and I've walked the streets and, you know, so forth and so on. I would say yes, it's more difficult because black folks are just not helpin' each other the way they used to, we don't love each other anymore, we don't reach out to each other like we used to. You remember when I told - let's go back a little - about the era, Doctor Martin Luther King? That was a lovefest. We helped each other, we were proud of each other, we reached out and helped you. If a family member went down, the other family members surrounded that family member, and you ate at your house tonight and maybe Aunt Lucy the next night. There was no such thing as welfare, and you bein' thrown out, or whatever. You got your things, if I had to store them at your house - my things are stored at my grandmother's now - but that's what you did. And some relative, if all of them couldn't stay with you, Uncle Ben - you understand what I'm sayin'? - they stayed over here with Aunt Lucy. But the family was kept together. We don't do that as black folks. African-Americans, black Americans, we don't do that anymore. We don't love anymore, we don't reach out and help anymore. It's me, me, me. We live in the I, the I generation. And yes, in that respect, yes, it's difficult because we've lost, we've lost what the others died for, we don't have it. We've lost the name, we've lost the heritage, it's failing, and this younger generation is just totally not interested. So I would say, in that respect, yes. In other respects I would say no, because it depends on where they are, and what part of town they're in, or shelter, or center.

What about women? Do you think it's harder on women than on men?

A man can get by and hustle and bluff his way through, but a woman is taken advantage of, so it is difficult. And I'm thankful to the Lord for this ministry, for this center, because to be out there alone roamin' the streets or possibly bein' knocked over the head, your ID stolen, relatives not even knowin' where you are, whether you're alive or dead, it's rough out there, so I'm thankful for this ministry. I hear complaints about the food, the this, or whatever, but like I told them, my relatives haven't invited me to dinner, and I notice yours haven't either, so be thankful for the ministry. ·

What do you think about the whole issue of homelessness? Some people say there should be more programs to help the homeless; other people say we are already doing enough. What do you think about all that?

Okay, well I have to add this also: There's some people out there that are classified as homeless that really enjoy livin' the way they are. And that's here, too. They get in here, they cry and kick and, "Oh, I don't have any place to go. Take me in. I don't have anywhere to go, so you let me in." I stay there for awhile, I get comfortable, the rules and regulations, all of a sudden, I don't want to abide by them. Well that's everywhere, but some of the persons that have been classified as homeless enjoy that type of lifestyle. They don't want to be anywhere where they have to abide by rules and regulations; they want to come and go as they please. Some of them don't want to work, never have, never will. Some of them are just so - the brains are burnt out from the crack and other drugs until, you know, the thinking processes have diminished, and they enjoy it. So for those, that's A-1, that's what they want. And for others, I don't like the stigma, I don't like to be labeled, because stigmas, sometimes they travel with you, even to your grave. I don't like to be labeled, stigmatized or stereotyped because sometimes people don't want you - or will not allow you - to forget, the stigma, the stigma of that word homeless.

Now, as far as services, Miami really is not that interested in the homeless. I don't know if you've read it or not, but Coconut Grove has stated that they don't want them over. That goes for other people also, including relatives. You know, it's always, "I don't want to be bothered." But when the bottom falls out for you, you reach out to everybody, you want somebody to help you. But right now, I don't see that coming, so I don't want to be bothered. And it may never happen, but you never know. So no, there are not enough services, there are not enough services. There should be more ministries like this one. I would like to see this expanded. Just like, when I was a social worker, we used to develop and write home studies for foster and group homes. Well, I think the same thing can happen with the homeless also. We deinstitutionalized places in Orlando and here in Miami, and started placin' them in group and foster homes. The same thing can be done with the homeless. You know, one of my pet statements is, "Everyone wants to help the homeless, but no one wants them in their homes." That's sort of ironic. "I'll do anything for you, but nooooo, you can't come in here." Which, now don't get me wrong, you have to be careful. But there are some cynics out there, they'll come over here and preach that story about we wanna help the homeless, and then they go on to their mansions in Miami Lakes or wherever. And that goes for black leaders also. I talk about both, not just one. This isn't hatred; I'm just bein' factual with you. That goes for all of them. "It's easy for me to talk about it because, after all, I don't live in this area, and when I leave here, I don't have to see you, I don't have to think about you, I don't have to smell you." You understand? And the bottom line to that is that more ministries like this one should be opened, and I think it's a necessary evil and a necessary blessing. It's an evil and a blessing in some respects.

I haven't lived this type of life since college days, all girls, Spelman College, dormitory, and then after my freshman year I got a private life - I mean a private room - and a private life, you know. So this is dormitory. I can deal with it, see, I can deal with the getting up, even though I'm tired of it, I can deal with it because I haven't done this in over 20 years, since I left college. But I can deal with it. But I'm ready to move on now, ready to get a job and continue with my ministry and continue with my life, and if the Lord is going to send a companion, whatever, I'm ready for all of that, I'm ready to move on. I'm goin' through my healing process and so forth, and I'm just ready to tackle that other hurdle. I'm not holdin' any grudges or animosity in my heart because in order to be forgiven, you've got to forgive, and you can't get anything accomplished by walkin' around with anger and animosity in your heart. That would only set you back. But I have so much that I want to do, and other things that I have accomplished and I want to see accomplished, possibly me havin' a home or whatever, or openin' a facility. So I can't allow animosity and hatred and prejudice and all those little illnesses to affect me. I have to keep a clear mind so that I can move on and do what I have to do, or what I've been called to do, or will be called to do.

Has this experience changed your political orientation with respect to elected officials or how you look at how the system works or fails to work?

My eyes have been opened not only to my family, but people in general. We don't help and love each other like we used to; it's not there. And I guess some people are sayin', "Hey, we're just tired. We're just downright tired." Okay, but some of them have to realize that persons like me, we're not all out there lookin' for a handout, but a hand, not a handout, but a hand.

If all goes well, what will happen in the next six months or a year?

If all goes well, I will get a dynamite job, and I will get me a little place, room or whatever. Oh, and possibly marry, maybe adopt children or have, or whatever, and just continue to live and help others. I've always worked in the helping profession, and I think if I had to live where I couldn't help or do somethin' for someone, I don't think I would want to live, really.

Job, housing, get in my prayer closet, havin' my own little space, clearin' my mind, getting myself together, you know, going through my healing process, and then movin' onto another dimension, maybe a spouse, maybe just a good companion, maybe just friends. It may or may not be marriage, you understand? But a companion, someone you can talk to and relate to, and movin' on from there.

Is there anything else you'd like to add?

I thing what you're doin' is necessary because I think people need to know. And I think people need to know that there is another side to being, for lack of a better term, homeless, quote unquote. You know, they just see one picture, probably someone out there that's drugged out or alcoholic or dirty, hair dirty, not combed, unkempt, or whatever. But the bottom can fall out for anyone, and it can happen today, tomorrow, tonight. You never know. You can be wealthy today and a pauper tomorrow; it has happened. And don't judge, don't just group, just because what you see under the expressway as just the quote unquote homeless, okay? Check the situation out. Donate to centers like this, because it's very necessary. I can see what's goin' on here, and I think it's a beautiful ministry, and what is donated is used worthwhile, it's not abused, okay? And continue, because you have children that will have to outlive this traumatic experience. Draggin' a child from pillar to post, and from one place to another, it's not a pretty sight.

How do you think the children are holding up in here?

Some of these children are extremely lost, I'll just be honest with you, they're lost. And we'll just have to pray for them when they leave here, or whatever.

Chapter Five

Addictions

About 27 million Americans use an illegal drug at least once in the course of a year, and approximately 103 million consume alcohol at least once a month. The vast majority of these people are not addicts, but some users eventually do become addicted. About 336,000 Americans use cocaine on a daily basis, and close to 500,000 use the highly addictive crack form of cocaine in a given month. Many addicts manage to live relatively normal lives for years, or even decades, but for some drug users the addiction ignites a chain of events that ends in the streets. Most of them lose their jobs and the health insurance that goes with it. Consequently, they are unable to enter private drug treatment programs. Those who want to enter publicly funded programs may find themselves on long waiting lists.

Ralph Lazorra, 46, is a native of New York City. He was interviewed in Jacksonville at the Trinity Rescue Mission.

How long have you been in Florida?
Three months I've been here; I came specifically for this place from New York. I've been homeless before. I was homeless in New York, but it's different in New York than it is down here. In New York there's a lot of agencies, a lot of different places to go to, you know, there's different categories of homeless. It's real different there. I came down here for the program 'cause I came to Christ, I'm a born-again Christian. I came to Christ in '84; it's been up and down, up and down, up and down, and I wanted to get right with Him. And I heard about this place, I called up

from New York, and they told me to come down, she told me to come down, I hitchhiked down here. It took me seven days to hitchhike down here and I've been here ever since April, April 10th, something like that (the interview was conducted in June).

I was homeless in New York, but like, in New York, like I say, it's a little different. There it's just different. Here it's like, I don't know, it's just totally different here. I wouldn't wanna be homeless out here.

Over there, when you sit down to eat, you don't eat like you do here; over there it's like a penitentiary type atmosphere in any of the shelters. Like, "Eat it and beat it; move out." Soup and a piece of dried bread, you know. Over here we have a clothing room in here and people fortunately get some clothes and they get to pick their clothes. Sometimes they act like they're in Burdine's (a department store), you know, and you gotta give them one shirt, they don't want that one, you give 'em another one. Over there, you tell them shirt, they write it out on a slip of paper, your size, and they come down with maybe Jackie Gleason's old pants, or all different mismatched clothes. Here they're very fortunate over here, ya know?

I've lived in cardboard boxes, like I lived in one, a refrigerator box, for almost a year-and-a-half. I had it covered with linoleum, I had the top window I cut out, and I used to push it off and see the snow, and then I'd go back underneath. I survived. I was a drug addict; stopped shootin' drugs in '80. I got that habit in Vietnam.

What kinds of drugs?

Heroin, cocaine, together. I don't consider myself an alcoholic, but when I do I'm not a park bench drinker or anything like that; I like to go to nice bars, especially sports bars. I like sports bars. I go to them, and I don't leave. If I go in with $100, I'm lucky if I leave with 10, you know? I've been to college, got a degree.

Where did you go to school?

Cooper Union university in New York City, fine industrial arts. I worked for a medical advertising company; we used to do all the art work for the American Medical Journal, you know, transparencies. I've done all sorts of work. I've always let like outside things affect me.

My mother and father died this past January, and that was almost a bottom point, but I'm so used to death, that she's been working with me for three months now, because she's close to what my mother's age was.

Who?

Mrs. Willinger (a mission staff member). You know, she has certain key men here. There's like 10 guys in the program, there's three that are her key men. I'm one of them.

These are people that she trusts and that she depends on. She's really surrounded me with a lot of love, more so than my mother; my mother and I used to drink together. I guess I got the bar room and restaurant thing from her. She was a retired bank worker; we used to go to clubs and Italian restaurants and just sit there and drink, you know?

I feel now, my plans now, like when I was in New York I used to sit on park benches, you know, and sit there with - I loved marijuana, you know? I hope that it stops. Like right now, I've been clean - about a month before I came here, so about four months I haven't done it. And I hope I can continue that. Since I've been here, I came in here 160; I'm 205. I'm goin' back big spiritually and back big physically. While I was there, I always had a quiet respect from the guys in my neighborhood. I come from an outrageously tough kind of neighborhood. There's a lot of hard-core punk rocks, there's a lot of gentrification, a lot of that and a lot of drug addicts, a lot of everything. But everyone gets along, blends pretty well.

Where were you living?

The lower east side in New York City. I don't know if you've heard of Tompkins Square Park, well right across the street - that's on Seventh Street - I lived right on Seventh Street overlooking the park. I was there the time they had the riot, you know, and there were policeman, you know, they beat up. I got some photographs from that. Anyway, I've always sat in that park smokin' a joint, with a bottle, witnessing, you know, Jesus loves you [demonstrates holding his breath in the way that marijuana smokers do] and then spittin' it out. And they're lookin' at me. Then, these same people that I'd be witnessing to about Christ, about two or three weeks later I'd see them all dressed, with a Bible, changed, shaved, haircut. I'm still on the bench and I said God, what's going on? What am I? Made out of wood? You know, what's goin' on with me? Where's the change you're promising me? But He wasn't gonna change me 'cause I was still drinkin' and smokin'. And I realized I had to give that up, and since I've been down here, it's been awesome, it's been a total change in my life. Not just from Christ, but the way I feel about things.

Like they have a rehabilitation farm here also, and the day that I was supposed to go - I was here two weeks before me and this other fellow that came here was supposed to go. And the day that I woke up, I was supposed to go, I already had packed, and I felt strange, I felt like weird. I said to Mrs. Willinger, "I don't know what it is. What's goin' on?" She said, "You know what it is, Ralph? God has a ministry for you in the streets of New York, and He wants you to stay here to prepare for that with the people comin' in here; pray about it." So she let me stay another day here. That night, the whole night I prayed: God, what do you want me to do? The next morning I said, "That's what it is." Ever since then I've been here; the other guy went to the farm, but I've done my time here. And then this clothing room is unbelievable. If you wanna see somethin', stick around for after church, you're gonna see somethin' unbelievable. These guys, they are demanding, it's a thankless job, they don't appreciate nothin'. But like I look out on them and I gotta care for them 'cause these are the kind of people that I wanna reach with God's word. I wanna reach them, let them know that you don't have to be homeless. If they're lookin' for what the devil has to offer, that's just what they're gonna get, what the devil has to offer - a lot of crap and a whole lot of pain, misery. And that's the way it's been. I know from firsthand experience. I've seen a lot of death, I've seen a lot of misery. And I'm cold to a lot of things. I mean I've seen people fall dead right in front of me and I would just look at them - I mean, it's happened, I've seen it, you know? It's gotten me a little callous. I hope God can deliver me from that; I'm sure He will. I want to get some compassion. Deep down inside my character is not to care about nobody. I couldn't care less. But I know there's something else there, 'cause there's doubt now. Sometimes it worries me. Am I too soft? I know we're not talkin' about homelessness, but this is all part of it.

Sure. When you were homeless in New York, was that because of your addiction?

Yeah, I would say that it was primarily because of my unwillingness to stop and seek the help that I needed. I was goin' to a Vietnam vet center and they were tellin' me, "Go here, go here, go there." I'd say, "No, I can do it by myself." Then I'd walk out and say, "I'll do it tomorrow." I'd be drinkin' and smokin' reefer 'cause that got to be a massive habit for me, man. Drinkin' and marijuana gives you a third head; the two of them together make a third head. It was massive for me. In New York City you can walk around smokin' a joint and drinkin' beer. I used to walk around and cup the joint and smoke it, drinkin' beer, and just float along, you know? And I lost all sense of responsibility; I just didn't bother with nothin'. I would hang around the parks during the daytime, whatever, go pick up my unemployment check, go sit in a bar half the night. I'd go take a shower at Holy Name Society - for homeless people - then I'd go to a bar at night time. It got pretty awesome after awhile. I found myself walkin' totally by myself. I was always by myself. And it got to the point where I started feelin' sorry for myself. Why am I homeless? I used to see people walkin' hand in hand, even when I used to see homosexuals walkin' hand in hand - I'm not gay, I'm just concerned with the love for people - all I would see was the love, not the gender. I'd say, "Wow, man, that's awesome. Where's mine? Where is mine? Where's my other part, my other half?" That'll come, that'll come eventually.

I feel a lot better now. I feel a lot better with respect to a lot of things now. What I gotta do is continue believin', stay in the Bible. It's just like, I'm not a fanatic, like "Jesus, hallelujah." But if you wanna talk about Christ, we'll talk about Christ. If I see you and I pinpoint on you and I see that in your face, that there's misery and hurt in ya, I'm gonna approach ya, "Hey man, you know you don't have to be like that, brother." I don't have to come to you like I see a lot of Christians [switches to a falsetto voice], "Brother, do you know the Lord loves you?" You know, like pious; I'm not pious. I'm from the streets, and that's how God can use me. I can reach people. God uses three-piece-suit Christians with people he can reach. He made me individual like he made you individual. There's certain people that I can reach that nobody else can reach. I know a lot of prostitutes, I know a lot of mafiosos, and I know a lot of guys that are like wise guys, that's what they call them, wise guys, young hoodlums that are just like borderline. They don't know what they're doin', they just want the name. I know a lot of drug addicts, I know a lot of crooks, these are people that I know how to bob and weave with them. And these are people that I think God's leadin' me right to. And they're not stupid; they're not ignorant people. They're smart people; they're just in a bad space. And I think that's the tool that God has given me. 'Cause I think everybody should do somethin' for the homeless, you know, even if it's donating a dollar, even if it's this, whatever. Everybody should take a turn at it, 'cause it's not getting any better. I know you've done some research; it's not getting any better at all. And then with crack, forget about it. Crack is a monster; it's the worst thing.

Do you have a place to live there when you go back?

Well, like here, what it is, next week I'm gonna start lookin' for a job. Hopefully I got a couple leads that are really like promising. Mrs. Willinger will let me stay here another month-and-a-half, two months, you know, whatever I need to get enough money to get an apartment, a phone hooked up, food in my thing, maybe a couple month's rent paid up, to give me time to look for a job. The first thing I'm gonna do when I get there, I probably will go to the YMCA in Mount Vernon, New Jersey, which is where my old fiance lives. She don't live in the Y; she lives in Mount Vernon. It's a nice neighborhood. It's very, very nice; it's like kind of a preppie town, you know? With cherry blossoms, outdoor cafes, it's really nice. It's a college town, that's where Mount Vernon State University teacher's college is. So I'll go there, and I'd really like to move into a carriage house. I lived in one before, so maybe I can do it again. I'll get another little Volkswagen and just go from there.

Are you going to move back to New York City eventually?

I think I'm gonna stay out of New York City as far as residing there. That's where I'll be walking, I may even be working there. I think I have to sever living there; I'm gonna hit New Jersey for awhile. I'm not really crazy about New Jersey 'cause I like a lot of steam and I like a lot of noise and a lot of action and a lot of people, you know. But I'm gonna stay there. I'm gonna hook up with a church in New Jersey, and maybe work in the city, and after work go on the streets, and maybe my church has a street ministry of some sort, go from there.

What kind of work are you looking for? Commercial art?

Well no, here I don't wanna get tied with something where I'm gonna be dependent on someone or they're dependent on me, like I'll be here and just leave them. One of the fellows just started a job today. He's in this program; he just started a job today. He's a CPA and he got a job - janitorial work, cleaning offices at night, they just picked him up. His addiction is compulsive gambling, so he has to be humble and take that job, $5 an hour. So whatever I can get, man, whatever job I can get, $5 an hour, $6 an hour, whatever it is, where I'm not in the position where they have to depend on me to be there all the time and to stay forever, something where I can work and get money and let them know a week ahead I'm gonna be leavin'.

Do you think it's easier to be homeless in New York because there's so many social service agencies up there?

Oh definitely, no doubt, you know like in New York City you can get money, you can get clothes, you can get to eat, you don't have to be hungry, you can take a shower. I mean, it's unbelievable, they have so many places you can go to. You can wake up in the morning and go to Holy Name, take a shower, they'll give you clothes, you can walk around, kill some time, you know what park to go to if the Hare Krishnas are gonna be there servin' food, or if this lady who used to come around with fried chicken, she's gonna be there. You know the labor pools you can go to get a job. They give you a subway token. A whole lot, there's no comparison. The only problem there is that there seems to be a big influx of psychiatrically recovering people on the streets, like a lot of psychiatric hospitals just put them on the street, so you got them there, then you got the addictive homeless, then you got the ones that have come out of jail, then you got the ones that are there paying dues for somethin' they've done wrong, as a result of their lifestyle, and then they got the ones that just don't care. Then you got the ones that got burnt out of their house or somethin', got no place to go, but they usually stay a little while and then they leave. You can see in their faces who's been out there, who's satisfied with it. Then some people that are homeless, you don't even know they're homeless. That's the way it was always with me, man. I used to go take a shower every day, shave every day. I used to get in line, and a lady told me, "This is only for homeless." I said, "I am homeless." There's a lot of people walking around like that. It used to surprise me how many when I used to go stand in lines at some mission. I'd see the same people walkin' around, whoa, this guy, I thought he looked like he had a place, but I do too; he must have thought the same thing about me. I'd start talkin' to them, just realizin' that somethin' has happened. A lot of people use the pills. You gotta deal with the addictions, that's the whole thing, the alcohol and the drugs, that's what does it. It robs everybody of everything, *everything,* not only material things, it'll rob you of everything. It gets to the point where, no self-esteem, no nothin'. I mean, there's absolutely nothing left. You become totally dependent on somebody else. Then you have nothing, and then you demand everything. "The food stinks." "I don't want them clothes." In the meantime, you don't have no food and you don't have no clothes. It's pretty bad, it gets pretty bad.

How long have you been homeless all together?

Well, I would say the longest period I was homeless was about a year-and-a-half that I was actually out on the street. But I would say maybe about three years, here or there. The last time before this time was in 1985.

I thank God, you know, because I tell ya, there's so many times I could have gotten killed because I've been in situations - bein' homeless - in situations where I could have really got hurt, and I didn't, and God has watched me, and He's given me a brain, and I'm grateful for that. He's kept me like really in good shape.

This has been a blessing here, man. This isn't a fancy place; it's an old place. It has cockroaches and all that crap. It isn't the prettiest place in the world, but there's a lot of love here. If somebody wants to really, really stop what they're doin' and get a good life started, get a foundation, instead of hanging up in the air like somebody holding up a tree in the air, plant it, start blossoming, this is the place to start. I'll never forget this place, ever. Her, she's unbelievable, 80 years old. I mean, she takes my heart. She really does, she really takes my heart. She knows it. I tell her, I say, "I believe you do love me." She tells me she loves me; she tells everybody she loves them. I say, "Mrs. Willinger, I've never believed anybody in my life, but I believe you." I would do anything for her, anything; she knows it. She's sweet. When I first came here, I said, "Oh my God." I pictured what this place looks like, wall to wall rugs or something, marble here, pool table, swimming pool. I came here, "What the hell am I doing here?"

But after a week I said, "Oh well, I'll give it a shot." It's been like day by day by day.

Do you see any big differences in how people wind up on the street, comparing New York and Florida?

Oh yeah, I always tease people about it. I call 'em pussy cats, 'cause like in New York they're rough, really rough. They fight, they yank ya out of line. You could be standing in line all day waitin' for something and they come right in front of you, smack ya. They don't do that here, they're soft.

For the most part, it's really smooth here. In New York there's a lot of strife, a lot of anger, a lot of fightin'. It's totally different. There's a lot of people, a lot of homeless people. There's a lot of rippin' off, a lot of hurting people. That's why I said God has really protected me, man, 'cause I've been in situations where I'd be sleeping on a bench and somebody down on the other bench is gettin' beat up, somebody over here is gettin' beat up, I just go back to sleep. I got like painted with the blood, like the Passover blood, and they just pass over me. I never got into the problems at all. So I thank God. Yeah, there's a big difference, a big difference, in everything: food, services, and everything else.

So in some ways it's more difficult up there, but in other ways it's easier because there's more social services available.

Yeah, right, exactly, if you're having a problem with certain agencies up there, you go downtown, that's totally different, you go out by Chinatown, that's totally different, it's a little better out there; you go midtown, that's rough. Go Times Square, that's serious. Walk down by Harlem? Forget it, you gotta be black. You gotta go where you fit in.

Donna Robinson, 27, is a native of Morganton, North Carolina. She was interviewed in Zellwood at Anthony House, a family shelter, where she was staying with her children: Tyler, 4, and Talisa, 2.

How long have you been in Florida?
For about 13 years.
What brought you down?
My mother brought me down here to live with my father. I was a hard-to-handle teenager. [laughs] So she brought me to live with dad, hoping that would settle me down a little bit, but it didn't work. [laughs] It didn't work too well. I've more or less been on my own since I was 15, living with friends; I'm in my second marriage, and I guess what really brought me here was I've been working on getting my life straight. I'm a recovering drug addict, been clean for six months now. I lost my children

to HRS and regained custody last December, which is when I came here. I came here November of '90, and I've been here since. The program here has been really helpful to me in more ways than just having a place to live. The staff has been really great as far as counseling, or just somebody to talk to, or advice. It's helped me to learn a great deal about gratitude. [laughs] By coming here I was able to get my children back. I was in a residential rehabilitation program for 30 days in October of '90, and upon leaving the residential center - to try to get my children back - so that they didn't go into a foster home, I was unable to get a job right away. And I was out three weeks prior to coming here, and once I decided to come here my HRS case worker told me that with three recommendations she could recommend to the judge that I get full custody. So that worked out, and through the process of things, you know, once I got the kids back, I was able to go to school through an HRS program called Project Independence. And I just completed that program last week, last Tuesday, and things are really starting to look up for me. Anthony House has a new program, it's called Measure of Independence, it's a six-month program, which I was able to get into, and as a follow up, I'm goin' to be goin' into another six-month program, but I'll be leaving the Anthony House and getting into a place of my own, for the children and me. And they have found a sponsor family for me through one of the local churches in Apopka, it's the Presbyterian church of Apopka, and they are going to be makin' visits to the house - it's gonna be a trailer, two-bedroom trailer - they're gonna be making visits weekly, and helpin' me work on a budget, and the objective of this program is to help me get to where I can be self-supporting, you know. I had to write out what my goals are, and what I want to do for myself, and the top of the list is my independence and bein' self-support-ing, for myself and the kids.

I don't know, I never really checked on any of the other shelters; I've heard of them, and I've heard things about them, but the way the Anthony House is run, I can really appreciate what they do. You know that you've got a place every night, it's not like you come on a daily basis and take your chances to whether or not you get a bed that night. As long as you follow the rules, and as long as you're willing to help yourself and willing to do whatever is needed by you here to maintain the place - which isn't a lot - if you've got your own place, you're going to work, you know, you're going to maintain that and it's a lot more work. [laughs]

Are your children living here with you now?

They live here; during the day they're at day care, yeah, I've been job hunting. It's a court order that they attend child care for at least one year, that's one of the rules through HRS, one of the stipulations to my getting custody, and they have to attend at least eight hours a day during the week, which is really helpful to me because, you know, that gives me time; I was in school. And now that I'm looking for a job, that gives me the time to do what I need to do, so it's really helpful. Before, I would never have thought about puttin' my kids in day care.

Did you come to Anthony House directly from the residential program?

Well, no, my sister-in-law has a house with a little upstairs apartment, and she let me stay in that apartment; I was there for three weeks before I came to Anthony House, so there was a little time period there when I was more or less on my own.

What originally caused you to lose having a regular place to live?

My addiction, drugs.

Where did you live before you were in the residential program?

Well, we stayed with my mother-in-law for awhile. We were in and out of places a lot. Okay, so, you know, when you're on drugs, especially the drug of my choice, which was cocaine, it's really devastating; you lose your sense of any kind of responsibility or direction. And they've been really helpful here, I mean I've been on restriction since I've been here, and I was kind of resentful of that because I thought I was being judged for my past, but it's really been to my benefit. It's a tough program here, and it's really hard, but it also determines who really wants to do something for themself. And it determines who wants to help himself and who expects something to be done for 'em. It is hard, and it's been hard, and it's going to continue to be hard, but you just do what you gotta do.

Did you ever have to live outside for awhile?

Well, years ago I had, when I separated from my first husband. Now, I have a older son, he lives with his father, my ex-husband. Let's see, I've got to think back, how many years - nine years ago I slept in a car with him for, you know, a few days. So I know what it's like to really be without. And there are people that are worse off, that don't even have a car, that are really out in the street. So I'm really fortunate in a lot of ways, even now, that I have family members - in-laws - that have helped me a lot. I guess I would be one of the luckier people in this situation; I really consider myself very fortunate because I see a lot of people that have it a lot worse than I do.

How did you get separated from your children?

They were taken by HRS.

How did that happen?

Through the course of my addiction, which, I was on that particular drug for five years. It originally started when my daughter was born; we were under voluntary protective services, which meant an HRS case worker made, you know, unannounced visits to our home. And we had moved, and that case had not been closed.

Our being on voluntary protective services was drug-related, so when they had another call an investigator came, and she filed her report, and then the supervisor said that we can't take it under voluntary again. So we either had to find a family member to take the children or they would take 'em; they took 'em and placed them in a shelter, an HRS shelter. Let's see, they were taken last June. So there again, I'm really blessed that I got 'em back when I did.

How long were you separated from them?

Six months.

Were you in that residential program the whole time?

No, I didn't enter. As a matter of fact, it got worse when the kids were taken. Because that responsibility - what little bit I did do - the whole responsibility was taken away, you know. I didn't have to cook for 'em, I didn't have to bathe 'em, I didn't have to make sure they had clothes on. So when that responsibility was taken away, the illness really progressed a lot.

I used up until the day I went into the residential center. And even on that day, I had a girl friend was taking me down there, and the whole ride I was biting my tongue 'cause I wanted to say turn around and take me back, turn around and take me back. 'Cause it was really scary. But I bit my tongue, and I made it, and I'm still making it. [laughs] I'm really proud of myself; I really am. I've got six months clean and I've really accomplished a lot in that time. I've had a lot of support; I still go to outpatient classes, and I'll finish that program at the end of this month. But I'll continue with NA meetings, Narcotics Anonymous, for support, and my counselor says that I've done a good job of networking through coming to the Anthony House, with Herb (Herb Aguirresaenz, the shelter director), with his contacts, and then getting into the programs that I've gotten into, so I have a lot of support. The help is out there if people want it; it's there, I'm learning that. I used to feel like nobody gives a damn, you know, but even with my past, people have accepted me for what I'm doin' now, and are willin' to help me.

What was the Project Independence program you mentioned earlier?

That's a schooling program. They paid for my schooling.

What kind of schooling?

I took data processing at a vocational school. Now I've got to find a job. But it's really good because, you know, it broadens the field as far as any kind of office job; there are a lot of different types of jobs you could get

with that knowledge, it's just a matter of finding somebody that will give
you a chance to get some experience.

*Have you found that employers are reluctant to hire someone who lives
at a shelter?*

Not yet, but the address that I give, I give the street address, which is
6215 Holly Street, and unless somebody were to really ask, they wouldn't
know the difference, you know, so I guess I'm lucky in that. Unless it were
right around here, somebody might know, but I've been concentrating on
- there's not much around here [laughs] - so I've been concentrating more
around Orlando and Altamonte (Altamonte Springs), just what I see in the
Sunday papers or through the job service. But I'm not ashamed of it, and
I'm not reluctant to tell somebody that that's where I'm at. It really doesn't
bother me I guess, but some people are really judgmental, and see a
homeless person as a bum, which is not necessarily true. There are people
that are victims of circumstance, and there are people that choose to be
that way too. I wouldn't say I'm a victim of circumstance; I don't know
what I would say. I don't choose to be homeless, but my past choices got
me here.

*What was your living situation like before you had all this trouble with
the courts and so on?*

We moved a lot from place to place, you know, pay by the week. The
duplex that's next door [points to a house that is on the property adjacent
to the shelter] - prior to the children being taken away, we had lived there;
it used to have lights and water, and we lived in one side of that. It's an
abandoned building now; it should have been when we lived in it too. We
lived there for, let's see, I don't know, about eight months. And I guess
you would say that's where we were when everything came down; when
the HRS investigator showed up we were packin' to move, but we were
really just runnin' again, you know, we weren't facin' up to our problems,
we were runnin', as we had done a lot of times before. We lived in
rent-by-the-week places out on Lake Apopka, which were dumps that
should be condemned. But that was not necessarily by choice.

Were you working?

No, I worked for about five or six months when Tyler turned a year old;
I worked in a dry cleaner's. But other than that I stayed home with the
kids.

*Were you always able to get enough of the basics - food, health care
and clothing?*

Right, well clothing - a lot of things were passed down through the
family. Like, my children have cousins that, you know, my in-laws would

give us clothes. So clothing was pretty much always there; for myself, I just made do with what I had. And I had friends that gave me clothes.

A drug addict really doesn't care much about appearance, you know. We were clean, we'd shower, and we washed our clothes; sometimes we'd go for a month before we washed our clothes. I washed them out by hand a lot. That's an insane world, it's an insane world.

Did you lose having a regular place to live directly because of all that?

Well, all of it really centers around - because of the drugs.

I guess everybody says you have to hit a rock bottom, and we definitely hit a rock bottom. They say that you have to hit rock bottom before you can ever look for help or really want to get help. And I believe it; I mean that's what it took, that's what it took.

Some politicians think there should be more programs for homeless people, and others say we're already doing enough. What do you think?

I really don't know. I mean I know there should be more programs like this one, because I don't know what the other places do or how they're run. From what I understand about shelters in Orlando, it's like, you know, okay, you come in by such a certain time in the afternoon and you get meals and maybe you'll get a bed. And then first thing in the morning you're out on the street. In that type of situation, I don't think I would have made it. Here, you have as close to a home-type environment as you can get, without having your own home. Sure, you share a room with strangers or whatever, but you know that your place is here. And you have people on staff that really take an interest in helping you, *if* you want to help yourself. Programs like this, I would definitely recommend for somebody, I really would. I've seen more volunteers comin' in. Two nights a week they give out clothing. I've seen a lot of people donate items here: clothing, furniture, different things. And I'm really touched by it. My husband and I, we used to say that we really wanted to help homeless people, that we would like to do that someday. This was like, another one of those other big dreams - if we hit the lottery, you know. But I would really like to do it, maybe not necessarily with money, but with time, 'cause I don't have no money now, but with time I would like to help. Maybe in some other ways in the future, when I'm more situated, I would like to help.

I've never done any type of study or research, so I really don't know what all is available. But I don't think there can ever be too much help for other people, you know. It also boils down to people that want to help themself, but sometimes people in this situation need some encouragement, they need to know that somebody cares and is willin' to be some kind of support - not necessarily financial support, I don't mean that - but a shoulder to cry on or somebody to talk to. I think that's real important to most people. Because I know I've needed the people here a lot. I've gone through a lot of changes since I came here, and I've grown up a lot, learned a lot about myself, and I've built up my self-esteem and my confidence and learned that no matter what I've done in the past, that I can still pick up and carry on, and I can make better for the future, and do better. And other people being there for a support system helps you to learn this about yourself. I don't think there could ever be too much of that. You can never help others too much; everybody needs somebody at sometime for whatever reason.

Do the people who are staying here look out for one another?

Yeah, it's like a big family, and you see members come and go, or I have, you know, and there are a couple other women being considered for the new program, and I'm really anxious for them, because I know how it's helped me. I know where my place is, at least for six months, and that's a good amount of time to work on getting it together and savin' your money, whatever income you can get. You can save virtually every dime of it outside of whatever expenses - if you have a car; I'm lucky enough to have a car. It's not much, but it serves a purpose, it's gotten me from point A to point B and back again. It costs money to operate one and maintain one, but that's just a necessity. But some people don't have it, and have to make do. But they've got a new van, it's gonna be to provide transportation just solely for that purpose, for helping people to find jobs or get to work or get to HRS or to school or whatever. Herb has done a lot with this place; I really have a lot of respect for him. He's tough, and there's times that he's made me *really* angry, but he speaks the truth. [laughs] What he said is true; I might have been mad 'cause it was true and I just didn't want to face it, but I have a lot of respect for him. He's done a lot with the programs and everything here, and everybody works together, people livin' here, we work together to maintain the place, to keep it clean, and we share our problems, we share good times. The older kids help out with the smaller children while the mothers might have chores to do or like, for cleaning up after dinner, or just whatever. So it is like a big family, it's really nice.

Some people staying in shelters in Orlando have said they encounter a lot of hostility from outsiders. Have you encountered any of that?

No, I haven't. But I would believe that because people are judgmental about how somebody looks. I've done that before. I mean I've never been hostile, but I've been judgmental of other people because they might be dirty or something, or look, you know, which isn't right. And I try to watch myself now because I'm not any better off than they are, or I'm not any better. I might have a little more to my advantage, but I'm not any better.

But yeah, I believe people would do that. When I was in school, and I would talk to some of the other women there, at first it would be, a couple of them would kind of like give me this funny look when I said I stayed in a shelter, but they were never nasty towards me. But I like to think I'm a nice person, and I get along with other people, so maybe that's why. I don't know. They continued to talk with me when we'd take our breaks and everything. But I'm sure that does happen, because people are mean. It's a dog eat dog world.

Have your recent experiences influenced your religious beliefs? Have you become more religious or less religious?

More, more religious, more belief, well, let's say more faith than I've ever had. I never had faith. I mean when I grew up I did not have any idea really of the concept of God - or God as I understand Him - everybody's got their own idea, and, you know, Jesus Christ. I'm from a Baptist background, but I really didn't know anything. My husband grew up in I guess what you'd call the all-American family, whereas mine was totally opposite. And he grew up in the church, and really, you know, very active in the church, and he used to always tell me, he said, "Donna, if anybody can help us beat this, God can." And he used to tell me that a lot. And I took that to heart whenever I went into the treatment center, and I started to read in the Bible, and pray, and as I started learnin' and understanding some of the things in the Bible, and I started tryin' to turn it over to God, and have faith, things started workin' for me. So I really believe in it. I've always believed in miracles because of my two children, the younger ones that are with me, they are truly miracles because I was an addict when I was pregnant. I did quit eventually, but they are really miracle babies in every sense of the word. They were both born on a Sunday, and I always said that just by them bein' normal and healthy and having a good mind and intelligent kids, they are miracles. And I'm a miracle. I never thought of myself as being a miracle, but me bein' alive today is a miracle in itself, because I was committin' a slow suicide, was what I was actually doin'. I have more faith in God today, and the NA program is really centered around seeking a higher power and turnin' the will of your life over to God as you understand Him, and I think that's the hardest thing, is saying, "Okay, whatever your will for me is." That's the hardest part 'cause you always want to say, "Okay, I know how to do this." But I'm working on it, and I know, I *know*, that when I just say, "Okay, God, here it is, guide me in what I need to do, lead me in the right direction," that He leads me in the direction to go. Just like, comin' here was an answer to a prayer. I prayed a lot because I was afraid - when my sister-in-law mentioned it to me - I was afraid to come here because, number one, we lived right next

door. I said, "I'm not strong enough to go right back to where I came from."
But I prayed about it for two weeks, every night and every day, I'd say,
"Is this the right thing to do?" It's like, when I quit prayin' and I was sitting
there, I was just: What am I going to do? What can I do? And the first thing
that came to my mind was Anthony House, so I called up here, and it turned
out to be the best thing. It has enriched my belief, strengthened it, because
before I had no faith at all. And it's made me more conscious of things that
I do or say, whereas before I just didn't care, I'd just do what I wanted to.

Do you think being homeless is harder on women than on men?

Definitely if they have children, I would think so, yeah. It's hard to
generalize like that because I think it just depends on the individual,
because some men could be just as devastated by it. But overall, in general,
I think it would be harder on women, especially if they have children,
because with things the way they are, it's like: How am I gonna provide
the next meal for my children? A lot of women tend to forget whether or
not they eat, or not care, just as long as they've got it for their children.
It's depressing, to say the least.

*Has this been hard on your children? Do they understand what's going
on?*

Well, Tyler is at a point - he's four - he's at a point where he talks about
being in our own home, and he looks forward to daddy coming home.
(Robinson was not living with her husband at the time of the interview.) I
don't know, you know, it's been hard on them from the beginning, really.

Them being taken away just like that, and then comin' here. Well they
were in a shelter, and then my sister-in-law got temporary custody of 'em,
and then from being with my sister-in-law they came here with me. So it's
been hard on them, the whole thing, but they didn't come right from being
in a home with security to being in this. But I know it was hard on them.
When we first saw them after they were taken from the home, they had
regressed and withdrawn. Tyler was really bitter. He was three then, not
quite four years old; you could tell that there was a lot of resentment and
anger, and there are times when I can sense his resentment, and I'm not
sure where it's directed.

I'd like to work on whatever deep down inner resentments he has and
get 'em out, because that had a lot to do with my addiction; I've learned
that it actually started when I was young, it started with food, and when I
got to be about 12 years old is when it turned to alcohol and drugs because
I didn't know how to deal with the angers and resentments and the hurt
that I felt from things that happened to me as a child, you know. And you
never want to see your kids go through all the painful things that you went
through, and I would hate to see any of my kids go through the hell I went

through with drugs. I know you can't control it, but education I think is the main thing. And Tyler knows that I've been in treatment.

So it is hard on kids. And I've seen kids come in that, they experience a lot of behavioral problems, and mothers experience problems in discipline because they feel guilty about what's happening. I know I go through that sometimes - guilt - but you have to learn to put the guilt behind you because you can't make up for the past; it's just impossible to do that.

Do you think there is anything you could have done differently to avoid this situation?

Yeah, but probably not, because I didn't have the knowledge or insight I've got now. You know, I could have worked toward my independence at a earlier age.

I think a lot of things go back to being children because a lot of hurt children grow up to be adults full of anger. So I think children are very important, and educating them and lovin' 'em and carin' for 'em, and being there, being a friend to them, as well as a parent, which, it's really sad that a lot of people don't do that.

For myself, it's hard to say; I really don't know. I had a chance at one point to really try to become independent, but I let myself depend on other people, so I never really worked at it. I always say if I knew then what I know now, it would have been different. [laughs] So I don't know if I could have changed it or not. I don't think I would want to because I've learned so much about myself and about life and the quality of life and the value of life, and I've also learned the ways that I can help other people, which is real important to me, you know. If I could help one kid decide not to use drugs, that would mean a lot to me. Or if I could convince one teenage girl to think twice before she has sex with somebody and gets pregnant - my first son was born when I was 17, just turned 17 - and then right after he was born I got married, which was two mistakes right on top of each other. All your bad experiences aren't so bad if you learn from 'em, and if you can help somebody else through what you've learned, then it's alright.

So if all goes well, what will happen in the next year?

In the next year? Well, let's see, within about four weeks the children and I will be movin' into a trailer. I will have steady employment, hopefully. You know, I would like to get in with a company where I can advance and learn more. I would like to talk at schools about drug abuse and addiction. I would like to help the homeless, I would like to help with the Anthony House, if not other organizations - but one step at a time. [laughs] But I do have a strong desire to help with the Anthony House in some way. I will be self-supporting, myself and the children, and just livin' life to the fullest, makin' it the best I can for myself and for my children.

And bein' able to communicate and keep the line of communication open with my children is really important to me. Because, hey, I can't teach them everything, and I can't control their lives, but it's important that they know that if they've got a problem, maybe they feel that they can come and share it with me, and maybe I can help them, or maybe I can lead them in the right direction...just bein' more independent and secure in myself in the next year.

Leroy Walker*, 37, is a native of New Orleans, Louisiana. He was interviewed in Miami underneath a highway overpass where a number of homeless people were living.

How long have you been in Florida?
A year.
Did you come directly from Louisiana?
Yeah, I come from Louisiana to Miami.
What brought you down here?
I don't know, just from state to state I guess. I really can't say.
Were you looking for work when you came here?
When I got here I was lookin' for work, but I guess work - I don't know. You know, I come here lookin' for a job. I had a good job here, and I blew it. I had a good job.
It didn't work out?
I didn't work out. The job was perfect. It was me, it wasn't the job, it was me.
What happened?
I'm a junkie, and a junkie can't keep a job. That's it; I'm a junkie. I've had beautiful jobs, it's just that if you a drug addict, how do you expect to hold a job? So that's what my problem is.
What kind of drugs were you using?
I'm still a drug addict. I'm a drug addict, I'm a junkie for heroin, cocaine, crack. Mostly cocaine and heroin. I have a good education. I'm just a junkie. You know, I have a good skill - refrigeration - but I'm just a junkie. I can even make 35 grand a year. I'm just a junkie and I can't hold a job.
How long have you been living outside here?
For over a year. I became a junkie in '87, been down on my ass ever since '87, when I turned junkie. I come out with a broke back; I'm crippled now. See my back? [He is shirtless, and turns to reveal a series of scars along his spine.] I got a bad foot, went through a whole lot of changes. So now I couldn't get a job if I wanted to. Who would hire me now? 'Cause I'm just fucked up, man, just fucked up. I'm just fucked up.

You can't work because of your back?

Yeah, you see my back all fucked up. So I just messed up, just blew it, you know? Sometimes you win, sometimes you lose, and I lost. [laughs] I'm a loser.

Have you been living outside ever since you came here?

Yeah.

What about New Orleans? Were you living outside there?

I had it together in New Orleans until - I told you - I turned junkie there in '87. Like I say, when you turn junkie, there's nothing else left. You be up so high, and then once you turn junkie you fall so low you have to go. You know, you can't be around no friends or nothing, once you been up. It's like, if you'd lose your position, you'd go somewhere else. You don't want nobody to see you in the gutter. So that's what I done; that's what happened. If you turned junkie, you wouldn't want nobody to see ya - after you'd been a writer and stuff. You'd leave; you'd go somewhere else. Wouldn't you? Wouldn't you think so? So that's what I done; I just left. I'm here, same damn thing here, but I don't know nobody. You know, it doesn't matter who sees ya, who don't see ya. I don't know nobody, so it don't really matter. But I had it pretty good; I've had a pretty good life, a beautiful life, but I just messed up, something that we all do.

What do you do to get food?

All I can't steal for I go to jail and get.

But where do you go to get it?

To get what?

To get food.

Anywhere I can get it, [points] this dumpster and that dumpster, or I steal and make money. You know, any way that I can get it, any way, that's survival, that's what we do, that's what I do.

Do you ever go to the soup kitchens?

That's so far to walk with a broke back and no foot, you know. Sometimes I catch 'em, sometimes I don't. But that's a bad thing to depend on, them soup kitchens. I'd rather depend on me. I try to keep a few bucks, you know. If not, I roll with the punches; whatever comes I get. If I don't, I don't get it. Like I hadn't eaten in two days till yesterday, but finally I made three bucks and I got a meal. You'll get it. Things will break; you will get it. Somebody will slip and you will get it.

What do you do to make money?

What do I do to make money? Whatever comes up. Whatever I see I can pick up [laughs] or whatever, anything.

Do you go to the labor pools?

I can't work, between my back and my feet.

You can't work for a whole day?

I can't work probably an hour. I probably can't walk eight blocks. It would take me from here - this is 36th Street. From 36th Street to 20th Street, hell, that'd take me over an hour-and-a-half. It's a long time, 'cause I'd walk two blocks and I'd sit down for 10 or 15 minutes, I'd walk three blocks and I'd sit down 10 or 15 minutes. You know, it's hard to walk. But I get there. I have a van. I usually keep a van. I got busted over the weekend in a drug hole. You know, where they sell drugs.

In a house?

No, just in the street.

The police ran up, and I didn't have proof of insurance and driver's license, so they took my van. I got a van right now. I bought the van. I get disability. But now I'm broke, and now I'm tryin' to figure out a way that I could steal something to get it out, which I'm gonna get it, get it or go to jail, you know?

[laughs]

Now you're laughin' at me. [laughs] Well, that's just the truth, you know? I gotta get it out. And I gotta steal. I don't have any money, and so, they're not gonna give it back to me, so I got to lay around, see if somebody slips, see what I can spot to steal. That's what I'm waitin' on, see what I can spot to steal for a hundred and some bucks to go get my truck. And I'm gonna get it. Or go to jail.

So you had a van?

I still got it, but it's in the tow yard.

Can you live in your van?

That's what I was doin', that's what I was doin'. That's why I have these screwdrivers. See these screwdrivers? [pulls two screwdrivers out of his pants pocket] See, I wanna go home, and that was my intention, to go home.

Back to New Orleans?

Yeah. See like, this month, I get my check transferred from here to New Orleans, my Social Security check, and it done got lost in the mail. I don't know what done happened, but somebody done got it. [laughs] So, that fucked me up. I guess if it wasn't for bad luck, you wouldn't have no luck, right? And so it got me all delayed. So, I'm fucked now. So anyway I gotta figure a way to get it out, to get two or three hundred bucks, you understand? And go home. See, I gotta go home. I got tired of this; everybody's goin' to jail, everybody's goin' to prison, now they're killin' everybody around here, man, you'd be surprised. It's time to go, you know? It done got really, really hard. It used to not be this hard, it really didn't. Man, it done got rough.

Out here on the streets?

Yeah, it got rough.

Because of the police or because of other people?

I don't know. I guess life, life is changin', world is changin', man, things is changin'. It got pretty rough, man; it didn't used to be. I guess that people have gotten so bad now that everybody's strung out on drugs and stuff, and everybody's doin' everything to support their habits, so I guess it's makin' the world bad, you know. It's not only the police; they've got to do their jobs, you understand? Just like you got a job to do. Everything is gettin' so bad, man, everybody's getting bad, everything's gettin' worse. You understand what I'm tryin' to say? It's gettin' to be *hell*, man. Even the people are gettin' rough, so that's makin' the polices get rough. You used to walk down the street and hustle five or ten bucks. Nowadays you walk down the street, and if you're walkin' down the street, you see 30 policemen, you're gonna see 30 security guards, it's just not there no more. So either you gotta live right, you gotta change your habits and live right, I guess, because it got rough, man.

Were you staying out here before this weekend?

Yeah, there's a lotta places I stay. I stay under this part, I'll go stay out there on the beach at the other bridge, I'll go stay back up here on the hole up here, anywhere. I'm a loner; I go alone. Anything I wanna do, I do it by myself. I feel comfortable that way.

How many people are staying here at night?

Shit, sometimes five, sometimes 10, sometimes three, sometimes 20. You never know.

How have the police been? Do they ever help you out or bother you?

They don't help. I'm gonna tell you what. I don't mean to say it like this, but the only time the police ever bothered me is when I'm tryin' to break the law. I hate to say it like -'cause I hate fucking cops. But they ain't never bothered me for really for nothin' that I didn't do. If I'm fucked up in a bad neighborhood or walking through this lot [gestures toward a restaurant parking lot nearby] trying to spot something to steal or something, and they look, catch you, or you look suspicious or something, they start with you, but other than that, they ain't never really bothered me. I've been all over, all over, all over. When I catch hell is when I'm tryin' to break the law, and anybody else who'll tell you the truth will tell you the same damn thing. So it's not too bad, it's just the person, it's just me, it's just like it is anybody else. If you're livin' this life, it's what you expect, what you expect. If you're a crook, you're a fucking crook; I don't care how you look at it.

Have you been able to get enough clothes out here?

No, I got these clothes out of a dude's bag today. [gestures towards piles of clothing and bedrolls nearby] Me and him might get in a fight when he get home today. [laughs] Yeah, really, it doesn't matter, no big deal. But I got his clothes out of his bag today. My clothes, they stink so bad, they stand up by themselves; I had 'em on for a month.

What do you do about medical care?

I've been to the Army, I go to the VA, or I can go to Jackson Hospital, whatever.

So you don't have to worry about that?

I don't have to worry. I never worry. If I get it I get it, if I don't - I just never worry. The only thing that worries me is about getting my van, 'cause that's my home, I have a nice bed. So I get it out, I got my own bed in it, everything. I got a good one, you know? I get a check every third of the month, all except this month. And I just let it go, you know. I don't have any complaints. I just need to get my shit together and kick this habit I got. Everybody you see on the streets is a junkie; he's a junkie or he's crazy. Believe that. You know that, don't you? Everybody on the street is either a junkie or he got a mental problem, 'cause nobody would be out here if it wasn't for that, nobody. The guys you see out here now [gestures], look at how healthy he looks and stuff, look at how healthy this guy looks, see how healthy this guy looks and stuff? Now, do you think he would be out here if he didn't have a drug problem, or crazy?

Well, some people lose their jobs or whatever.

Yeah, well you know why they lose it, don't you? You haven't lost yours, right? Okay now, either you're crazy as hell or you're a junkie, man. It just that simple.

Do these guys [gestures] stay out here with you?

I don't say much to them. Yeah, they stay here sometimes. I think I'm a loner. I don't say nothin' to nobody here; nobody says nothin' to me.

Are the people who are out here pretty good about looking out for each other?

I'm a loner. I don't get involved with other people. Man, you can get killed out here; you gotta mind your fucking business. Your friends is the ones that can get you. A stranger can't hurt you. Someone might come up, they say you told somethin' or any fucking thing. You lay out here at night and get your fucking neck slit. So I'm a loner. Everybody you see is by theirself. [gestures] See he's way over there by himself, see that guy is by himself, you see that one is over there by his fucking self and you see that one there is walking by hisself, and I'm by my fucking self, so you can look at it and tell, everybody's by themselves. Out of five people out here you don't see nobody together, nobody.

Is everyone here by themselves, or are there some families staying here too?

Everybody's a loner. Some families sleep outside, the husband and wife and children. You see a lot of that out here. But they givin' away shelter now, you know? They be givin' it away for 90 days; 90 days is up they'll be right back out here, you know that. They're junkies or they have mental problems. Ain't nothin' nobody can do. You can cry that they're homeless, they can donate millions and millions of dollars. It's not gonna - what it's gonna help? You can feed 'em every day, and they gonna be a junkie every day. Just gotta kick that junkie habit, man. It's the only way out. Believe what I'm tellin' ya.

Have you tried getting treatment at a drug treatment center or anything like that?

I haven't used now since Friday (the interview was conducted on a Tuesday). I was tellin' myself I was gonna quit. I really would. I done had the chance today and yesterday and the day before, but I haven't used since Friday. I'm gonna quit. I don't know how true it is, but that's what I'm tellin' myself. I could use it every day, I believe. I could get it. I could get it; if I wanted it, I would get it. You know that, don't you? If I wanted it, I could really get it. But I'm tellin' myself I'm gonna quit. I don't know. I've gotta quit, *got* to quit. You're gonna quit or die. Either two things are gonna happen. You're gonna wind up in jail all your life, or somebody gonna kill ya for takin' their shit. So, you gotta do somethin'. There's not but two ways to go. There's death, or you're gonna wind up in fuckin' jail all your life. Which other way can you look at it?

Do you think you're going to head back to New Orleans?

If I ever get my van out of storage, I'm on my way. If I got it out this 20 minutes, I'd be on my way, I'd hit the road, talkin' about straight, I'd never stop.

Do you have a family there?

Yeah, I got a mother and a father and stuff, but I've asked them for so much. You know, they would give me the money, but I've asked for so much over the years, and I'm 37 years old. Sometimes you get so that, hey, you just feel embarrassed of yourself, to keep on askin', to keep on askin'. I could get it; they would give it to me. I have a very tight family. I could get the money, but I feel so fucked up that I'm the oldest son, and all I ever did is ask. And so I be askin' so god damn long, it make you feel - you understand what I'm sayin'? You don't wanna ask anymore. I've asked and I've asked, and they have gave and they have gave. They still would give, but god damn, you get older, older you get, say damn, you're asking, you're the one that should be giving instead of begging, so I don't even ask no more. I could get it. I could call them. Matter of fact, they would even send me a bus ticket. Yeah, they would, yeah. I could go home.

There's somethin' about it. I never destroyed my relationship with my family, even everything that I did, I never destroyed, and I have a very close family. I could call them right now, even let you speak to them, and they would tell you theirselves. As a matter of fact, my brother would come here and get me, he'd fly here and get me, and get my van out and we'd drive it back. I guarantee ya that. I don't know, I'm just, got old, man, I'm gonna do it for myself for a change. You know, I'm a junkie, man. It's time for me to do it for myself. But they would do it. I don't have to be out here. I don't have to be on these streets. As a matter of fact, let me tell ya somethin', there's a lot of other cats out here that don't have to be on these streets. Ya know, they feel that they just fucked up so bad and so long that...

I was intendin' to rob her [gestures toward a woman in the adjacent parking lot], not rob her, but I seen something I was intendin' to get earlier, but I felt it wasn't for the best. I said I better keep my shit together and just lay back. [laughs] I feel if I take it easy - okay, today is Tuesday - I feel if I take it easy I will have that hundred and somethin' bucks by Friday. So, you know, it's already about 110 bucks, 105, 110. I feel if I just mess around, and don't rush it, a good lick will come through. You know, if you rush things, things won't happen. But if you just lay around and try to stay free, somethin' will happen for you. It will; it all comes to ya. You know, I'll get me a lift. I'll get a hundred-twenty-thirty-forty dollars, I can go home. And that's what I'm waitin' on. Or either Dade County jail will get me and take care of me. [laughs]

You were in jail over the weekend?

Yeah.

They didn't keep you very long, huh?

Four hours.

Do a lot of people get arrested on purpose just to get a place to stay and rest up for awhile?

Yeah, I went to jail, I went to prison here for four months because I was wore out. I didn't weigh 100 pounds.

What did you get busted for?

What'd I go to prison for? Car burglary.

[Looks toward some people in the adjacent parking lot] It's like if I'd a knew back then, something that I seen earlier, if I'd a knew they had one of those telephones in their car, I would have gotten it. But now, standing around, I see they did, and they have it in their hands, and they left it in their car, and I didn't know it, see I would have my car, my van out.

But you know what? I don't like takin', because people work hard. You know, you get out and you go do 10 or 12 hours a day, and then some fucking head, junkie come along and breaks into your car and takes all your stuff that took you six months to work for, and he takes it in less than six minutes. You paid 5,000 for it, and he goes sell it for 150 bucks. It hurts, man. So it's just not all in me in doin' wrong. It's not good. So I just gotta kick this habit, I just gotta kick it. Because you just can't go around hurting, hurting, hurting people, not just to support your habit. You gotta give it up. It's not gonna work, man, it's not gonna work.

Do you think there's anything you could have done differently to stay out of that whole scene?

Yeah, I had a dynamite job. I tell you what fucked me up. I used to deal it. And I had about 28 or 29,000 dollars cash, with a job. And then, after you get to think that you got 25 or 30 grand cash, you think that you is Howard Hughes. You think you got as much money as Howard. You understand what I'm sayin'? You're a tough guy then, you know, you got 30 grand, you ain't never had shit in your fucking life, and you got a new ride and you got a big old neck full of gold, you got diamond rings, and you're lookin' sharp. And you go to work, get off, seem like every corner you turn, this chick wants ya because you're lookin' slick, you're dealin' the drugs and everything. When I got to 30, 35 grand, then I was tough. Then I quit my job. I was makin' money sellin', I was makin' a grand a day. That's just by sellin' - you know, I'd get up at 10 o'clock in the morning, and five or six o'clock in the evening, I already done made me about a grand, so I'm ready to party. Hey, I was married, I got a wife and two beautiful children. Yeah, so I'm ready to party. And those bitches started me to smokin' that shit; that's what started me. Like I told you, you think you're Howard Hughes. You got 30 grand, you think you got 30 million. You understand what I'm sayin'? And this is what I got out of the deal: a broke back, a maimed foot, a separation from your wife, and a junkie in the street. This is all I got out of it. This is it. But once I had it. [laughs] Once I really had it.

Do you think you'll be able to get back together with your wife when you go home?

Once I lose something I don't want it anymore. I don't know, I don't even want it anymore. It's gone, it's over, I say fuck it. I don't even think about gettin' back together. It's over and it's gone. Let it go. Let it enjoy.

Man, I tell you, I just fucked up. You don't know how I fucked up. You just don't realize how I fucked up, man. I done really fucked up. Every job that I worked at, I used to get me like 1,800 a month, and I didn't have to pay no rent. I used to have a three-bedroom apartment, no rent, no nothin'. And I used to give out air-conditionin' cards, and all the parts and stuff that I needed to repair them on the street was there on the job, so I didn't have to buy shit. And I turned to be a fucking junkie. I don't know, I just believe once, you know, it's funny, you get too big of a play in life and don't really know how to handle it, I believe you blows everything. I believe that's what happened. I believe I had too much goin', I had a lot goin'. Sometimes I'd get off work in the afternoon, and make five or six hundred bucks within two hours. Maybe your compressor's bad in the unit, you know, get an air conditioning call. People would see you workin' for an apartment, and they would stop, and ask you to come by there and fix theirs that afternoon, you know, to keep from callin' an air conditionin' company. Yeah man, I got off a lot of days, man, I swear to God, man, and would go out, I'd get off at four o'clock and at five o'clock I'd have made four or five hundred fucking bucks profit, yeah. And I turned junkie; I just can't believe that I did that. I ask myself that: What the fuck did I do? I can't believe I did this. I gave it all up to come to live under a fucking bridge. That's hard to believe, man. I don't believe I did it, man. I mean, I don't believe I did it. Fucked up, man.

Have all these experiences influenced or changed your religious beliefs at all?

It must not be because I'm still out here. So if it had changed anything I wouldn't fuckin' be out here, right? So it must not have changed nothin' yet. But I told ya I haven't used drugs since Friday; I told myself I was gonna quit. That's what I told myself. And I don't know, man, I gave up a whole life just to fucking come to be a pile of shit. That's all it is. [points around at people close by and their small piles of possessions] Look at the shit he's livin' in, look at the shit he's livin' in, look at the shit he's livin' in, look at the shit I'm livin in. We're livin' in a pile of shit. Hey, what the fuck can ya say? Must not changed too much; still out here in this fucking shit. You understand me?

Have you ever stayed in the shelters at all?

No.

How come?

I don't know. I be askin' myself that. What good is a shelter when you know you're just a junkie and you're gonna get right out? You know, you can only fool yourself. Like fooling yourself? So why fool yourself? I know I'm not gonna stay in it, 'cause I'm a junkie. I know I've got to get out and get my medicine. So why give the people the hassle? When you're ready to do right, that's when you go into a shelter. When I'm ready to do it right, I'll go into a shelter. And when I'm ready to do right, I can go home. I can go home to mom and dad. I got five sisters and a brother. When

I'm ready to do it right, I can go home. I have all the help in the world, all the help in the world, a place to live, a place to eat, a car to drive, they would let me drive their cars. But I'm just a fuck up. You know how it is when you're just a fuck up? [laughs]

But don't you think you could turn that around?

I could. You know, my life could be as good as yours, if I would quit usin' drugs.

Do you think you'll be able to stay clean on your own, or will you go to a treatment center?

I don't think I need a treatment. I see a lot of my friends, god damn it, they turned around. I know a dude named Turbo, he's at Camillus House (a shelter) now; we went to prison together. That was my cell partner; he just got out. Now he done went clean. And there's another one of my friends there named Roscoe, he's a counselor now, he's down there in the clinic, he went clean. And these are the guys that you can talk to that went clean, and we all was junkies. They didn't go to no fucking clinic. They quit, they quit. Turbo just got out of prison. He can tell you about that prison life. He just got out; he ain't been out but two months.

What prison were you in?

South Florida. I've been all over. These are guys that ran the streets and did drugs with me. These guys are clean. These guys are clean. These guys are clean. Matter of fact, I seen several partners that ran the streets with me, man, I seen one of them drivin' a Cadillac; I seen one of them with a *beautiful* woman, I'm talkin' about a beautiful girl, I'm talkin' she was like a star. And so you don't have to get a treatment. You got to put in your fuckin' thick head that you're through with it. That's all you gotta do. And be through with it. What can a treatment do? It still gotta be up in here [points to his head] for you to stop, right? This is your mind, so a treatment can't control it. You're the one that's got to control your mind. And so, there's nothing a treatment gonna do, not shit.

So if all goes well, what's going to happen in the next year or so?

If I quit usin' drugs, twelve months from today I could have a wife, I could have a brand new car. I get 600 bucks a month. And I get it on the third of the month, I swear to God that on the fifth of the month I don't have a dime. It's fucked up, man. It's pretty bad, it's pretty bad. You know what all I could do? I could work part-time. Actually, I could live a hell of a life. I could get six hundred a month. I could meet someone's makin' a thousand a month. I could get out and get a truck, pick up scrap iron or whatever for the other $400 a month. That's 24 grand a year. Me and the other person could live pretty well fair. Don't you think so? With 24,000 a year? It's all easy there to be made. But I'm not all fucked up that I can't get a chick, you know what I'm sayin'? [laughs] I hope not anyway. [laughs] I still got the nature. [laughs] But I don't know, it's just bein' a junkie. There's so many ways you can live. Oh man, if I quit usin' drugs, a year from now, who knows? I'm a vet, I could get a small business loan, there's so much I could do. I could get a small business loan and get a truck, a wrecker truck, like that wrecker truck there. [points] There's so much I could do, but I'm a junkie. There's so many guys out here that could get their shit together, but they're junkies. Some of them out here got college educations, man. You know that? But they gotta put that dope in their arm, got to put it in their arm. And that's fucked up. And you'd be surprised at the people that's homeless. You see a lot of these guys walkin' down the street with suits on, with shiny shoes and shit, and you'll see them under the bridge over here about one o'clock at night, or settin' over in a little hole somewhere asleep, don't wanna be seen. Believe that. You'd be surprised. You'd be surprised. You see the guy sometimes in a car, they have nice cars, but they're somewhere sleepin' in it. I got a beautiful van, a 1980, metallic blue, beautiful. You'd never thought I'd slept in it, but that was my home. When you saw me out here you'd see I'm all fucked up, but when I was drivin' that truck you'd never think I was homeless: well he got a good job. And I ain't got shit. [laughs] A lot of guys, you'd be surprised, you'd really be surprised. And a lot of these guys, don't you wake up, neither. Don't wake up these guys. See these guys asleep? It's not too good to wake 'em up. Don't wake 'em up. Might start a very, very bad - call you things you don't wanna be called.

But you know what, man? I swear to God, I could live a life as good as you're livin'. You can't fault nobody. Like they say the white man kept the black man from gettin' an education, and you know, blah blah this and blah blah this, but it's not. Everybody got the same opportunity to be any fucking thing they wanna be. I could have been anything I wanted to be. You know that? Any fucking thing I wanted to be. All of us could out here. So I just feel we just fucked up, we just *fucked* up.

[gestures] This white guy goin', I was gonna get you to catch him. He's all fucked up, too. You see that white guy over there? He slipped off. He was there asleep. He slipped off while we was talkin'.

Once you're out here, do you think it's harder to be out on the street if you're a black guy?

It's harder for a black guy to be out here. Because, I tell you what we can do right now, and I can make it a known fact, I'll make it a known fact. If the police wouldn't get us - I wish you had that kind of power - me and you could walk off this lot and panhandle right now, and I bet you you'd have five dollars before I get a dollar. I bet you you will. And I'd bet you what we could do. I could ask one man for a quarter, and he'd tell me no, and I'll bet he could walk around that corner, you could ask him for a quarter, he'd give it to you. I've seen it done too many times; I've seen it done. I'll tell you what I did do. We got the paper right now. This morning there was this old white man, he was gettin' a paper out of the booths out here. I say, "You gonna get a paper?" He said, "Yeah, I'm gonna get a paper." He said, "Why?" I said, "I wanna get one when you put your quarter in." He said, "Get the fuck away from here!" But the white guy got one, this paper layin' right here. [points] But I couldn't get one. Now see, that was fucked up. If I'd have caught him in a dark alley I'd have split his head and took everything that he had. That's what I would have done to him. [laughs] I'd have fucked him up; I'd have robbed him.

Have you tried panhandling to get money?

I don't like beggin'. I might ask you to buy me a soda or buy me a dinner. See that's why I'm goin' to the store. Sometimes I got to buy me somethin' to eat. [laughs] But I hate to say it because I hate for you to tell me no, and I know that you got it. I know that you can give me two or three bucks, I know you can do it, and then you tell me no. That's fucked, that bothers me. But it's your fucking money. You earned it, you worked for it. And that's a bad way for a person to be, to get mad about what's yours. [laughs] It's bad, man. If I ask you for three or four bucks, and you tell me no, and I get mad about - but it's your money, it's not mine, it's yours. You understand? You know, so that's fucked up, for me to get mad about what's not mine, get mad about what's yours, that's bad, that's fucked up, it really is.

Do you feel safe out here?

I don't never feel safe on the street, never. There's too many sick people. People come through, and you might look like somebody. You understand me? Like you had a dude killed under the bridge over by the Camillus House; he looked like somebody, guys fucked him up.

But in this immediate neighborhood the other guys know you, and they're not going to bother you, right?

You don't know nobody. This is do or die, this is survival, brother. Nobody's your friend, never believe in that, nobody's your friend, nobody, nobody. This drug gang, man, they will kill you for five bucks just as quick as you bat your eye. I tell you what. I would be scared to go to sleep over here with 30 or 40 bucks in my pocket. Matter of fact, I wouldn't go. I wouldn't go to sleep with 30 or 40 bucks, not even if one person knew. I wouldn't go to sleep if one person knew. He wouldn't do it, but he'd tell the other guy, understand? It's like, if I knew you got $1,000, I might not rob you and take it from you then, but I'd say, "Hey Joe, he got that cash on him." And Joe is gonna get it. Do you understand? And that's half is mine. Don't trust any son of a bitch out here, not a one, not one, not a *one,* nobody. If you got 50 cents, you don't let nobody know it, nobody.

That's the way you keep livin'. Any other way you might die. That's the way you keep livin'.

This guy that got killed under the other bridge down there, how long ago was that?

That ain't been more than two months ago. Somebody jumped out of a van and beat him to death. You should have saw it. It's been all on the TV. He might not even have been the guy. You can look like somebody, right? Yeah, I can look like somebody; he could say, "That was him." Just like last Friday night - the last time I smoked crack was Friday. And this guy told me right here I saw you was goin' behind a white girl down the freeway right here. I said, "No, you did not." He said, "Hell, I did." I said, "No, you did not." And he insisted it was me, but god damn it, it was not me. I did not walk down Biscayne (Biscayne Boulevard) Friday night behind no girl. He said I was followin' the white girl, and it was not me. Now what if something had happened, and the girl come up dead, god damn. He'd have said, "I saw him walkin' behind her." He's a god damn liar, and it was not me, but he still tells me, last night, it was me, and it was not me. See, something could have happened, and I could have got something that I didn't even know nothing about. It was not me. It was not me, man. But he's still tellin' me it was me, and it was not. That was not me. I don't know who in the hell it was, but it was not me. But he still tells me it was me. See, people can accuse you. Out here in the street it's dangerous; it really is. You go to prison for 10 or 15 years for somethin' you don't even know what in the fuck is goin' on. You have people get arrested for somethin' they didn't do. Now see somethin' could have happened, I don't even know what in the hell he's talkin' about. And I could have went to jail for five or 10 years. All these guys, man, everybody in the street, is dangerous. So you always be aware of that.

What do you think is the worst part about being out here?

The worst part is lookin' like a pile of shit. [laughs] That's the worst part of it. You stink, you're nasty, that's the worst part. Other parts I think is not that hard. The worst part is me. Hey, you can't comb your hair, you can't wash your face, you can't keep a shave. Your appearance, your appearance is the worst part of bein' out here in the streets. Everything else you can cope with it. If you could keep lookin' decent, you could make it, but your appearance. It's like you see these guys well dressed and everything, you know what I'm sayin', but they be homeless. But if you could keep yourself lookin' like those guys, you could make it.

John Curtis, 55, is a native of Tallahassee. He was interviewed in
Tallahassee at the Haven of Rest Rescue Mission.*

How long have you been staying here at the mission?
Well, I've been here several times, Phil, but just recently I've been here,
oh about a month I guess.
What brought you here?
Well, just no place to go, really. I had been staying with this girlfriend
for awhile.
Alcohol is what brought me down; never fooled with any drugs other
than alcohol, but that's a killer. I don't know, got a pretty good education,
went to Florida State (Florida State University in Tallahassee).
When did you graduate?
'58.
What were you studying?
Business. And I worked for the federal government for years and years,
but I don't have any income at all. If I did, I probably wouldn't be here -
well, I'm sure I wouldn't.
What kind of work did you do for the federal government?
I was an administrative officer in financial management, accounting and
auditing, anything a business office would do - inventories, budgets,
purchases, worked on computers 12, 14 years. Everybody says, "What in
the world is he doin' here?" You oughta see my resume. But it's been my
case recently, last several years, I haven't had much trouble gettin' jobs,
be it minimum wage or above, but I'll get a paycheck or two and go get
drunk and blow it. If I was makin' a million dollars a day, that wouldn't
work. So I decided that, after the assistant (the assistant director of the
shelter where he was staying) called me and said, "Will you come back?"
I said, "Yeah." So here I am. How long I'll stay - he's always tried to get
me to stay quite a length of time, six months or longer - I don't know. It's
a fine place, a great place, but, you know, when you've had responsible
jobs, you've had your own lifestyle, make your own money, it's hard to -
not adjust - that's not the word, but who wants to live in a mission for the
rest of their life? I certainly don't. So I've been thinking seriously about
quitting this time, or trying to.
Quitting...
Drinking. I'm a beeraholic you might say. I never drink any wine, don't
like mixed drinks, but a beer, cold beer, on a hot summer afternoon or
anything else, you drink a six-pack and say, well, you better quit, but I
don't. I wanna continue till I'm broke or something. Basically, that's the

reason I'm here. If I had a retirement or anything like that, I'm sure I'd
have an apartment or something.

Did you lose your job as a result of your drinking?

Well, indirectly, I mean I resigned, I wasn't fired, but yeah, I'm sure if
I hadn't resigned they probably would have initiated, you know, termina-
tion.

Were you missing work and so on?

Yeah, it got to the point, right there toward the last, I'd get up and drink
some, you know, even before goin' to work. It's a progressive disease they
say, and I believe it is. I mean I never did that for years and years, never
drank anything on the job or anything like that, always after work. But
right at the last there I'd get up 4:30, you know, in the morning - sometimes,
not every morning - drink two or three beers and go into work at 7:30. You
can't do it, not on a job like that.

So when did you leave that job?

Oh, it's been seven, eight years; it's been a long time. And I've had
[sighs] oh security work, and minimum wage, a little bit of office work,
things like that. I haven't been really - oh, I don't know what word to use
- but competently employed or steadily employed, for quite some time.
It's all because of the business of the drinking, not that I lack the
qualifications and the experience. And I suspect if you talked to most of
these guys in here, they'd tell ya the same thing. A lot of them don't have
the education and experience I got; I know that.

Were you married?

Uh-huh.

Do you have children?

Yeah, I have a daughter and a son.

Most of my friends, really anybody who cares about me, they're glad
to see me here. I mean I could be out on the streets, dirty and still tryin' to
drink, this and that. So this is a great place if you let it work for ya.

Are you still married?

No, no I've been divorced quite some time, years as a matter of fact.
Just one time, I never tried it again.

We were middle income, we both had jobs, made pretty good money.
We were just, I guess, upper-middle class, not that much, I mean, but, you
know, new car every two or three years, nice brick home. And then we got
divorced, and I suppose that's when I really started drinkin' even more.
Women tend to slow ya down [laughs] when ya drink. She definitely did
me, and when we got divorced I of course moved into not a nice apartment
to begin with, had to work out finances and this and that, child support
and everything else, but after that I remember I bought a new Grand Prix,

one of the old bigger ones, bought new clothes, had a federal job. Let's put it this way: I got invited to a lot of parties. And I'd drink, two or three o'clock in the morning, go home sometimes, keep on drinkin' a humongous amount.

I recall my mother years ago - mother and daddy never drank anything - she told me, she said, "Son, don't ever fool with it. It'll get ya if ya fool with it long enough."

Well, I see kids - I've been in detox a few times over the years - I've seen kids in their 20s and early 30s in there. It didn't get me till I was in my late 40s really. But it got me. Happens to a lot of people - on crack and marijuana. I suppose if I'd been born a different time I might have done the same thing. But when I was a kid all we had was alcohol, and I never liked mixed drinks much, just beer. You go fishin', ride down the coast or anywhere, there's always a little store, stop and get a cold beer. But I've paid dearly for it. And physically, it's punishment for your body, too. I can feel this old body startin' to ache and crack a little bit more as I get older, for sure.

So it's been a few years since you left that job. Where have you been living in the meanwhile?

Oh, I stayed with this gal nearly a year one time; we almost got married. And I've stayed with her off and on since then. I've stayed here three or four times before for a month or two at a time, just different places really.

Have you ever stayed at another shelter, or had to live outside for a time?

Oh yeah, I've been in the Green Leaf Motel quite a few nights. Have you ever heard that expression - Green Leaf Motel?

No.

That's the bushes. [laughs] Yeah, I've been out there a few nights; it's no good. But, you know, without havin' a place to live, and no money, the alcoholic - I'll tell ya somethin', in case you don't know - the alcoholic puts gettin' another beer ahead of anything. So you'll spend that last dollar for a quart of beer, but you won't buy a can of food, so generally, not havin' enough money to stay in a motel. I would naturally stay in a motel if I had the money. I don't enjoy the bushes. You eventually get dirty and this and that. When I say the bushes I'm talkin' about just on the edge of the highway, I mean not out in the woods, just to keep the cops from seein' you when they drive by or something. But it's no fun, I assure you. So I don't know, I've decided this time, Phil, it's been about seven weeks now since I had a beer or anything at all - beer is what I always drank. I'm gonna try very hard. My son and my daughter both want me to quit. I mean if I had a retirement coming it would be an entirely different thing. Well, more than likely I'd have an apartment or somethin'; I wouldn't be here. But it's no fun with no money in your pocket, at my age and everything; I'm not gettin' any younger.

When you were out on the streets, were you always able to get enough food?

Basically, I guess, most of the time. I've never been out any real length of time. I'd maybe go drink for a week or two, and then the old body starts - you know, you're not eatin' much, or at least I don't - I mean, really, you're poisoning yourself, is what it amounts to. Toxic means poison, of course. So when you drink so much of it, what I'm saying is you get sick, I usually get sick a week or two weeks, dependin' how much I'm drinkin', how much I've eaten. So I've never been out like some of these guys, get real dirty, beards and moustaches and stuff, I suppose they live in tents and stuff. I've never done anything like that. I just go out and get drunk for a couple of weeks as best I can, as long as the money holds out. And then, oh I go by and get cleaned up, shower, with the girlfriend, and I got another couple of friends that let me stay with them a night or two, something like that. So I haven't had any experience like some of these people; I guess they stay out all the time. So I've always really basically had enough food. I didn't weigh this much [laughs] when I came here a month ago, but around here the food's very good.

I had a good, happy marriage for years, beautiful wife and everything.

Do you think your drinking is what led to the divorce?

I believe it had quite a bit to do with it. I denied it for a long time, but I think it probably did; I just wasn't payin' the attention to her that I should have, I guess. We hardly ever went anywhere.

I don't really know, to tell you the truth, Phil, what caused it exactly, but I'm sure the drinking contributed to it. She never drank much, very little.

I know my life has not been full of roses, but on the other hand it's been nothing that would cause me to drink. But I mean, I started drinking when I was 16, in high school, we all did, a lot of us did. And I know kids are still out there drinking today, too. I drank in high school, I drank when I went to FSU (Florida State University), drank when I was in the Marine Corps for a short while, it just seemed like that was always the thing to do. And everybody I knew, or most people I knew, they were drinkin' too. And, I don't know, it just finally got pretty rough there. And I got disgusted, too, you know? And it's pretty easy to hang it up when you're disgusted along with them tryin' to hang you up, too. I mean, if I could do it over, I'd make some changes for sure, wouldn't do the same thing.

In terms of the alcohol?

Well that plus the job. I mean, my God, I could have retired, right now I probably could have retired on 1,800 a month plus all that government insurance and everything else. We had a good retirement. And I've been in management and on the other side of the fence, supervisory and non-supervisory. I wasn't makin' all that much money, oh 25 or better, I guess, eight years ago, which I suppose would be about 35 now. So, I mean, I had a fairly good job, I was satisfied with it. I didn't have to worry about where the next sirloin steak or the next six-pack was comin' from. I had a nice apartment.

If all goes well, what will happen...

If all goes well, I'll stay off the beer, because I haven't even had a mixed drink, never smoked any marijuana or anything like that, or crack, not even once. And if all goes well I'll stay off the stuff for a few months, a year or so, and hopefully be employed within a short time, several months or so, with the state or the federal government. I've got so much federal time I really need to get back with them. Had very little state time. I feel confident, I mean I know a debit from a credit; I know computerized accounting. I've got the experience, and I still feel that I could accomplish a good job at accounting - well, any office type work. The thing that's thrown me is just simply I'd get a job, whether it be a small pay or what, but you know, I'd go get drunk in a payday or two or sooner. So if I stay off the booze, I could see, still even at my age, because of my past experience - when you get this age, if you don't have some education and some training here, you're out of luck. It's hard enough as it is. But I noticed too a trend somewhat, it seems like a lot of the people want mature workers now, or at least to some extent.

So I can see good things just if I'm able to stay off of it. If you ask me whether I'll be drunk again in six months, to give you an honest answer: I don't know. I wouldn't tell ya one way or the other right now. There's a good chance, and there's also a chance I might not. But I'll get a job I think sooner or later. I never had much trouble gettin' jobs. Luckily, I don't think I've damaged myself mentally - seen some people I guess on drugs and all - I still think pretty clearly. I'm not tryin' to brag, but I always had a high IQ, things like that. And somebody suggested one time too that drinkin' beer is sorta like dilutin' the stuff. I mean, I drank a lot, but it's not like the concentrated form of straight whiskey. I don't know if that had any difference to do with it or not.

What do you think about the debate about homelessness? A lot of people say there should be more programs to help the homeless, while others say we're already doing enough.

Well, that's a two-sided coin, really. Of course, I only know what I've seen here at the mission, and from my own experience. I think a certain part of society has forgotten the homeless, like I used to. When I had a good federal job I'd drive down the road in my new car and see some guy, dirty and unshaven on the side of the road, and I'd say, "Boy, look at that bum. Why don't he get a job?" And unfortunately [laughs] I found myself in that same situation a few years later. I believe that possibly some more help would be helpful, but you'd have to have some checks and balances built into whatever you do. I mean, you'd have to find out whether a man really wants to help himself. If he does, I'd help him, or try to. But you'd have to weed out the ones that just wanna go along for a free ride, and want government to take care of 'em. So I don't know how that could be done, but it could be done to a certain extent. A lot of people on welfare, some of 'em probably deserve it and need it, but not all by any means.

Is there anything else you'd like to add?

I've never been on anything other than alcohol, but in my opinion there's nothin' any worse. Just encourage kids to not really ever start it I guess. I can remember the first two or three beers I ever drank when I was 16. I thought it was so bitter; it's terrible tasting. But, you know, it's dangerous. I don't know, people don't listen to advice, especially when you're younger, you tend not to listen. If I had listened to my folks and all, I would have quit drinkin' about 40 years ago, never really started. But it's so much fun to have a party and everybody gettin' about half high, this and that. I couldn't see ever losin' a job; I was gettin' pretty close to retirement in a couple of years or better. And I never thought I'd wind up in a rescue mission. You might point out, yeah, it can happen to you. That's very true. And the first time anybody ever told me I was an alcoholic, I was ready to fight 'em. But I suppose really I am; I know I am. But you just never think it's gonna happen to you; you just can't see losin' your income and your job. The only salvation I see for me is the simple fact I do have enough training and experience. If I don't drink, I think I can get a job. I mean I'm single now, my kids are grown, I don't have any credits, I don't have any bills. I could even exist on minimum wage. I don't need that house on the hill that I once fantasized with, $100,000 house sittin' on top of the hill, or $200,000 in this day and age, I guess. [laughs] But it can happen to anybody that fools with these drugs. But, you know, as crazy as it is, who's to say? I might be loaded three months from now, three weeks from now. Now, I'm gonna try not to. I don't think I will. But there's a certain insanity out there, I mean crazy, crazy. But anybody that drinks or does drugs is missin' somethin' in life. I just got used to it. I've talked to people in here that started drinkin', some of them, seven, eight years old. Their daddy was an old bootlegger or moonshiner or somethin'. So I don't know, but you really pay a price. I mean I don't enjoy livin' here at the mission. What happened to me, I had a good federal job and lost it due to drinking, no other reason.

Darryl Anderson, 26, is a native of Rochester, New York. He was interviewed in Orlando at a shelter run by the Christian Service Center for Central Florida.

Did you come here from Rochester?
No, I just came from Miami.
What brought you down to Florida?
My drug addiction.
How?
Well, I was working for some people, and I misappropriated some merchandise and money, so I didn't wish to face the consequences, so I came down here to Central Florida. That's why I'm here today.
Was that in upstate New York?
Yes.
So you went down to Miami first?
No, this is my second time period in Orlando. The first time I was here I stayed about four months. My drug habit got real bad, and I moved to Miami, you know. I was under the impression that if I changed locations, things would be better. But I still took myself along with me regardless of where I went. Then I went down to Miami, I did a little better, and my drug addiction got worse all over again. Then I was sleeping on the streets, I was fightin' and stealin', then I went into a treatment program.
Then you came back up here?
After I got out of treatment I was supposedly goin' home, and I was with a friend of mine, and I relapsed, and I didn't want to face the embarrassment of my friends, you know, because I'm the type of person people always get high expectations of me. So I came to Orlando, and I've been here about seven-and-a-half months, and I haven't used in seven-and-a-half-months. I guess what they say, relapse is part of recovery, 'cause my head was swelled up, 'cause since I could walk back in the drug areas and not use, and I didn't get the craving for a hit or whatever you wish to call it, I thought I was cured. But I still have that type of personality, you know what I'm saying? So I must put things in their proper perspective or I'll be right back out there in the streets again. I don't wish to live like that anymore. It's unfit for a man to live that way.
When you came back to Orlando, were you on the street all that time?

Oh, I'm a old hand at how to find somewhere to stay at. I came here and I worked two-and-a-half months at the labor pools, and I couldn't seem to get a regular job through the labor pools. So many things have changed in Orlando since the last time I've been here, so I finally got tired, and I checked into the A-R-C, the adult rehabilitation program the Salvation Army has down on Colonial. I figure I get me some nice clothes, put a little weight on me, you know, get my face to shining back over again. Because you don't even have to use drugs, but just have a certain amount of vitamin deficiencies in your diet, and you look just like you're using drugs. That's why their skin is no longer shiny, because they have a deficiency. So I got my head together, I got a little philosophy, you know what I'm saying? I got a little more open-minded, you know. And I came down here, talked to Reverend Holmes (Vincent Holmes, the shelter director), and told him it was time for me to make a change.

I'm only 26 years old; I have to reach for the stars right now 'cause by the time I reach 35 years old, 40 years old, the train is going to start coming to a halt. If I don't start getting some type of education, and meeting people that's trying to do something with their lives, I'll be like a lot of these older guys you see out here on the streets, 40, 50 years old, they don't have any family, they don't have any money, they don't have any education, they don't have *anything*. I don't want to wind up like that. They have no motivation today in life, you know what I'm saying? Because I could go out today and I could see them out there on the streets, and I tell myself I don't want to be like that, you know. I see the clothes they wear, I see that they don't take baths, their personal hygiene is at a all time low. And I have a hard enough time dealing with society as it is when I'm doing the proper things, let alone dealing with drugs and have to deal with society.

What kinds of drugs were you taking?

Well, before I came down here I was freebasing, but when I came to Orlando, I started smoking crack, and that was an experience, you know.

Now that you've been off for seven months, do you ever have problems being around drugs when you're on the streets?

Seven-and-a-half months is just a drop, one tear drop in the ocean. You know what I'm saying? It doesn't even count. [laughs] You know, I'm serious, I'm 26 years old; I hope to God I have at least 26 more years to live on this earth. I'm very new in recovery; there's a lot of things I must relearn because I have a lot of old ways about me. Just being in the streets of Miami, I see how I tend to be aggressive on certain things. And I'm basically a very mild-mannered person. You really have to keep rubbing me the wrong way for me to go off, but it's just like, I need my space. I don't like anyone to like bother me too much. [laughs] Even my friends, it's just the environment I came out of, and I have to slowly change these things. It's not going to happen overnight. But I apologize to people when I say things that aren't right, and I try to be on my best behavior at all times. But you know how life is: it's ups and downs.

When you came to Orlando, were you able to find a place to stay right away or did you have to live outside for awhile?

Well, when I first came down to Orlando I only had a small amount of money. I slept outside maybe three days, but I think it was for the best because it gave me more motivation, because it showed me that I didn't want to exist the way I had before, you know. See sometimes, I believe God places us in certain situations to give us fortitude in life.

There's good and evil. You know what I'm saying? And there's good and bad. So it's all in your perspective, in the way that you look at it. So I try to take things in life today as a learning experience, so I can be smarter today. I tend to over-analyze things. That's kind of bad, because it puts me in a trip bag a lot of times because of assumptions. That's one of my character defects, I'm going to have to work on that one, but it's doing me more good today than it's doing me ill, so I feel better, I talk better today, my thoughts are clearer today. I don't smoke cigarettes anymore, I don't eat any red meat, it's been 10 months since I had a drink. And I don't forget where I came from, because I know today even though I can go in there and change clothes three or four times a day, seven days a week, it's a nothing, because if I go out there and use drugs today, where am I going to keep these clothes? Where am I going to take a shower? It's very demoralizing when you're in a shower with eight other guys; you don't even know who these people are. It's almost like you're cattle or something. It makes you a very hard individual. People tend not to realize these things. When you're in an environment that's cozy and warm and friendly, you are like that, but when you're in an environment that's hard and callous, you must be that way because you have to stuff your feelings aside, man, or they'll be trampled on. And no one wants to be trampled on.

You mentioned that you had to live outside for a few days. Where did you sleep?

There's some railroad tracks around.

Before, when I was out in the street - I'm a loner now, you know, I wasn't with that congregational crap - if I'm gonna be a bum or whatever, I'm going to do it by myself away from everybody else. Some of these individuals just *wallow* in it. Even though there's been times my addiction has made me sleep outside, that doesn't mean I've got to flaunt it in front of everyone. I still have a small amount of pride and dignity, but I slept by these railroad tracks. They had high weeds back there. I think it was about three days, three or four days, 'cause I came here on a Friday, so I had Friday, Saturday, Sunday, and Monday I started working for the labor pool, so I got blessed in that.

Where did you stay after that?

On OBT (Orange Blossom Trail) they have a place called Industrial Labor, they have a bunk house right next to the labor pool. Another one of those great ideas, you know what I'm saying? I stayed there about two-and-a-half months, then I got tired of going out to work every day, and workin' hard - because I try to take pride in whatever I do in my life regardless of if I'm a drug addict or not - and it wasn't appreciated.

I just got tired. I had been in the A-R-C down in Miami for about a month-and-a-half, so I just went there one morning, I went there early enough, and I checked in, 'cause a friend of mine was there, and I had seen him at the plasma center. He had his moustache all trimmed, hair cut well, face was shining, clean clothes - he looked like a million bucks. Everybody else in the place looked so dull and gray, you know, but he looked bright, he looked like he had life inside of him, and that's the way I wanted to look. I said, "That's for me." [laughs] So I had to go there. So I went there and I dealt with that situation for about three-and-a-half months. If I had had me some family here, I probably would have left sooner, but I didn't want to go from bad to worse. So eventually God led me to this place right here.

What was your life like before you left Rochester?

It was more hectic. I didn't have too much family there; I was stayin' with my sister. But I had some good hustles that I could just - have you ever lost a large amount of money before?

No.

Well, let me tell you what truly, desperation is. When you have $300 to $400 in your pocket, and you have responsibilities, and you have just smoked up every last *cent* of this money, it's four o'clock in the morning, and you can't go to sleep, you know what I'm saying? And you're worrying about what you're going to do next, because all the money is gone. That is truly desperation, and it was just an endless cycle for me, you know, because I was always able to get money there. I was raised in Rochester, I had connections.

But see, the things that I had going for me at home were all illegal. I don't have no work experience but hustlin' and sellin' things. If I get into sales, I'll be excellent because I'm so used to selling things to people. Anything to do with people I'll be great with because, with me being in the streets so much selling people things, selling people dreams, you know. At home it was so bad I used to tell people - they used to ask me, "What do you have?" I used to tell them, "It's not what I have, it's what you want. You tell me what you want, and we'll agree upon the price, and then I'll go get it for you, by the order." And I was gettin' pretty good, but I guess it wasn't the will of God for me to have gone farther in that type of endeavor, so some chain of events happened. I went to jail, and when I came out, my little soldiers had forsaken me, all my little hustlers.

All my old connections were kind of shaky to deal with me. You know what I'm saying? What was the real surprising thing about it, that I could have told on some other people, and they could have came to jail also, but I didn't.

I used to do a lot of things to be a self-serving person, to be someone who I wasn't. That was basically why I was a drug user anyway, not being able to deal with my emotions, so I put up a facade of trying to be somebody who I wasn't. But today I can just be myself, and if you don't like it, that's your business. I kind of hate to feel that way sometimes, but I have to because I have to do it for me today. If I go back to living for somebody else, I'll be back on them streets, because for me it all boils down on that drug usage.

My mother owned a two-family home; she had it renovated to a one-family home, but it was in the city, you know what I'm saying? We had a car, we had cable, telephone, carpet through the house. I knew people who had less than we had, I knew people who had more than we did. So it wasn't so much on my home environment was the motivating factor for me to go out there and be a drug user. Maybe I just didn't have any direction, so I just went hog wild. I think a child needs a direction - when they are coming up, needs some type of focus. Otherwise, there's too many things out there in the world that are distracting, that can pull you astray, and I didn't have that focus point. I can't blame my mother for that. I should have had a little bit more, I don't know, gumption about myself or whatever. [laughs] But I think it's for the best. I like the person who I am today. I don't *have* too much; I really don't worry about that because I try to be a spiritual-minded person today. And I say spiritual-minded, I don't mean bein' dogmatic. I knock no man for their religious beliefs. Whatever belief that you wish to believe in, great, but I don't like to be dogmatic. To me there's something wrong in being dogmatic because sometimes you miss things that you shouldn't have missed by being dogmatic. These are the things I think about day-to-day. I try to think of philosophies inside my head. Maybe in five more years I'll be somebody in the community; I don't know, I'm feeling all right today.

Some people think there should be more government programs to help homeless people, and others think homeless people should just help themselves. What do you think?

Well, coming from a homeless person, I really don't have too much compassion. There should be some sort of program for an individual who wishes to help theirself, but as a program that's givin' 'em too much it should just be like this. This place is actually meant for somebody comin' off drug addiction, but Orlando has no halfway houses. I would rather be in a halfway house because I don't like to be around people in addiction. Addicts are foul people, man. They don't have any manners, no courtesy, no nothing, because you can't have no courtesy out there. It kind of makes it bad. Most addicts don't want to be clean, man, I'm telling you. Like when I was in treatment, they said out of 100 people, 90 percent were going to relapse. Look at that number: 90 *percent*. It's incredible. And with odds like that, it's almost like, why should I help these people? If you truly take a good look at it, but if you're a humanitarian person, your hearts will still go out to them. But if you take it strictly on the mind level, on dollars and cents, it's not gonna add up correctly 'cause your gonna cause more harm on yourself than good you're going to do. I don't really have any type of comparison. I don't care if they have programs or not, because the program I went through in Miami was self-supporting. They weren't aligned with any government organizations or anything. Basically, the programs need to come out of the neighborhoods. How can you get somebody to start up a program, to place people in a program, to help people they can't even relate to? It's kind of backwards. You get people out of that type of background, then maybe you can do a little changing.

If a person really wants to change, they should; I'm a living example. I'm 26. For five years I was smoking base or crack cocaine. Since I was 16 year old until I was 20, I was an alcoholic. With these type of odds, I'm supposed to still be out there, but by the grace of God today I'm not out there, and I'm all right to sit here and talk to you. Basically, they can have a million programs out there, because this program right here, this open door policy, you can get kicked out real fast, but you're back in two weeks. It kind of like self-defeating. If I know I can come back in two weeks, I can mess up.

When you were living on the street, did the police ever bother you?

No, because what's the word? Recluse? Does that mean to be off to yourself?

Uh-huh.

Well that's what I was.

Chapter Six

The Long-Term Homeless

Some homeless people manage to get off the streets in a very short period of time, but for most the process takes months. Many shelters set time limits - often as short as two to five nights - on how long people can stay, forcing the homeless to move from one shelter to another in an attempt to avoid sleeping outside. Shelters that do not set strict time limits report that the average stay is 30 to 45 days, and many people take from 60 to 90 days to find employment and save enough money to get into permanent housing. A relatively small proportion of the homeless remain on the streets for years, or go through periods of stability followed by another round of homelessness. An even smaller number choose to remain homeless, preferring a life that is free from the responsibilities that most people take for granted.

Shirley James*, 30, is a native of Arcadia, Florida. She was interviewed at the Miami Women's and Children's Shelter.

What brought you to Miami originally?
I left Arcadia, I come with my sister, my sister was livin' here. And then I left and went back home, and then I left again, with my children's daddy and I come here, and me and him couldn't get along, so I stayed here and met another man, and I married. I'm married 13 years now. He's in jail. That's the only reason I'm to this shelter now, 'cause if he was out I wouldn't be in a shelter. He'd give me a place to stay.
Are your children with you?

No, no my mother have my kids. I have four. My oldest daughter graduate this year.

How did you lose having a regular place to live?

It burned up.

It was a fire?

It was a fire, electrical wires caught afire and burnt the place up, and I just had nowhere to go, didn't have no money. And the man that own the building, he didn't give nobody back no money, nobody seen him. The place got burned up; nobody seen him. So we just out here.

When did that happen?

About two weeks now, today'll be two weeks it's been like that.

Was it an apartment building?

No, a hotel.

How long had you been living there?

For about three months; it was nice.

Where did you go when that happened?

I wandered around in the streets. My husband's in a wheel chair. I just push him in the wheel chair and we sleep where we can sleep until he gets money. When he gets money, then we get us a place to stay. He get a check. We keep somewhere to stay because we get a check, but it's like he's in jail now and I'm alone, and I can't get the money, so I hafta do like I do now, go into a shelter. I'd rather be into a shelter than to be on the street. If I could pick up his check, I would be in a place of my own and wait until he get out, but I can't pick up his check, so I stay here rather than bein' back out on the street.

So you were staying outside for awhile?

Yeah.

How long?

I was stayin' outside for about a week.

With him?

No, not with him, by myself. He's in jail.

How long has he been in jail?

Two weeks.

What is he in jail for?

I'd rather not even just put it on the tape. [laughs] I don't wanna put it on your tape. He gonna be out pretty soon.

So that's short-term, he's in and out?

Yeah, and this is short-term for me, bein' here. I'm only here for seven days. They only let ya stay here seven days out of a year. Do that make any sense to you?

I don't know. It seems like sometimes they'll let you stay longer, right?

I don't know. It's my first time ever into a shelter, never been into a shelter before, but it's nice here, at least I got a bed to sleep in upstairs, I got a shower, take up a shower, and I can eat when I wanna eat, and that's all that counts.

So you were living outside for a week or two?

Uh-huh. Oh, I have lived outside before now, for months and months around the Camillus House (a shelter, soup kitchen and medical clinic for homeless people) before they ran us away. And then I moved. I didn't move up under I-95, but I moved somewhere else to sleep outside. I have slept outside a lot of times.

But you were always with your husband?

Uh-huh, this is the first time I had to sleep outside without my husband, so I'd rather come into a shelter than to be out there dying. 'Cause I know with him nobody'll try nothin', but without him somebody will. Like the other morning I woke up and this man was standin' up over me, you know, and I knew it was time for me to leave then, so I come here.

Are you working during the day?

No, I haven't worked in 13 years. I don't have to.

What do you mean?

My husband get money every two weeks, enough money to take care of him and me for a whole month, and to pay our bills. He's just in jail now, so I can't get no money.

Have you been able to get enough food?

Too much food. [laughs] Too much food. You know, when you're outside and you're homeless, and you're sleepin' under those bridges and things, people think about you, you know? A lot of people think a lot of people just drive by and look at you, say you're poor, but it's not like that. People think about you. We eat better outside - you might not believe it - than we do at some of these here missions. They feed you better. People come by with food; people come by seven days a week and feed you. Sometime we eat hot meals; people feed you outside. It's not like you don't get no food, 'cause the food is there. If they say they go hungry in Miami, that's a lie; nobody never goes hungry in Miami 'cause there's always somebody comin' to feed you. All times of night you get food. They wake you up to feed you. I know because I used to sleep on Miami Avenue. Seven days a week you got food; somebody always comes along with food. So anybody like, you don't have no food, "I'm hungry. I can't get no food." That's a lie, 'cause people feed you, they comes to feed the homeless. But you know, a lot of people, they homeless 'cause they wanna be homeless. See, a lot of young people today, I can understand all these people bein' homeless because somebody else givin' them money, but us young people, drugs are why most people are out on the streets - young, like I am, homeless. You understand what I'm sayin'? My husband made me think about that. See, I really didn't think about that. A lot of people are out there homeless because they want to be. They smokin' crack. If they got enough money to pay rent, they say, "Well I can take this $200 here and smoke this up, and I can always go to the Camillus House to get me somethin' to eat." You understand what I'm sayin? That's what they say. See, I used to smoke crack, too, no more crack for me. I don't smoke crack no more. See, I know how they think 'cause I used to do the same thing. I don't smoke it, but I know what crack will do for you. Crack took my children away from me, crack made me lose my car, crack made me pawn my rings.

How did you lose your children?

Smoking crack I lose 'em. My mother come and took 'em away. All I wanted to do was get that other hit; I didn't care nothin' about no kids, and my mother come and took 'em away.

And now I sit back and I look at some of the people, just thinkin' how that could have been me, you know? I think about it.

Are your children with your mother now?

Yeah, they with my mother. I talk to 'em. Matter of fact, I called 'em today, I talked to 'em today. I call them and I talk to them. When I get lonely sometimes, I call. When I wanna hear they voice, I call. They alright.

Is that the reason you were living outside for awhile - because of crack?

Yeah, 'cause I would take my money and I would buy the crack with it. What the hell I wanna take and get me a place to stay for when I can sleep outside and eat free to the Camillus House? See, I think everybody else thinkin' the same thing. I was thinkin' like that, too, but no more. No more, you never know who gonna walk up there and cut your head off, or cut your ears off while you sleep. See, while I'm sleepin' outside, I hear everything. I don't get enough rest like that. Every time I hear somethin, my eyes are open, 'cause I woke up one mornin', this man, he was just standin' up over me, and I left and came over here 'cause he could have killed me. I just left and came here, and I been here ever since.

Do you think it's harder to be out on the streets for a woman than for a man?

No, not for a woman, for a man, not for a woman.

Why?

'Cause a woman can make money. A woman can always make money when a man can't make money. See, that ain't my type of lifestyle, so I'd rather be in here than to be tryin' to make that money that some girls do to get a place. I'm not like that. That's not my lifestyle. I don't do nothin' like that. You understand what I'm sayin'? I'm not like that. It's easier for us than it is for a man. It's easier for us to get anything we wanna get, 'cause we got what they need, but I'm not like that, I wasn't raised like that.

Were you always able to get enough clothing?

No, I really wouldn't. I used to wear my clothes for like a whole week, and I used to smell, and I used to just take 'em off and wash 'em with some soap or something and put 'em right back on wet, you know? And then they still smell, 'cause I don't take a bath and I still smell. But I got tired of that too, so I got to the point where I just didn't care, I'd just get up under a water hose in front of everybody. I had to take a shower. I knew if I could smell myself, somebody else can, too. Then I started to think, I said, "That's not ladylike; I'm a lady." I said, "What I do? I just leave." I was on Biscayne (Biscayne Boulevard). I just left and come here. And my friend Gert, she just come down here today, they had been looking for me. They didn't know where I was; nobody knew where I was. I just got on the bus, ended up here. Nobody knew where I was. She came, and she said, "I been lookin' for you." "You been lookin' for me?" And she said, "Yeah, nobody knew where you were at." I don't want nobody to know where I'm at, 'cause they gonna pull me right back. I know it, I know that's what they gonna do. I'm hidin' out here, I'll stay here. I hafta leave here every morning, but there's another shelter you can go to, it close at five. But see, I have to be back here at 4:30, so I goes over there in the morning time, and I stay over there all day. I look at TV, I make my phone calls, I call my husband, or he'll call me, and we'll talk for awhile, I eat, I sleep, until it's time to come back over here.

What's the name of the other place?

Women's Place (a day center for homeless women). It's a very nice place for women. You eat, if you wanna eat, they got a kitchen there. They got a little old lady in there, but she show you what to eat, you know. You show her what you want, she'll get it for you. It's nice over there. It's better than bein' in the streets all day.

What do you do about health care?

Camillus House got a free clinic, so you can go there and they will help you. They will give you a referral to go to Jackson (Jackson Memorial Hospital), you won't have to pay. Like my friend, she got a referral right now to go get her teeth cleaned; she don't have to pay. Jackson, or you go there to Camillus House, they got a free clinic. They got doctors there, nurses. So we're very well taken care of - homeless people. You know, you're homeless 'cause you wanna be. But really, I don't wanna be. If my husband was out, I wouldn't be in this place here. That's the first time I ever stayed into a shelter. I had rather slept on the streets than stay into the shelter because I wouldn't let my pride, my pride, you know? But now, after that man was standin' up over me, I knew it was time for me to go somewhere, 'cause he could have killed me, so I just come here. I only got five more days in here, so after my five days here I'm hopin' my husband get out jail so I can go get me a place.

Do the police ever help you out or bother you?

They bother me a lot. Yeah, when you on Biscayne, they bother you a lot. 'Cause they think you a whore or somethin' 'cause I hang around Biscayne. I hang around Biscayne because if I want somethin' to eat. On Biscayne, down on Biscayne, the part that I was, people don't come. There's a lot of homeless people down there a lot of people don't know about. There's a park down there, there's a lot of homeless people sleepin' in that park. I went through there the other morning, and I seen a lot of homeless people. The people that come through there and feed you, they don't know about these homeless people there, 'cause if they did they would go by there and feed these people. See, when I'm there, I panhandle my money. If I'm hungry, I'm gonna go and ask somebody for something; I'm not gonna take it. I'm gonna ask 'em, "I'm hungry. Could I have 50 cents to get this? Could I have a quarter to get that?" If they tell me no, I just go along to the next person, ask the next person, till I get enough to get me somethin' to eat. I'm not gonna take nothin' from nobody, 'cause I'll go hungry before I take anything.

How do people react when you're panhandling?

They call the police. They want me off their premises because I'm harassin' their customers. So when they call the police I just ask the police for money. "I'm hungry. Would you buy me somethin' to eat, I can get off these people's premises? I'm hungry."

What do the police do?

He will buy me a piece of chicken or a soda. I got two policeman, they are my friends, and if I catch one of those - if they call the police, mostly one of those mostly come, 'cause they know who it be. So they come there, give me some money to get somethin' to eat, and tell me to leave. They alright. I got two friends be policeman. But I had one policeman, he was so mad he wanted to take me to jail. But I didn't care if he take me to jail because if he did I would have had a bed there and had food to eat. That's all that counts. I didn't care about bein' locked up. I done been locked up several times; it didn't bother me.

What have you been arrested for?

Bustin' people in the head, fighting, one drug case, I done sold cocaine to an undercover cop. That was the biggest case I had. Other than that, just misdemeanors.

Have you found that other people who are out on the street look out for each other?

Yeah, they do. They do, they look out for each other. 'Cause if they're out on the streets, if we out on the streets and we got somethin' to eat and they don't have nothin' to eat, we'll try to share what we got with those that don't have nothin' to eat. And our clothes, we try to share our clothes. We share everything when we're out on the street. They do, they look out for each other. They have to. 'Cause if not, there ain't nobody gonna look out for 'em.

What about other people - who aren't out on the streets? How do they treat you?

Like trash. You know, they ride by, they throw eggs at you, they throw balloons with water at you. You be layin' out somewhere, they throw eggs at you, crap like that, cursin' us out, callin' us homeless and all that. But I look at 'em. They ride by and take pictures of you. Next thing you know you're sittin' up in the newspaper, you don't know nothin' about it, you're in the newspaper. They took your picture while you sleep. There's a lot of stuff like that goin' on. See they never do me like that 'cause I would sue if I see my picture anywhere without my permission. I would sue the hell out of 'em.

What's the worst part about being out on the streets?

Well, not bein' able to take a bath. This is the worst part; the rest I can deal with, but not bein' able to take a bath. I like my body to be clean, and I can't deal with it. And it worries me. Like I gonna have a nervous breakdown 'cause I can't take a bath. But other than that it's alright.

So what do you think will happen in the next month or so? What would you like to do?

In the next month I'm hopin' my husband be home, and we have our own place.

You'll have to find a new place, right?

Yeah, it won't be no problem, though, as long as he out. I'm just kinda lost now. See, I been with him 13 years, and this is the second time we ever been separated. I'm kinda lost. But other than that, it's fine. I like it here because of these people, you know? They're decent people. They don't think that because we are transients that we are trash, 'cause the ones that come in and stay overnight, they are transients. They don't think that we are trash. They treat us just like we live here. And I like that.

Is there anything else you'd like to add?

Just don't put my name down on that paper. [laughs]

Rick "Preacher" Brown, 38, is a native of Germany. He was interviewed in Orlando at Our Daily Bread, a soup kitchen run by the Christian Service Center for Central Florida.

Where are you from originally?
Germany.
That's where you were born?
Yes sir, lived there about 15 years.
Are you an American citizen?
No, sir.
How did you get to the United States?
My dad was in the service. I was in the service for about three-and-a-half years, and went over to Vietnam, and they said, "Become an American citizen," and I said "No." Because whether I become an American citizen or not, I'm still gonna be German.
So you have German citizenship although your parents were Americans?
My dad was American, my mom was German; she became an American citizen in about '72.
How long have you been in Florida?
I've been here in Orlando about 15 years.
What originally brought you here to Orlando?
I was in New Smyrna (New Smyrna Beach), I've got two sisters in New Smyrna, I just come up here to go to work, just stayed.
Where are you staying right now?
Up at the church. It's I think the Nazareth church, sleep on that property. On Fridays and Saturdays I sleep in front of a building. When I get up in the morning, you know, as long as I clean up the area, it's okay. 'Cause Fridays and Saturdays, you can't sleep on the church property.
Oh, that's the Methodist church, right?
Methodist, yeah, it's their church.
You don't like staying in shelters?
I did at the beginning because of the fact that it was off the street, but it's too many headaches, you know, the drugs that come in the shelters, they have fighting and stuff like this. If you go to the church you're a little bit more peaceful, you can sleep where you want to, you don't get up as early, you get up about eight o'clock. I'm more or less by myself. That way you don't get in trouble.
How many people are staying out at the church now?
I would say a good 200, 250. There's a lot of people around there. The whole church, the whole property on the inside and around the edges of the church, people are sleeping.
How long have you been homeless?
I'd say about 10 years. But it was my choice.
I have a habit of inviting people over, and they think there's not enough room for me.

Then I get another place, and go back to work, and keep invitin' people over. This way, if I go to church, everybody's already there, so I don't have to invite nobody over.

Have you been able to find work?

Yes sir, yes sir.

What kind of work do you do?

Anything from making fireplaces - well, labor pools, labor pools got a lot of jobs. In fact, right after this little conversation, we're going to the convention center. It's just, you know, if you go to the labor pools, there's a lot of time you don't get out; there's a lot of people in front of the window, a lot of headaches, they have their choice of people. But if you're at the church, and you're just walkin' around, people come up to you and say, you know, there's 150 people needed at this labor pool, and there's 100 people needed at this labor pool, so you got a pretty good chance of gettin' out because there isn't that many people around, you know, in the afternoon.

Can you get steady work?

Steady work? Not really, because it seems like in Florida, they don't want to pay that insurance, you know for that workman's comp and stuff, so they go through the labor pools; it saves them a lot of money. I mean that's their choice, and a lot of times, like we put up the Sunbank, and across the street from the Sunbank, that Woolworth's store, it's an old Woolworth's store, and pretty soon, they're supposed to tear that down and go up with it, it's supposed to go higher than Sunbank, so there will be a lot of jobs, say within the next month, so you just gotta hang around for another month. So I mean there's work around, it's just, a lot of the people make it bad for the rest of the people because they're pretty well tied up in that drug scene. You know, they work and they want the money and then they get drugs and they work, and they're a little bit hopeless because they can't work, they're all worn down. It makes it a little bit bad. A lot of the labor pools have sold out because it's gotten that bad. You know, because they had about 13 labor pools in town; now they only got about seven. But I enjoy working at the labor pools because of the fact that you do different jobs. It's not the same thing every day. You learn a lot. I can build everything from a house, from the bottom up, it's just, you know, electrical work I don't do - afraid of getting shocked.

Do you prefer that to a permanent job?

Yes sir, yes sir. I mean I enjoy lawn work now, if I can get lawn work, I enjoy workin' outside. But as far as inside, factory work, stuff like that, no, I let that slide. I do like workin' at a labor pool because they put ya in a factory one day, the next day you might work outside, the next day, you know, you do a different kind of job; I like that. But as far as a permanent job inside, I don't like it.

Do you prefer living outside at the church to having a permanent place to live inside?

I do only because the work is not guaranteed every day. And a lot of jobs, when you get rained out, you don't get paid for the day if it's rained out. So therefore you have a headache, you know: Where am I going to get the rent money? Where am I going to get the discounted money for the telephone? And this and that. So I'm saying, if you live at the church, you don't have to worry about that. The church is never going to go anywhere. So you're always gonna be there, and then, you know, you've got different places where, if a friend invites you over, that's fine, go over and stay with them. So I'm saying, as far as a permanent address, I like the church because you don't have to pay for it. And if you work the labor pool, the money that you get, you can eat good, you can go take a shower, go to the movies, enjoy it, enjoy life, instead of worrying about bills.

Do you find that people who are staying out there are pretty good about taking care of each other?

No, I've been here about 15 years, and 10 years of it's been on the street, and it's what they would say is like a back stabbing variety of people. Like you can eat with somebody six days a week. You know, every day at lunch I come up to you and say, "Hey, let's go eat lunch." And then one day you say, "Hey, my buddy's coming over, I'm gonna feed him." And he'll tell on you, get you in trouble, so you can't eat by yourself. Everybody's attached to somebody who's got money. If you come to church, you got $100, you got 100 friends. As soon as that $100 is gone, everybody's gone. If you go there with any kind of change in your pocket, just keep it in your pocket and live your own life. It's very comfortable and it's very satisfying as far as, like I say, you don't have to worry about bills and stuff.

You mentioned that you're a Vietnam vet. Have you found that a lot of the other guys who are out on the streets are vets?

I would say maybe one-fourth of the people that are down there are vets. A lot of people say they are, but just their attitude and the way they talk, they're not. A lot of people use that for clout, and it ain't right.

Have you always been able to get enough food?

Oh yes sir, yes sir. They have their dos and don'ts, but there's about three good places that serve lunch. You got lunch, you got supper, and then you got like, about seven o'clock, you eat again. So that's three times a day. And if you luck out, somebody has doughnuts, somebody'll have coffee. You know, you could walk around this town and make a little cigarette money, make you a little coffee money, this and that, just helpin' people. You can make it in this town, but if you run around with a lot of people, no. If you're by yourself it's pretty simple. You get up at eight, walk around, you see somebody emptying their garbage, help them take their garbage out, they'll give you a couple dollars, there's coffee and toast. That's pretty nice, pretty comfortable.

Do you have a bed roll or something?

Yes sir, a sleeping bag and a blanket and pillow.

Where do you store that?

Right next to the church there's a couple bushes. I've got a plastic wrap, put that in the bushes with the plastic wrap around the sleeping bag and stuff. Just at night when I get ready to go over church I go pick it up. It's been over there about eight months; nobody's bothered it.

What do you do about health care?

At Salvation Army you take showers; here at Daily Bread you take showers. Like I said, I've been here for 15 years so I know a lot of people, get cleaned up there, brush your teeth, whatever there, take showers.

What do you do if you get sick and need to see a doctor?

If you go to the Orlando Regional Hospital, in the back they have a clinic, free clinic. And if you explain to them that you're homeless - like right now I have a card in my pocket - and you tell 'em that you make no money, they give you a health card. And it's free, free medical. So whatever happens to you, you know, you go in the hospital, no problem. In fact, about a month ago I had bleedin' ulcers, and I was staying with some people, and I went to go to work, passed out and woke up in the hospital. And they said that your body has 15 units of blood, and I had four is all in my legs, my stomach, my lungs, and the hospital took care of it. But that was a dynamite situation; I didn't even know it. So they take care of you; you get a health card.

Have you found that employers or people who work at social service agencies are hostile toward you because you're homeless?

Well, a lot of the places, like for instance food stamps, see, the homeless people here they consider tramps. But I'm saying if a tramp goes to the food stamp office, we are guaranteed to get food stamps because of the law now. So when you go up there and *take* the attitude that they give you, which is real, real rude, you know you'll keep it. But if you're rude back to them real quick, they'll give you your stamps and you can walk. It's just whatever attitude they have, just throw it right back in their face and they can't understand it. And you get what you need - you know, what the law says - you get food stamps, you'll get 'em. I get food stamps, I get VA pay, so I'm comfortable, you know; just a couple days a week I go through the labor pool for the exercise, and it's very comfortable. Again, you know, a lot of these people, they buddy up, they get a lot of buddies, and then the beer comes in, the drugs come in, you know, and then when they want to go for food stamps, you've got 15 people with ya; now they can't handle everybody. So if you're homeless, you kind of stay by yourself. It's very, very comfortable.

Do the police ever bother you?

They used to. But now it's to the point where, you know, they come up, give you the peace sign, "How you doing, Preacher? Is everything alright?" Yeah, they talk to me, or if they have a problem, and there was a stabbing here, or somebody got shot here, "Do you know anything?" And if I find out, I'll tell them. So, when I first come here, my appearance, with the long hair and stuff, was like, I was harassed a lot. But now, pretty good, "Preacher, want a ride?" "Can I sit in the front seat?" "No, you sit in the back." "No, I'll walk." It's pretty comfortable.

You say things seem to work better if you're on your own?

Yes sir.

Do you ever feel isolated or lonely?

Not really, because when you get tied up with the different people around the church, they've definitely got some problems, you know, and if you listen to the problems, you feel like you've got the problem. And then when you think you've got the problem, then they forget they had it, then you've got the headache and they don't. So if you just like, "Yeah, yeah," just shake your head like you're listenin' and just go on about your business, it's a comfortable life if you can do it. There's no headaches in it if you just go with the flow, as they say. But I'm saying if you try to push the system or get mad at this guy, mad at this guy, yeah, it can be a headache. Then again if you're runnin' around with a lot of people they make a headache for you, but by yourself it's pretty comfortable. The attitude is nice; you can do really what you want to. You know, somebody comes by, if you don't feel like workin', you got no money in your pocket, you don't have to work. You got a place to stay, you're gonna eat in the morning; it's pretty comfortable. If I had it to do over again I'd do it the same way, 'cause of the fact that Orlando is a busy town, and there's two types of people. We're the tramps that built up the city, and then when the city's already done, and they have some time to kill as far as workin', they come down on us pretty heavy as far as the police, just harassment, but like I said, I'm by myself, so they know me, and they just tell me to take a walk. So again, if I was with a lot of people, they would harass me. Because it's not just you doin' it, it's these three guys doin' it and you hang around with them, you're a part of it. It's a pretty comfortable town.

If you couldn't come here for lunch, would there be anyplace else to go?

Lunch, no. You can wait until four o'clock at the Salvation Army; they feed. At seven o'clock they feed at the Coalition. So they have different places, but I'm sayin' this is more or less a breakfast for the tramps, you know, the first meal of the day. And it's pretty simple. You just wait in line and come on in. Food's good, real good, and if you work for 'em, clean up after everybody leaves, you get a little bit more. So, you know, one hand washes the other. But I'm saying if you miss Daily Bread and you miss the Coalition, okay, if you ain't got no friends to give you a couple dollars or this and that, yeah, you just gotta wait till tomorrow. But it's not that bad. Everybody once in awhile will get a sandwich or get this, or take a couple sandwiches outta here. "Hey, Preacher, you want a sandwich?" And if you're hungry, you say yes. In the morning a lot of times at the church somebody'll get a bag of doughnuts and just leave it there. You go by, see a bag, pick it up and eat it. You know, because it's all good food, and what a lot of people do here - and it sounds bad - like the sub places and stuff, where they make the subs, that night they throw 'em out. But if a tramp goes up there and knocks on the back door, says, "Hey man, instead of throwing that stuff in the garbage, put it in a plastic bag." Then you go there the next night and you'll have, 20 or 30 sandwiches you can give to your friends. You know, because it's like daily service at the subway shops, and whatever sandwiches they got left, they throw out. So it's pretty nice.

You've been on the street a long time. Have you noticed changes in the number of people on the street, or why people are on the street?

I'll tell you what it is, it's the labor pools are startin' to cut down on work. There's a lot of drugs, cocaine, the rock. A lot of people are involved in that, so when they get paid, they ain't got no money after that to pay rent. The attitude is really, really bad because, you know, they're all broke, sweaty, dirty. They didn't have time to clean up because by the time the party's over it's about eight, nine o'clock. Where you gonna get cleaned up now? You gotta wait for in the morning. Then in the morning you come to Daily Bread smellin' bad, so you might be able to take a shower if you think about it; the shower's here, they tell everybody to come in first and take a shower if they want to. But yeah, people - about the last three years - have really, really changed for the worse. Especially when you see families out there. They've got families out there with kids; that's a little bit sad, you can take your kid and give it to a relationship or a friend, let them not suffer. When you get on your feet, you go back and get the kids. But you go out there now to the church, you see kids and stuff with their families. I mean it's fun for a couple days, but not as long as these people have been out there.

Jill Marie Gramig, 50, is a native of Louisville, Kentucky. She was interviewed at a shelter in Miami.

How long have you been in Florida?
Well, I've visited Florida before, but I haven't been here for about 10 years.
When did you move here?
Yes, I just moved here.
How long ago?
Last week.
Did you come from Kentucky?
No, I was in Texas.
What brought you to Florida?
Well, health, my health, having health problems and a lot of problems of, you know, I wouldn't know how to explain it, really, no help, receiving no help for a homeless person, I was receiving no help.
Were you homeless in Texas?
Yes.
For how long?
Almost the entire time, really. I had an old trailer to live in, but I had no electricity or water, just a place to sleep.
Where were you in Texas?
In Houston, Texas.
How long were you there?
Nine years.
How did you get here?
A bus, Greyhound bus.
Are you traveling alone?
Alone, and the trailer that I had was given to me by an old man that had sympathy for the homeless. Sometimes people have a particular care for others, you know, and he seemed to have a particular care for me, which was a blessing, because no one else did.
So what happened when you got to Miami? How did you wind up coming here?
Well, how did I wind up coming here? I planned to come here. I called Crisis, Crisis Hotline, at the bus station.
And they told you to come here?
This place and the other places. They gave me about five different places. But it was late, and I called them all, and no one answered. It was near 12 o'clock, I guess, and no one answered. So the lady I was with advised that I call maybe about seven in the morning, and I might get an

answer. See, I wasn't receiving any answers. So I called in the morning, and I called this place first.

We're in a world of stony-hearted people that hate the poor, want to destroy the poor, people like me.

The poor are the chosen ones of Christ, and they're not to be hated, they're not to be despised, and they're not to be destroyed. We're livin' in a destructive generation, full of violence, drugs, destruction.

So you came here the next day?

Yes, uh-huh, and I could get very little help, like downtown, not even the bus drivers could help me get up here; they didn't know how. I asked people on the street, mostly people that I could see were in the same situation I am, stranded or homeless, where this place was, and some of them, I guess I could say they gave me the best directions. I would say people of the city that had some kind of financial status were very cold, didn't even wanna talk to me, didn't even wanna give me any directions. And when I told them I was homeless, they go, "Get away from me, get away from me." You know, like I had the plague, a plague of some kind. There's a stigma, a terrible stigma in this country, with other people that are not homeless. They just don't want nothin' to do with ya, nothin'. Like I said, you'd think they were gonna catch a disease or somethin' if they just talk to ya. I mean, this country used to not be like that. It used to not be that way. When neighbors saw one another or needed help, and they were less fortunate than they are, they gave them help. They didn't turn their back on 'em and act like they had a disease of some kind. They pitched in and helped 'em, helped 'em get on their feet, didn't knock 'em down some more, say, "I don't want nothin' to do with them people, they're broke, they're poor." There's always been the certain ones in the city, you know, mostly the ones that have the authority, to snob the poor, but usually neighbors didn't do that to one another. They do now.

How long do you think you'll be staying here?

Oh, I'm gonna stay here as long as possible, 'cause I have a lot of things to do. I have no money, I have nowhere else to live, my ID has been stolen, I have no food stamps, I have no money in my pocket, so wouldn't you think it be good idea to hold on tight if you were in that situation, 'cause you were facing the street, and the street's no fun place to be in?

Have you applied for food stamps here?

You can't get 'em without an ID. My ID has been stolen.

When did that happen?

Well, several years ago, really.

Have you tried to get help from the police?

The police? The police don't care for the poor either. They'd just as soon lock you up and throw the key away. They don't like poor people. They don't like homeless people, and they threaten to lock you up if they see you on the street. You have to hide from the police. The police are not friends of the homeless. I don't know why I should have to tell you that.

Do you think you'll stay here now?

Oh, I'm definitely gonna stay here. I have nowhere else to go, unless they wanna throw me out in the ocean, drown me. I'm stayin' here.

What else would you like to add?

That's it, that's about it. There's not much help for the poor except Jesus Christ. That's about it, not too much help for the poor. Without Him none of the poor are going to make it, because the system is very inadequate, really, to take care of the poor.

Dana Shannon*, 35, is a native of Long Island, N.Y. She was interviewed in Fort Lauderdale at a family shelter run by the Salvation Army.

When did you first come to Florida?

When I was 21, when I first graduated college. I was 21; that was 1977, I came down to Florida.

Where did you go to college?

Cortland State University, upstate New York.

What did you study there?

I was a psychology major and an education major, and I came out with a teaching degree.

Did you come down here to Florida for a teaching job?

[laughs] Well, that's what I thought I was gonna do, yeah. That was what I believed I was to do, and I ended up coming down here and started waitin' tables in a nice French restaurant, and I got into the restaurant business for a little while.

What originally brought you to Florida? You just finished college and wanted to go someplace else?

Uh-huh, mostly the climate; I wanted to be in a nice area. I hated the cold weather in New York; I hated it. It was just very uncomfortable. The climate is what brought me here.

You lived in Palm Beach County for awhile?

Yep, first when I came to Florida I moved to Dade County; I lived in South Miami. And that place was real, real busy - it's just like New York; I didn't like it too much. So I ended up relocating in West Palm Beach.

Then you moved here to Fort Lauderdale?

Yeah, I came down to Fort Lauderdale strictly because I was put into a psychiatric hospital this past October. It was in Hollywood, and I went in there; I was put in for a diagnosis. I'm a drug addict and an alcoholic, and I'd been seeking help for that in a treatment center, and then they wanted me to get further help, psychiatric help, so I was in a psychiatric hospital, and that's what brought me to Broward County. And I ended up finished in the hospital, one thing led to another to another, and I ended up being discharged to here, to really nowhere. [laughs] You know, I can't say this is nowhere, 'cause this place has been real, real good, but it's temporary. I'm supposed to be leaving very soon; I'm not quite sure exactly where I'm going.

Before you were in the hospital, where were you living and what were you doing?

Well, in West Palm Beach I had the same apartment for four, maybe five years. I was an exterminator with a well-known company for three years, and I had two cats, I lived alone with my two cats, and that was my pride and joy - I liked having my apartment, it was on the water, we had a pool, and I just started getting into the drugs - again - I used to be in AA and then I left AA - and I started getting into the drugs again, and then I ended up losing everything I had, a brand new car. And I'll tell you something else: most of the people who are in here, in the Salvation Army, almost all the people I meet are in here because they've got a drug problem of one sort another. Do you know that?

I've heard that.

Yeah, quite a few people.

What kind of drugs were you doing?

I got into crack; two years ago I got into crack, and even at my age, I came out when I was sober in AA, I got into it and I got, in that two-year period of time, I ended up losin' everything, including my apartment.

Including your job?

Yeah, well, I still had my job when I came for help, but I did somethin' to lose that too. I'm gonna lose everything, I guess; I have absolutely nothing.

How did you wind up going to a hospital? You were looking to go to a treatment center?

I was in a treatment center already - in West Palm (West Palm Beach) - they sent me to a hospital. They sent me down to the Hollywood Pavilion for psychiatric evaluation, 'cause I tend to get really upset easy, and if I don't take medication I'll never sleep, I won't sleep, I'm extremely anxious. Right now I take 300 milligrams of Mellaril. And I also take Tofranil. Between the two of them - one's an anti-psychotic, which helps me with my mood swings, my temper, severe temper. And the other one's an anti-depressant, keeps me from being depressed, 'cause I get depressed a lot.

Did you go to the drug treatment center on your own?

Voluntarily, yeah.

Were you ever in trouble with the law because of drugs?

Years ago, well, years ago I got arrested for an armed robbery with a toy gun - back in 1982. I was robbing the drive-through stores with a toy gun, and at one point I got caught; you know, someone said they realized it wasn't a real gun, and I ended up getting arrested for it.

[Reacting to a noise in the room] What was that?

I don't know. It sounds like something swishing through the pipes or something.

Strange.

Yeah. And did you have to go to jail for that at all?

I ended up having time served. I went to jail, sure. They arrested me, took me to jail. It was the only time I ever stayed in jail. It was the fourth time I had been arrested, but the only time I really got behind the bars. I wasn't bailed out. I got out on my OR, my own recognizance, and I ended up going into a treatment center, 'cause I knew that I needed help; I went to a drug program up in West Palm. I stayed clean for two years. I've had sobriety, I've been clean before. It's been rough recently, I'm havin' a hard time - just I don't have access to the meetings and to the things that I need to go do. I volunteer here, I help out. I'm waiting to get into a program. There's a program that we're looking at that I'm supposed to go into, it's for mental illness and addiction problems - it's for both. From here, that's where I'm supposed to go. It's just that there's a lot of preliminary work and screening and paper work, and I'm waitin' for all this to go through already.

Is that here?

Uh-huh, it's in Pembroke Pines. It's on the grounds of South Florida State Hospital, the psychiatric hospital; it's on the same grounds as they are.

Is it a residential program?

Uh-huh.

By the time you went through that drug treatment program, had you lost your apartment?

At that time, yeah.

Where were you living?

Well I had been living at my mom and dad's house in Boca (Boca Raton). They have a lot of money, and I was living with them in their house, really beautiful home. And I went to a treatment center, and when I left I left their house and treatment with this girl that I had met in there. You know, my parents told me if I go with her, you may as well just say you're gone. And I did. I packed up my car, I packed everything I could fit in there. And that's when I ended up getting arrested - for the robbery, the armed robbery. You know, I got my car stolen from me, everything got stolen from me; this girl I met stole everything from me when I went into jail. So I came out of jail, I got raped four days after I got out of jail 'cause I didn't have a car, I was hitchhiking rides, you know. I just got through a rape trial just now, two weeks ago...all in the name of goin' to buy some crack.

Was the person convicted?

No, I didn't have any witnesses. It was gonna be a tough case for me, which is usually the case in rape, you know. It's sad, but they tend to get away with it. The guy was on top of me choking me with both his hands, and I figured kiss this world good bye, that was it, I couldn't breathe, this was it. [sighs] What ended up happening, they gave him time served for the time he had spent in jail - a couple months. And he pleaded no contest, like he didn't plead innocent or guilty, he just pleaded - which is as good as saying you're guilty - he just pleaded no contest, time served, and he's got another felony conviction; he was in prison for 13 years for second degree manslaughter, so I know the guy would have killed me if I didn't give in to what he wanted, so I gave in to what he wanted, and, you know, in lieu of not getting choked to death.

Do you want me to get my roommate soon (for another interview)?

No. Where did you stay after you lost your car and everything? Where did you sleep at night?

When I got out of jail I was in a lot of bars because of my drinking, and I had met a couple of different bar owners in maybe two, three different bars that I used to frequent, and they offered me places to stay with them, so what I used to do, I used to bring like my bag, my travel bag and stuff over their house. I found somewhere else to sleep 'cause like they wanted to sleep with me in exchange for me havin' a place to stay. I used to stay up in the 24-hour laundromats; sometimes, I remember this place that opened for breakfast at five in the morning - I'd stay in a bar all night and go for coffee with somebody at this breakfast place. I tried my best not to have to depend on anybody because it was always the same thing, "If you stay here, sleep with me," or whatever they wanted from me. So I had a lot of 24-hour laundromats; I used to get a lot of my sleep at the beach during the day. This was in Lake Worth.

So sometimes you had to sleep outside?

Yeah, or I wouldn't sleep at all. Some nights I didn't sleep at all.

How long were you out on the streets without a job or anything?

At that time, it was about six months. And I met a real nice couple when I was in JFK hospital, I had something happen - I cut my ear and got a real bad infection and all this shit - I met this nice couple who lived in Lantana; I went to stay with them for a couple of months, they let me live with them. They were into group sex, is what they were into. I stayed with them.

I ended up going into C.A.R.P. (Comprehensive Alcoholism Rehabilitation Program) program in Palm Beach County. C.A.R.P. is the county-funded, state-funded rehab center in West Palm Beach. I went in there and I stayed in there for seven months. It was good; I needed it.

And from there you went down to Hollywood?

No, this was back in 1982. From there I ended up getting my own apartment, which I had for a few years. I've had time with being responsible, stuff like that, but every time I've lost everything or became homeless it's because of the drugs or the drinking.

So you've been homeless several times?

A couple times, yeah; I don't really see it like that because usually there's someplace I can go for a little bit, but yeah, I guess I have been.

Is it difficult to find employment if you give a shelter as your address?

I never have trouble getting jobs, nope. I've never had to use a shelter address for getting a job. No, jobs are easy to get; I don't worry about that. No, if you want to work, there's plenty of jobs. I've never applied for a job being homeless, okay, so I wouldn't know. But maybe it is difficult. I was thinking about it because once in awhile I go up and visit some of these kids, these friends I know who live in the woods. They're *really* homeless; I mean I've got a roof over my head here and a bed and a washing machine where I can do my laundry. But I know people who live out in the woods, and their attitude is the same as mine, you know, if someone's hiring it doesn't make a shit of a difference where you live or if you live or whether you take the bus, drive a brand new BMW or ride a bike, it doesn't matter. If you wanna work, you'll work. You know that.

Are you working now?

No, I do a lot of volunteer work around here just to keep busy. No, I'm not into work right now; I'm tryin' to stay clean, all I'm tryin' to do is stay away from the crack one day at a time, and it's tough, it's been tough. I've had a couple of spills. I told my counselor I've had a couple of spills since I've been here. It's all over the place. You look around this building during the daytime, they're dealing out there, over there; it's all over.

Outside?

Yeah.

So you're hoping to get into this residential program. Then what will you do?

It's a good year to a year-and-a-half. From there you go out to work, you know, save money, get an apartment.

You mentioned before that you had been assaulted while hitchhiking. Is that a common problem for homeless women?

I don't know; I don't talk to that many people on the streets. I would imagine. I don't know. I don't even like to talk about it; it's too emotional for me, I have trouble. I went to therapy today and I couldn't even sit for an hour and talk to my counselor - who I love dearly - about my feelings. I kept getting up, I kept getting water; I'm having trouble sitting here now. I get in touch with too many feelings, it's overwhelming and I just wanna go get high, so I just have to shut the feelings off somehow.

What time is it? I didn't put my watch on after my shower.

Almost five of six.

Five to six, okay. Can we stop soon?

Yeah.

Okay. I get nervous talking about too many things. It bothers me.

I understand. Is there anything else you wanted to say about what it's like to be homeless?

Just hang on to what you got [laughs] while you have it, because it's not easy being homeless. It's not at all. People run all over you, they take advantage of you - especially being a woman. They take advantage of you. It's bad. I never thought I would get this low or things would be this bad, but...I really do, I thank God that I have a roof over my head, a good dinner to eat - I'm not much for breakfast. Just to have a safe place to call home, you know? I've never been in a Salvation Army before, but this Salvation Army is the best, from what I hear from other people in here. Some people make a *habit* out of going to one Salvation Army to another to another to another. You know that?

I've heard that.

Yeah, well I gather from people I've met here. It's my first time in this situation - in this Salvation Army. But from the people I've met here, they'll say the same thing. Like one lady who was here recently, she says, "God, I know this lady who goes from one place to another to another." She was talking about herself, but she didn't want to say it was "me," you know, she wouldn't say me. She was telling how this lady she knew went from one place to another. I gather a lot of people make a habit out of that, from what I've heard here, because a lot of people will say, "Oh, the Salvation Army in Michigan that I went to, or Grand Rapids." Or they'll say, "The Salvation Army that I went to when I was in West Palm was really low class." But you wonder why they're always going to Salvation - I hope to God this is my last Salvation Army, the first and the last. You know, I need to get my shit together, and I don't want to be in this situation at all.

Can we end soon? I'm getting tired.

We can end right now.

Susan Holly, 46, is a native of Worcester, Massachusetts. She was interviewed at a shelter in Miami.

How long have you been staying here at the shelter?

In and out for two-and-a-half years.

But you don't stay permanently here?

Well, you're not supposed to. That's why I've been in and out. I'm finally starting to get back on my feet. I have a job on the Beach (Miami Beach) now taking care of a little boy. I'm supposed to be going back tonight. I don't know if I will because I haven't talked to the mother yet, but...

What originally happened that made you lose having a regular place to live?

I lost my home.

How?

I lost all my money. [laughs] I used to have money. Money, I mean, real money, you know, like, not like $1,000. I mean real money. My mother died in 1984, and she never taught me anything about life, okay? She taught me everything about money but she never taught me about life, so I trusted the wrong people. There ya go.

What happened?

I lost all my money, let them handle stuff that they had no business handling.

Who were they?

A guy that I know, who still wants to know where I'm at. I trusted him. I loved him; I still love him. I don't trust anybody anymore because of what happened to me.

Were you married?

No, but it was the same as being married, you know, we were so close, at least I thought so. I trusted him; I shouldn't have. Now I don't trust anybody.

So was he gambling?

I really don't know how it happened, but I trusted him to take care of my affairs, and he...

He had access to all your money?

Yes, uh-huh.

Did you own a house?

Yes.

How did you lose your house?

I couldn't keep up the payments because I didn't have the money to make the payments. And I thought that he was takin' care of things - dumb, dumb.

Were you working?

Yes. I was working up until 1987; I lost my job. And I knew it was coming, so I decided to make provisions for myself, you know, 'cause it was gonna take me awhile to find another job because I'm handicapped, see, and you can't find a job that easy. I can't find a job that easy anyway.

You're physically handicapped?

Yes, uh-huh.

In what way?

I know, I don't look it. It's my legs. [laughs]

Oh, you have trouble walking?

Yeah. So I decided that I would put my money in income property, and I hired him for my manager, nothing on paper, you know, just trust - there you go, that word again, right? So, to make a long story short, after a year-and-a-half, there was nothing left, couldn't make the payments on the properties, lost them all, lost everything.

How much money did you start out with?

Two hundred thousand. It makes me sick to think about it, but I'm tryin' to get through it the easiest way I know how, you know, starting from scratch again. And it threw me for a loop, so that's why I've been this way for so long. I didn't know how to get back on my feet again, I really didn't, 'cause I'm naive. I'm still naive, I still am, I'll admit it. I know money; I don't know people at all. So I don't trust anybody anymore, a terrible thing, terrible.

What kind of work did you do before?

Office, I worked in an office. For 15 years I had a job in an office.

For the same company?

In one place, 15 years in one place, I should have retired.

Did you get laid off?

No, I got fired. I made 'em fire me 'cause I wouldn't quit because I wanted to get unemployment out of 'em. See, I didn't need it then, but I figured they owed it to me, only they didn't wanna pay me unemployment. It's the same with everybody, it's not just me, but they didn't wanna pay anybody unemployment. I made 'em fire me so they'd have to.

You were going to get laid off anyway?

I was gonna get laid off, yeah, but I made 'em fire me.

Where have you stayed when you haven't been staying here? Where do you sleep at night?

Oh, I've been very lucky 'cause I've always had a roof over my head and something to eat, you know, so the Women and Children's Shelter. I started out at Safespace because I got hit over the head.

Is that a women's shelter?

For abused women - he hit me over the head.

Your friend?

Yeah.

Were you hospitalized?

Well no, not really, see, he didn't hurt me that much, but I decided to leave, 'cause I said to myself - when we were first startin' to get involved I said to him that I loved him and all this stuff, but the first time he hit me, I was out of there. I kept my promise.

So you went to a battered women's shelter for awhile?

Uh-huh, Safespace, and I can't get any help from anywhere, which is why I'm havin' so much trouble, 'cause I didn't lie about what I had, see? I'm not street smart, I'm not street wise, I don't know how to play the game, see? I met a guy in one of these places - it must have been Camillus House, you know, I was down Camillus House (a shelter, soup kitchen and medical clinic for homeless people), and we were talkin', and he was tellin' me that he has like $50,000 worth of assets in the same kind of thing that I have, only it's one of these things where he's not gonna get until five years from now, it's in a trust. I have a little money - less than that - in something just like what he has, but I told everybody about it when I went for help. See, I don't know these things, I don't know, I don't know how to play the game, I'm not street smart. So I told them everything that I had, they said, "You can't get anything." I can't get food stamps, I can't get welfare, I can't get disability, I can't get anything.

Do you have access to that money?

No.

It's in a trust fund of some sort?

It's an investment which is not gonna be up until like 1994, '95.

Is it in bonds?

It's a real estate trust, a real estate investment trust, see?

So you can't get food stamps or anything?

I can't get anything because of that.

But you can't get your money either?

No. If I could, I would take it and I would spend it, see? So then I could get welfare and food stamps and all the rest of that. No, but I don't want that. I wanna work, but I can't get anybody to hire me.

Why not?

Everybody looks at the legs. What I've been sayin' to myself is that God looked down and He saw that my cross didn't bother me, so He gave me another one, He made people think that I was an idiot because of the way my legs are, 'cause everybody, it's like you said, you know, "Oh, that's funny, you don't look like you're handicapped." Of course I don't look like it. I'm not, I'm not handicapped, except for down here [points to her legs].

Do you go to soup kitchens?

Yeah, I've always had enough to eat - well, maybe not enough, but, you know. At noontime you go to the bus bench, "Excuse me. Could you give me a quarter so I could get something to eat?" I hate that. I hate it, but you gotta do it. I hate it; it's awful. I keep saying to myself and to everybody else, I really don't know how anybody in their right mind would think that anybody in their right mind would like to live like this. I can't see it.

How do people react when you're panhandling?

I don't do that.

You don't do it too much?

I don't do it that much anymore because you can get arrested that way. They'll look right through you. People just look right through you when you're homeless. They look right through you; they don't even see you. This experience has been an experience, let me tell ya. My consciousness has been raised way up. I never turn anybody down when they ask me for money anymore. Since I have a little bit, I share what I got.

So other people generally don't treat you very well?

They look right through you, you know. You ask them, "Excuse me, sir, could you possibly let me have a little money so that I can get something to eat?" They walk right by you. They don't even say anything to ya, a lot of 'em. Some of 'em do; some of 'em are very good, but a lot of 'em just look right through ya, they don't say anything to ya.

You mentioned earlier that this guy you were with wants to know where you are...

He knows where I am. I don't know why he wants to know, but he does, so I just give up, you know, I don't know why. It's like I got somebody lookin' over my shoulder, you know, and it feels good, it's alright.

What's the worst thing about being homeless?

Having no identity, people looking right through you. Nobody has respect for you. To me, I was brought up that a person should be respected because they're a child of God, you know, whether you're down there someplace or the highest person in the whole world, but it's not like that. My consciousness is raised; it's not like that.

A lot of people say we need more programs to help the homeless, but others say we're already doing enough. What do you think?

No, we're not, we're not doing enough. All this business, what they're doing under the bridge, setting up trailers under the bridge for the social workers - they should set up trailers under the bridge for the homeless people, never mind spending all that money to set up the trailers for the social workers. It's ridiculous.

Has anything good come out of this for you?

No, but I keep saying that it will. It's made me stronger, I'm much stronger now than I was, and something good will come from this, I know it will, I know. But it was meant to be, okay? Because the reason that I ended up in the street, let me tell you my story. I was here in 1989. At the end, I think it was maybe about six months into 1989, I ran into some people that I hadn't seen for over a year-and-a-half. And she said to me, you know, she'd wondered what happened to me and all this, and I told her, and she said, "I was afraid of that." She said, "Come with us," she and her husband, okay? "You come stay with us. You're not gonna stay here. You stay with us." So I went with them, and three, four months later, she ended up in the hospital, she was this far from dyin', he tried to kill her.

Who did?

Her husband, her husband tried to kill her, and if I hadn't been there, he would have. He beat her. And I know that's why I was there; God wanted me to be there. I believe that, I believe that, that's what I believe. And I know that God wants me for somethin'. He's gonna save me for somethin' good. He really is. God will get me through this, that's what I've been sayin' ever since 1989, God will get me through this. And He will.

So if all goes well, what will happen in the next year or so?

Who knows? God knows, I don't, I have no idea. But I'm working on getting a job through vocational rehab, I'm working on that, and this little mini-job will get me through the rough spots, you know, and through this, I'll get a place to stay - when I get my job through vocational rehab, I'll get a place to stay.

Is there anything else you'd like to add?

It's just that you think that people care. See, I thought people cared. They don't care; people don't care. You know, I care, but nobody else cares.

They only care about themselves, and until they can see that today it's me, tomorrow it could be them, until they can see that, nothin's gonna change.

Chapter Seven

Home Again

Most people who are out on the street eventually manage to find permanent housing. Quite often they find themselves inexorably drawn back to the homeless shelters and soup kitchens they once frequented, where they work as volunteers or full-time staff people.

Maribel Lopez, 25, is a native of Mexico. She was interviewed at the Orlando Union Rescue Mission, where she was working.

How long have you been in Florida?
For three years.
What brought you here originally?
I answered an ad to be a companion aide, and I worked for a year-and-a-half with a family, and then I got another job as a live-in, and then I kind of had problems there, and came into the shelter.
When you first came to the United States, did you come directly here to Florida?
No, I stayed in Brownsville, Texas, for two or three years, and then I came to Florida.
That's when you answered the ad?
Uh-huh.
Did you come to Orlando first, or somewhere else?
No, to Orlando.
So this is where you were working originally?
Yes.

And then you went to another job?
Uh-huh.
The same kind of job?
Yes.
It didn't work out?
Uh-huh.
What was the problem there?
Well, I answered an ad in the paper, and the paper stated that it was to be a salesperson, and I answered the ad, they hired me, I trust the people that hired me, and they happened to be drug dealers, so I had to get out of the situation immediately.
Where was that?
In Tampa.
They wanted you to sell drugs?
Yes, in Miami, because I spoke Spanish, and they said I could do pretty good sales over there, so I decided not to take the job. [laughs] Like I didn't know till I was already there, in their house, and then I figured out what it was, and I didn't tell 'em I didn't want to do it, the only thing is that I just thought to myself: I've got to get out of the situation.

So I got a ride there at their house at 10 o'clock p.m., and that entire night, you know, I was worried about where I was gonna go, and where I was gonna stay, and luckily some people helped me in Tampa, you know, some people, when I left at six o'clock in the morning, because I told them I jogged every day when they interviewed me, so they expected me to leave the house and jog, and they had interviewed, and they knew I didn't have a family and everything, so they thought, you know, that they had me there, I was going to be there to do whatever they were going to tell me to do. But when I left in the morning at six o'clock, I jogged, and I didn't care, and I left all my belongings in their house, and I just left. And I jogged and I jogged and I found this man, luckily he was watering his plants at that early in the morning, and I didn't have nothing with me, my birth certificate, I didn't have no Social Security number, no nothing, just shorts and a t-shirt and my tennis shoes, and I told him that if I could cut his yard or do something so I could get money to come back to Orlando, and he goes, "Well, what is your situation?" And I told him that I was in trouble, and he goes, "Well, let me talk to my wife." And his wife came out of the house and I explained to her that I was having trouble, and I didn't have nothing with me, so it was just my word, and I told them that I was staying at this house and I was in trouble, and if they could help me out. So they helped me out, they bought my tickets to come to Orlando, and the only bus coming to Orlando was at 9 p.m., so I had like an entire day, and what happened was they told me they were too old to get involved in that situation where I was in, but that they were gonna leave me in the corner of the street, where the house was, and for me to go in and get my stuff, and then if I didn't come out by a certain time they were gonna call the policeman, because I've been in the street, and I have street smarts, when I walk in the house, they end up very happy, the people there were too busy getting things ready and everything, so I didn't feel it was the right time to tell them, you know, no, I'm not going with you, so when the guy asked me if I was getting ready to go, I said yes, but, you know, I never told him where I was getting ready to go. [laughs]

So it took about two hours, just pacing the whole house, you know, thinking how am I gonna tell him, and I was very worried and I totally forgot about the old people, because when you have tense, and you're worried, you don't know what's gonna happen. I didn't want to know any information of them, of what they were gonna do or how, because I think it would be worse for me, so I tried to stay in the bathroom and walk around and not be around them. Suddenly, finally, some people came knocking on the door, they just came in running, and they're cops, and they got me out. And the old people were waiting for me at 7-Eleven. So what happened, they took me out of the house, they took my clothes, they put me in the policeman car, took me to 7-Eleven, that's where I met the people, and the people thought, since this had happened two hours ago, they thought oh I was already killed or something, you know. So they paid my ticket to come to Orlando, and they were very happy to see me, and still I had a ticket to come over here, but I didn't have a place to stay, and I'm here like, what am I gonna do?

I called the people that I used to work for and they told me that because I had left without no further notice, and because of when these people talked to me they told me that it was a challenge that I needed to take, they were gonna pay me $500 a week, and it's a chance, you know, and they were gonna hire somebody else if I didn't go that day, that night. So I said, "Well, I'll take that chance," even though I had that feeling inside that something was wrong. I didn't want to lose that opportunity, and because I had the desire of making money, I left, and then I got in trouble. And the people when I called them, they said, "Well you just left us, so we're not gonna help you." And a fellow that I knew through them, I called him, see, but he wouldn't help me, and he goes, "I have a girlfriend in my house right now, and you can't stay tonight, but maybe tomorrow, but I'm gonna take you to this place where I know that they'll take you in just for one night, and then I'll pick you up." So he brought me here to the shelter, and when he brought me here I was like, I didn't have no idea what the shelter was about, I wasn't that long here, the whole time that I spent with those people was at their house cleaning and everything. It took him awhile to try to take me in his home, and he brought me here, and that's how I ended up in the shelter.

This newspaper advertisement that you answered, was that in the local paper here?

Yes, in the local paper.

In The Orlando Sentinel?

Yes, what happened was, you see that's how I came to Orlando because I answered an ad from Brownsville, Texas, they usually - a domestic - they always have like, call collect, you know, a nanny, they want to take in a nanny with children, I mean a nanny willing to move to Florida, that's what. And they usually have ads like that, sometimes in California, you never know where you're calling, and I called. That was the first time, I had never looked at an ad before, but what happened was I was going through a lot of turmoil in my family, 'cause we come from a poor family.

Did the advertisement for the job in Tampa say specifically that they wanted a Spanish speaking person?

Yes, they wanted a bilingual. And what happened was, when I came to here, to Orlando, Florida, I was livin' in Longwood where all the rich people live, and my belief was that everybody was rich because I was surrounded by rich. I lived in, what is it called? Lake Mary area, so it was all rich, Publix (a supermarket chain) was all gold cards and everything, and I thought, you know, I had just arrived from one place, Brownsville, bein' poor, and comin' to another place which is like total - so that's why I believed that everybody in Orlando, everybody was rich here in the United States. I just felt like wow. The reason that I answered an ad was because I didn't feel content with my job because I was doing too much, I was doing taking care of that man, cleaning the house...

Taking care of...

A man who had Alzheimer's. I had to do that, I had to clean the house, cook breakfast, lunch and dinner for the person, then do the yard work, which was, they had a lot of land, so I had to cut their grass and do all this, and I felt like it was not enough money that they were paying for me to do all those things, plus being in the house like 24 hours, so it was a lot. So I did have the desire to make money, and because of that, I saw an ad, it looked pretty interesting, you know, it said wanted to be a salesperson, live-in salesperson, be bilingual, in Miami, so I thought, well that's pretty good, and then it said pay high amount of money, so I thought well that sounds interesting, and I said I'm bilingual, so I called up those people and they seemed very interested when they heard me on the phone, my voice, and they said, well, we're gonna go to Orlando and see you that same day that I called, and I was very impressed. They asked me where I worked, what I did, if I had family, and I told them everything. So my problem was that I told them everything about me; I didn't have no family, I was staying with these people and all that, so they liked me, and they said, "We'll meet you at Red Lobster (a restaurant) at seven o'clock p.m. in Colonial Drive." They said, "We're gonna be in a Mercedes, and meet us there." They told me the description of the car, was color blue, and was two fellows and a girl. So we met there at seven o'clock; I was driving that people's car. We met there at Red Lobster, and because of their appearance I believed they were rich. That's why I was fooled.

They asked you to come that night?

Well they asked me what I did, my job, and I talked to them, and the more I talked to them the more they liked me. They told me right away, "We like you; we want to take you." And they said this is a golden opportunity, you know, before somebody else gets the job, we would like you to do sales in Miami. You'd be real good.

So you left that night?

I said, "Well, how much are you gonna pay me?" And they said $500 a week and more. And then I thought well that's pretty good, you know? So I said yeah, it beats 250 or 300 a week that I was makin' over here, I thought well that's a lot more, and I thought, well that sounds good, and because of the money value, that's why I decided to leave. They told me, you know, "We'll go and pick you up." And because where I was livin', I didn't live in the home, I lived, you know, kind of like a little house, and I left, that's how I got away; it's not like I lived in their home.

Was that little house on their grounds?

Yes, so I left and, well of course it was night time so they thought, you know, I was probably in bed, or I would come back late that night, which I never did that, but I left, I got there at Tampa 10 o'clock, when I had that feeling, you know, when we were driving over there, they started smoking and the girl took some pills, and she asked me if I wanted to do anything. [laughs] I said no, I'm not feeling well, that's my excuse, I'm not feeling well, but maybe tomorrow. And I started feeling bad, like oh no, what have I got myself involved? Their language, everything was not good. So when I arrived over there, forget it. I knew, it was a dump home; they had told me, when they interviewed me, I'd live in a beautiful home, you know, two-story home, they had beautiful plants from different parts of the world, every morning she got up and she just went up and smelled those plants, I mean they were just gorgeous. And they had acres of acres of land, with horses and everything, and that I would have to get her up to the horses, and I had to be physically fit, and all these things they wanted me to do, and I thought, well, these people are real rich, you know? I believed them because I lived in a rich area, so...when we got there it was a dump home, it was a dump, it was one of those places where they do drugs and stuff. And I tried to call back to my boss and tell them that I was gonna come in late, but they would not let me use the phone, and they would not take me back to Orlando. I told them, you know, I don't think I want to work here. And they said, "Oh, you haven't even tried it. You're with us now." So I thought, no way. So that whole entire night I was like pacing the floors. I said, "Okay, well take me to my room. Where's my room? I don't feel well." So they took me, I mean it was squeaky floors. That's when I went upstairs, writing all over the walls and everything, went upstairs, it was like a mattress on the floor, and they said I was gonna stay there. So I'm with all my stuff, and I'm thinking oh my gosh, what have I gotten myself involved in?

So how long ago did this happen?

This happened two years ago.

What happened then? Were you able to find work here?

What happened was, once I came to the mission, I had a lot of personal problems from my past and everything. I had a very negative attitude. I had to be very strong, and not cry and stuff like that, because I've been in the street, and you have to be tough, so I was very tough when I came to the shelter. I didn't talk that much to people; I was very reserved, and always doubt people, didn't have any trust at all, no trust at all. So when I came here they kind of had a hard time with me because I didn't speak, you know, and didn't want to say no information to them about past or anything because I was not too sure if I could trust them, you know? And when you happen to be in the street you lose your privacy and you lose a lot of things, so I had to share a room with one of the ladies here, and Miss Moody (the shelter director) came and talked to me that same day that I walked in. She said that I could go take a shower because I looked bad because I had jogged and everything, I was like, I looked horrible. She goes, "Go take a shower and then fix yourself up and go and eat and then you can go out and find a job." I have to find a job in less than a week in order to stay here, so I thought like where am I gonna go? I don't have a car, I don't have money to get in the bus to take me anywhere. I'm just gonna have to walk to a place to work, which I didn't mind, but I was just like, I hope they hire me, you know? I didn't have no references. The references I had was not that good, the people I worked for, so I was like, when you're in this situation, you don't have references, it was kind of hard to find a job.

So Miss Moody goes, she talked to me the word of God, the same day that I walk in, I went to eat, and it was so funny, they were serving tacos, so she goes, "You must feel right at home" because she knew I was Spanish, she goes "You must feel right at home." I didn't know what she was saying at that time when she said that. And I went to sit in the very back of the dining room, and she came and talked to me and she asked me if I knew Jesus, and I told her I knew about three of them but they didn't know where I was. Jesus is very common in Mexico. So I told her I knew three of them, but they just didn't know where I was, and she goes, she was referring to Jesus in the Bible. I said, "Oh yes." And she talked to me about if I had ever been saved, and I said, again, because I was not raised in a Christian home, I didn't know what she was talking about, so I said, "Well, if you put me out on the street I'm probably not be saved, but if you leave me here for a short time I could be saved for a little period of time." And she decided she knew that I didn't know much about the Bible or anything, so she says that if I was willing to be in a discipleship program, which I didn't know what that was. She asked me to pray the sinner's prayer, we talked about the Bible and everything else, and she helped me out.

What happened was, I had a job to do here, I had to cook three meals a day for these people - for staying here. I was gonna get a small check: $35 every two weeks. And when she told me that I said like from $500 to $300 they're paying me $35. You've got to be kidding. [laughs] But she told me that I had to trust God, that He would supply all my needs. And I didn't have no trust, thought yeah right. So I said well I'm just gonna live here, I thought to myself for maybe a month, so I can get enough money to go to a hotel and see what I want to do. But that whole month that I stayed here I had to cook, and she discipled me a lot, not only through words, but they showed that they really, you know, that they cared for me, and it was a time where I could do a change if I wanted to. So she got me enrolled in Orlando Vo-Tech and while I was cooking here after I got finished cooking I would go to school, got my GED - that helped me out a lot too - and I'm attending now Valencia Community College, studying communications.

Went through a change, it was rough, but when you stay here, you meet a lot of people who are in the same situation, so you don't feel by yourself, and you look at other people, which, a lot of ladies that have children here, you feel worse than being a single person. And a lot of ladies come here, they have been abused big time, and they have been told a lot of things by their husbands, you know, "You're never going to make it; you're a failure," and they have children and they don't know what to do so they come in here and the people here, the staff people, they encourage them by telling them you can make it, they provide them with nice clothes, people like beauticians that cut their hair, they tell them what looks nice on them and everything, encourage them, and we encourage them so they can feel better about themselves. We also talk to them about the word of God and everything, what it has done in our lives. You know, I talk to a lot of the girls, I give them my testimony, and I know there's a lot of girls that can make it. And when they see, they hear, they not only see it, they see an example that we give them, they change. But a lot of ladies care, it's not easy to be on staff here because they all come with tough attitudes, they talk back to you, and they're rough with you, and you have to be like soft and really show that you're really a strong Christian, and that you really care for them, because a lot of girls that come here, nobody has cared, and they just give them like, well I'll give you this food or I'll give you this money or I'll give you this for right now, but they don't teach them the main thing about the word of God and that Jesus loves them and everything, and no matter what anybody has else done or thinks about them, Jesus still loves you, you know? So that was a big thing to me, was like wow, that my sins were forgiven, and that I could make it in life if I just think of the positive, think that God is with me and carries me through problems, but I have to do my part too. So that's the way we encourage the ladies, and then we do provide them with materialistic things like clothing, make up, soap, everything, and when they see this, all this is given, we tell them it's not from us, but it's God that has 'em here for a reason, to teach them something for a period of time, so they can see. And a lot of times God puts you in a situation like this to teach you a lesson, either to draw you back to God and say, "Hey, it's time for you to straighten up your life, or you could make it."

Are you on staff full-time here?

Yes.

And you're going to school too?

Yes. I just finished a semester. I'm not going to summer school. But I'm gonna attend September, but I'm gonna be in charge of the children this semester.

It seems like a lot of women who are staying in other shelters have left situations where their husbands were abusing them. Do you see a lot of that here?

Do we see a lot of that here? Yes. We turn away about 35 to 45 people a day. It's kind of bad. That's why we're trying to do another facility where we could help these ladies out, with children. We have a family here, a lady, she has beautiful children, they're so cute, and the husband was drinking and doing drugs and abused her and everything. Their children were in the street, I mean beautiful, blond, blue eyes, long hair, cute, and they were all in the street because of the dad, and we got her here. She came here and we told her that we could help her out, and she had to find a job and try to make it, not to go down with thinking, "Oh, all this has happened to me, and I have these children." You have to encourage her to go out and find a job so she can be strong for her children. And they usually come very depressed, because sometimes the women have been dependent with their husband for a long time, they've been married since like they were 19 or 18, and they never went to college, they never got an education, and got married, and then 20 years later the husband decides to find somebody else and drops them off. No education, no nothing, some just drop out of school to get married, and the husband goes with somebody else, he's the one that had the career and everything, and drops them off, and they're just without nothing, and then it's hard. And that's when we help them out here, in a lot of cases.

A lot of people that are out in the community, they think that homeless people are just lazy people, and they're into drugs and stuff like that. It's not true, 'cause you find all kinds of backgrounds; some people have had a good education and everything, and they've had like a nervous breakdown for some reason, some problems, or some have been abused and they need a chance. And some of 'em - let me tell you - some do come here and they just want to take advantage of the program. We've had incidents where they don't want to look for a job, they don't want to do nothing, they just want to sit around and get everything they can. We do find those kind of people too. Or they go from shelter to shelter to shelter, and they really don't want to do anything. That's the people I don't understand, why they don't want to try to do something with their life.

Roscoe Morey, 30, is a native of Greenville, Mississippi. He was interviewed in Miami at Camillus Health Concern, which provides free medical care for homeless people and is associated with Camillus House, a shelter and soup kitchen. Morey is a staff member at Camillus Health Concern.

How long have you been in Florida?
Since January the fifth, 1985.
What brought you down here?
My aunt. I came down here when I was in the military, and I liked it, so I came back after I got out of the military.
Were you in the Army?
Yes.

Do you have a lot of relatives here?

I had an aunt here at that time, but right now it's more like three of us here: my aunt, my cousin and I.

You were out on the street for awhile?

I was on the street from the middle of 1986 up until May of 1988, roughly about two years.

How did you lose having a regular place to live?

Well, I wasn't followin' my own, you know, instincts. I was really like listenin' to someone else. When I got here I got caught up in a thing of followin' other people, followin' other people instead of listenin' to myself. I tried pleasin' other people, and I got into the habit of usin' drugs and drinkin' heavily. And one day - my aunt - sorta got into like a small argument. She asked me did I wanna go back home, and I didn't wanna go back home. I was partially intoxicated at that time, so I just packed my clothes and I left. And I moved in with a friend, and from there everything just went downhill, from an efficiency to the streets. The efficiency wasn't well furnished at all, just a sofa here and a bed in the other room.

Were you working at the time?

I started out working in June of 1985, about five months after I got here, at the Hyatt Regency downtown. After about two months, they let me go 'cause of my alcohol and drug problem. I'd just go into work late. I'd get off like 11 o'clock at night and I would stay up till like three in the morning at the bars here, drinkin' with friends. I'm thinkin' I'm havin' fun, but forgettin' about that I had to go to work the next day like 10 o'clock in the morning. And it's hard to wake up when you're intoxicated - highly intoxicated, really. And so, they finally got fed up with me partyin' all the time, so they let me go. From there I started out as a part-time DJ job on the weekends, spinnin' records. It wasn't payin' much, and I wasn't utilizin' the money correctly, so it wasn't benefitin' me. And eventually that ended, and from there things just got worse. From the efficiency I went out to the streets. I started out in Little Haiti, from Little Haiti I drifted over to Overtown, and there I stayed for about another year-and-a-half. And from there I got incarcerated for four-and-a-half months. I was given more of like a choice. They said you could go to this program for 90 days, do 90 days and get out, or you can do five years in prison. So really it wasn't a choice; I knew what I was takin'. But my mind was made up when I went to jail for the last time, which was in May of 1988, that I wasn't gonna use drugs, I wasn't gonna drink anymore. And once I got out - on October fifth, 1988 - I came here. I talked to Brother Harry; the same day that I got out I talked to him. He told me he didn't have no beds available at the present time, so he told me just to keep checkin' with him.

I checked with him on a daily basis. But in the meantime I got me a job up to the Miami Arena, as a maintenance person. First paycheck I gave it to him to show that I was sincere about what I wanted to do. After Halloween day he let me in, and from there everything just started lookin' better for me. My head wasn't cloudy anymore; it started clearin' up. I could think better, and I got that self-respect back, and I wanted more out of life then, and it took me to where I am today, and I enjoy life more.

What kinds of drugs had you been using?

I started out smokin' marijuana about seventh grade, and I smoked marijuana up until I was 26 or 27. And I never used cocaine until I got here in Miami. I started snorting cocaine when I first got to Miami, and I started smokin' crack, I'd say the latter part of 1986. That was my biggest downfall, it took me further - all the way down to concrete, to sleepin' on the streets, you know. It really caused me a lot of problems. Also, around the same time - I used to consume a lot of alcohol while I was in the military. I started out like seventh, eighth grade, started out drinkin' beer and wine, and it just grew. When I was goin' to high school I used to drink like a pint of liquor every morning, me and my friends - between two or three persons, you know, before I'd get to class, before I'd eat breakfast. That was my breakfast. I thought I was enjoyin' myself, not knowin' that I was hurtin' myself all the time. I didn't know what the future held for me, until I finally realized that I hurt myself. I set down and I think about it. I did all this? I smile about it, but god damn, I had a hell of a life for the past 18 years. Everything that I missed out on, all because I was tryin' to satisfy someone else. I should have satisfied Roscoe. But I learn from that today.

You mentioned that you had been arrested. Did you get busted for drugs?

No, I was arrested for breakin' into my aunt's car - the same person that helped me when I first got here, you know. And I seen the hurt that was on her face, 'cause she couldn't believe that was me that had broken into her car. She couldn't believe that I was doin' somethin' like that to her. And to see the hurt on her face, it hurt me. And I knew right then and there. I started prayin' to God to help me stop usin' this, you know, stop doin' what I'm doin', 'cause I started hurtin' my family, and I never hurt no one in my family in my life. And my mind was made up from right there: no more drugs, no more alcohol, no more anything. It's time for me to get my life together; otherwise I'm gonna end up dead or wind up hurtin' everyone in my family.

Were you breaking in to take something?

Oh, takin' change or anything that I could find I could sell. That's what I was mainly takin'.

Where did you sleep at night when you were on the streets?

I started out in abandoned houses. From there I went down to this courthouse down here, the county courthouse. I slept up in there for about six months during the winter season when it was really cold, 30 degrees, you know, and I didn't have a blanket or anything like that. The only thing I had to cover with was a cardboard box. From there I slept across the street over here. When there was that abandoned building that was burnt out, I slept there for like six months. It was a variety of places. I slept over on Second Avenue and Ninth Street, right down from Biscayne (Biscayne Boulevard), stayed there for about three or four months off and on, anywhere that I could find, anywhere that we thought it was safe, me and my friends, we thought it was safe to camp out there. But really there's no way to be safe on the streets. It was hell. It was somethin' I wasn't used to. But until I could get somewhere, isolate myself and get my mind together - I know I would still be doing the same thing. If my aunt hadn't sent me to jail, give me time to think about what I was doin', I believe I'd still be out there.

Were you always able to get enough clothes?

Not enough, 'cause you can only carry so much. You could carry at least two changes of clothes. 'Cause when you go to the labor pool lookin' for work, you wanna at least be smellin' decent and lookin' decent, kinda decent. You won't look your best, but you will look presentable. The main thing was to make sure you're sorta presentable.

Were you able to make enough money by going to the labor pools? Is that what you mainly did to make money?

Sometimes I stole. Mostly every day, Monday through Friday, I would be at the labor pool, which didn't pay too much. It'd pay like minimum wage, I'd bring home 23. You'd make $27. They give us like a $3 advance pay to get to work and to get back here, which wasn't that much 'cause we had to buy lunch also, but they feelin' you should be responsible; if you work one day, and you know you goin' back out the next day, you should save you some money for lunch. But it wasn't enough to make a livin' on, 22, $23 a day, five days a week, that's not enough for nobody, not for a decent livin'.

And sometimes you stole?

Yes.

What would you do? Break into houses or cars?

And businesses, whatever we were able to take.

Did you ever have to steal food?

No. There was times when I'd be walkin', comin' from Little Haiti walkin' this way, that I was really hungry and I'd want to steal food, but it just wasn't there. If I wasn't high, I couldn't steal, 'cause the courage wasn't there. But if I was high and I needed somethin', I'd steal.

What was it like dealing with other people who were out on the street? Were people pretty good about looking out for each other?

You have like a certain group, you know? You pick your own friends. Certain people don't fit in with certain people. That's the way it was. Just like when you be in high school or you goin' to elementary school or somethin', you pick a friend. That's how it is on the street. You might meet 'em in a food line, you might just meet 'em on the streets, walkin', you stop and start talkin'. You might just end up in a line with each other every day, sharin' things.

How about outsiders? Did they treat you okay or ignore you or what?

The only people that treated us, you know, equally in some type of way was the church people. Most of the businesses, you couldn't go in there. And some of the pride that I still had left in me, I wouldn't go in there anyway, you know, 'cause I was afraid I might see someone that I know, and I felt I had lost respect for myself, and I didn't want anyone to see me like this. But they would usually turn their heads away from me, couldn't get too much out of 'em. I usually stayed out of their sight. I would just go to work in the day and at night time just go down to the courthouse or just lay out front here.

What would you do about rain or cold weather?

That was the hard part, that was the worst part, the winter season, 'cause most of us didn't have blankets. If we did, someone stole them though, someone would sit down there, watch us while we hide our blankets for the day and we'd go to work. When we'd come back, they were gone. And at night, when it'd get down to like 30, 25 degrees, 35 degrees, the only thing we had to cover with was cardboard. It was really cold. There was a lot of nights like that, like during the '87 season.

Did the police ever try to help you out or bother you?

They would come by and harass us sometimes. We got arrested one time for sleeping out here on the sidewalk, right out front here. They arrested us.

For loitering?

For vagrancy. They took us downtown like for three or four hours and let us go. It's more like harassment than an arrest, just givin' them somethin' to do I guess; they had nothin' better to do, you know, than come down here.

What was the worst part about being out on the streets?

Hygiene, you know, mother nature, the weather, and nutrition. That's the worst three things about it. You're fightin' three things. You fight against nature, you try to keep your health up, and you try to keep your personal hygiene up.

Was there any place you could go to take showers?

Here at Camillus House, for the most part. Or else just had to go jump out there in the bay. [laughs] They say salt water is good for anything. [laughs]

Were you ever sick? Did you ever have to go see a doctor?

I caught pneumonia one time, my fever got up to like 103, while I just got released from jail. I got sick in jail, I told them about it, but they just released me anyway. And I was walkin' back, and I felt dizzy, and it started raining. Time I got over here, I seen the doctor, he told me my fever was 103. But I had to go back out on the streets. They gave me some medication. I went back out on the streets, right across the street, laid back down.

Have these experiences had any influence on your religious beliefs one way or the other? Have you become more religious or less religious?

I always believed in God, you know. This brought me closer in touch with Him. I pray more, which is like every night, 'cause I don't wanna forget what got me here, where I am today. And it's because of Him that I have the strength today, that I'm a lot wiser and I'm a lot stronger towards people, places and things.

Has anything good come out of all these experiences for you?

It was a learnin' experience, you know. 'Cause when I first got here to Miami I used to pass by, I used to see these people. I'd say, "Man, what's wrong with these people? What are they doin' on the streets?" I'd never seen anything like that before. Where I'm from, people always stick together. And I never thought I'd end up out there. And I learned then, it was a learning experience for me, that anyone can fall. You learn a lot more about yourself while you're out there. You have a lot more time to think about the situation that you're in, 'cause I'd never been there before. I always had a place to live. It wasn't the best place in the world, but I always had somewhere to live, I always had something to eat, and I always had decent clothing.

Some politicians say we should be doing a lot more to help homeless people, and others say we're already doing enough. What do you think about all that?

I think it's a lot of hogwash. I don't think they're doin' enough 'cause there's a lot more could be done. Like they're sendin' a lot of money to these foreign countries; should keep the money at home and helpin' their own, you know. You got close to a million people that are homeless in the United States, and they're sayin' that they can't place them somewhere, that they can't help that. They ought to stop and ask themselves why, why you cannot help it. Is it because you can't, or you don't want to? It's all because of their greed, where you want everything all for yourself. You should always help your fellow man - not no more in the United States. Most people, if they see a man fallin' here, they walk away from him instead of tryin' to help him, tryin' to pick him up. I see it a lot. They're just caught up in politics. I can't see it. And they have a lot of empty shelters around here, HUD housing, here in Miami. They have all these apartments in Miami that are boarded up; they have families out on the streets that need homes. Why not take some of these government funds and place these people into these houses?

Make like a dormitory type, help create somethin'. Once you give these people somethin' decent to live in, nine times out of 10 they will take care of it. Once they see someone's tryin' to help them, they help themselves. You keep turnin' your back on them, they feel like you don't care anything about them. That push a person's pride down far, make him feel like he's worthless, he or she is worthless.

Do you think it's harder to be out on the streets for a black guy than for a white guy?

I think it's about the same, it's about the same, 'cause once you're homeless - homelessness, it doesn't have a color, could be black or white or Hispanic, you know, it doesn't make a difference. When other people look at you, they look at you as you are. If you're homeless, you're homeless. It doesn't matter.

So you're on the staff here now?

Yes, I've been on the staff for like two years. I've just been recently promoted from security and intake person to a social work coordinator.

What does your new job entail?

Like little, small things, I process people for food stamps, help them get Social Security cards, IDs. I might refer them to food pantries to help them get food and things like that, clothing. Small things that I can take care of, you know, instead of sendin' them back there to see a social worker, take up 30 to 45 minutes, I can take five minutes, I can write it up right there.

So you get to meet all kinds of people.

Oh, yeah. I enjoy doin' my work. I've always got a smile for everyone, man or woman, you know, old or young.

Rev. Vincent Holmes, 38, a native of Alexandria, Louisiana, is director of the Fresh Start program sponsored by the Christian

Service Center for Central Florida. The program is designed to provide temporary shelter and an array of services and counseling for men who want to get off the streets. Holmes was interviewed at his Orlando office.

What brought you to Florida?
Nothing in particular. It was the next place on the journey.
What was your life like when you were living on the streets? What were you doing?
Basically, trying to find answers. Not really knowing what the answers were, but trying to find them anyway. It's really hard to say. Running from myself.
How were you spending your time?
It varied, different cities, different things; work where you could, where you couldn't, you didn't - could always find a place to sleep - Salvation Army, the rescue mission, anywhere, but always could find food and shelter, and where you could find work, you worked.
How old were you when you started...
The quest. [laughs] Let's see, I'm 38 now, I would say about 23.
Is that when you left Alexandria?
Let's see, I left home earlier. I went in the Marine Corps, stayed in the Marine Corps about five years. Then I moved to New York. [laughs] That's where it all began - New York I was a drug dealer, sold drugs. I lived in New York until 1978, and then that's when the quest began.
Where did you go?
I left New York; I woke up one day, I realized that nothing was right. This is really what happened, nothing was right. The more I pursued, I felt really trapped by something we had created - selling the drugs, you couldn't go anywhere, you always had to worry about your territory, you had to worry about this, worry about that, so I just got tired, I got really burnt out with it all, and one day I left. I think I started in Philly, and that was the worst part of the quest, not knowing where I was going, but just knowing I had to go. It was like, the only way to stay ahead of everything was to keep moving, but what I didn't think about was I was taking everything with me each time I - so I went from Philadelphia to Washington, D.C., Washington, D.C. to Atlanta, Atlanta to Jacksonville, Jacksonville to Miami. That's when life began to really get weird. I encountered a man in Miami who probably was one of the most, I'd like to say, central figures in my life. His name is Joseph Tarver. Joe was a director of the Miami Rescue Mission, and when I met Joe we had a long talk, and, you know, he knew I'd been a player. And, first of all, living on the streets, you have

so many different kinds of people on the streets, and you can't categorize any. You can't say well he's this or he's that. You never know, you never know where the guy has really come from, so you kind of always have to leave it open at that. So, when I met Joe and we talked, I told him I was running. Basically, I was able to tell him that I didn't know where I was going, but I'm going - just, this is where I am now. And he said, "Well listen, won't you stop, and just rest?" I had no idea, I had never tapped into God, none of this. I mean this was totally away from me. So I stayed there with Joe, and that was the first place where I encountered the Bible, Christianity, any of that, the very first time, and it probably had more of an effect on me than anything else that happened.

Even though I stayed with him for a year in Miami, after that year I still ran again. I mean because I still didn't know what I was looking for. I didn't know what to expect, or what I was really looking for. So I left Joe in Miami, went to Houston, that was the next stop, stayed in Houston 10 months. From Houston to Phoenix, stayed there a couple of months, Phoenix to Los Angeles, the worst nightmare of my life; it was terrible. The drug problem there is really worse than anywhere I've seen - the Los Angeles problem - it's terrible, just terrible, it's a nightmare.

For you personally?

Well yeah, in a sense, because first, you've got to realize, I was running away from being in that business. At that point in my life, that was all I thought I knew how to do. You know, so here you are, you're running away from this, and you run right to it. I would work if I could find a job, but if not...

If I could, I would work, and when I couldn't I would buy me a couple ounces. Usually, wherever I went I kept money, always kept money. First of all, if you've been involved in the business, you try not to become a sucker - that's being on the streets with *nothing* - you always want to have something, something to fall on. You keep yourself a bus ticket in your pocket, or some cash, something; that way you can always stay ahead. So when I first got to Los Angeles, first thing I did, man, I couldn't find a job at all, I mean this place was terrible. In Los Angeles, every corner, there's a crack house. I mean in central city, almost every corner. Right outside the police station they have crack camps, I mean directly across the street. Everybody knows that they're selling, they're living there, they're smoking; everybody knows. So I caught myself, I bought me a couple of OZs, and I started, you know, slinging a little product, and next thing I know I was right back in it, right back in it, quite an adventure.

So what happened?

So I kept going. I stayed in Los Angeles I guess for about a year or so, a year-and-a-half. I kept selling product for awhile, then after that something kept clicking; I was a little more concerned about my self and about my life then. I mean this was because of the contact I had made in Miami, but yet I had no idea what had happened. And what had really happened, in essence, was my friend Joe had stimulated the spiritual side of me, something that had never been tapped into, and all of a sudden now it's tapped into. So I caught myself really having a struggle there, wanting not to get involved but yet involved, so then I got out. I ended up meeting a friend there, his name is Reverend Pullens, and he ran a place called the Disciple House. So I went there and talked to him and, you know, explained what I was feeling, the struggle going on. He just started telling me, said well, now you're coming in touch with something you had never come in touch with, something you were never in touch with before, so now you need to begin to look at this and deal with this, because there's only a couple of choices. And I mean I had been out long enough to know that there were only a couple of choices. Either I played this game, go right back to the same lifestyle, or I go ahead and try to begin to step out of this. So I tried. [laughs] And that was another quest, because then I really began to - I joined a church in Los Angeles, started really trying to get it together, and, I don't know, something happened, I just still couldn't hang in there. So one day I upped and moved - the middle of the night - I moved to San Francisco. And this was a pattern. The worse thing I've noticed about living on the street: it causes a pattern; it's like an indirect object of movement, you've got to keep going yet you don't always know why you're going but yet you're going. So then I went to San Francisco. That was the true nightmare. I could find no work. Everything was just bad there; I didn't like the place, I didn't like the people. I felt like I was really caught in hell; I really did, and I didn't see any way out. Everybody travels to California, especially street people. They go to the West Coast so they can get general assistance. All of them. And I never could understand that. Why travel a thousand miles just to go get on welfare? And man, these guys, they play the coast. They start from San Diego, pick up their checks and their food stamps, then they go to Los Angeles, do the same thing, then they go up to San Francisco, then up to Portland. And then they turn around and go back. So it's real crazy. But I stayed in San Francisco, and that was really the deciding factor for me to stop - my stay there. I mean I actually had enough. I had seen enough of - it was more than just homelessness; it was poverty, it was terrible, terrible. And the crack problem was terrible. But I got strong there. And then I began to backtrack. [laughs]

Where did you go then?

Went back to Los Angeles, I went to see Reverend Pullens, I went to see my pastor, told him, I said, "Listen, I've had enough, I don't know how to really do this, but I've had enough." You know, I really showed everybody that I was really sincere now. And they began to really work with me. I went into what is called a discipleship program, then I went into a Bible training center...and just stayed steadfast for awhile. Then that's when I really first began to start working - you know, here I am crossing over from selling the drugs, being on the streets, and now moving away from that and beginning to work with some of the same people who I knew, alright, and trying to help them. And it was interesting, it was really interesting. Man, I began to really see and learn a lot, and the more I got involved with this, the more I wanted to do something, because I realized that it's not who we were but it's who we are. And it's where we are; we can make a difference right now if we decide right now to start doing something about it. So I stayed in Los Angeles awhile, and then it was like God took me back through the whole - everywhere I had gone, He took me right back. [laughs] I called my friend Joe down in Miami. I told him what happened, I said, "Listen, man, I really got it together, I've been studying." You know, I let him know I had become a disciple, and my life had really begun to change.

But during this whole period, it was really strange, because I hadn't talked to my mother in 18 years. She and I just made contact a couple of years ago. And I mean part of this was myself, and I know now that part of it was God, because first of all, I had played so many games with so many people, that I didn't even trust myself when it came to saying well I'm really doing this. Because with me it was always I could take anything and be successful at it, but I had to really be sure within myself that it was genuine too. So I called Joe and told him, "Listen man, I'm really working on everything and trying to get it together." Life had really changed, man. If you could see me, you could see a change in me if you had known me. And so I told him, I said, "I'm thinking about coming back to Florida."

It's funny that Florida for me has always been that place that God has chosen for my life. I got saved in Florida, I returned, got married in Florida, went into full-fledged ministry in Florida, got ordained in Florida; everything happened here for me, and it's where God has me now. But when I returned to Miami, that's when I really got involved with homelessness, and working with it full-time.

And all along you were studying...

Had been studying, going to school, yeah. Had really discarded a whole lot of the trash, had begun to be responsible. I was making amends to different people; you know, some I just had to call and say I'm sorry, different little things, but yet being responsible for the first time in my life. And that was also the first time in my life that I didn't have to look over my shoulder. I knew I wasn't doing anything to hurt anybody, wasn't selling anybody anything, I was doing what was right, so it was a lot of differences then, a lot of differences.

Did you come here from Miami?

From Miami. I worked down in Miami about a year-and-a-half with Joe. And now it's like, always allowing God to lead me to wherever, and knowing that wherever He leads me, everything's going to be fine, because now, even though I look back on my wandering period, He always took care of me then. So now, when I move, it's knowing that wherever I'm going, it's because that's where I'm supposed to be. But when I came to Orlando, that was the only move I made that I wasn't running from anything, wasn't running from myself, nothing. It was just time to make a move, break away, and I came here and just got me a job the second day I was here. I was working at the Hilton; I worked there about a year. And one day I got a phone call, so I came here - started working at Daily Bread (a soup kitchen) first, and then I applied for this job.

So how long have you been in Orlando now?

It's just about three years. I don't know, I'm really at a point in life where I really know that if a man is determined, and he's had enough with playing with himself, pretending, even if he's on drugs or whatever, he can actually make it. But you've got to really be fed up with all the trash that you tell yourself, all the lies, neglecting responsibility. You can do it; it can be done.

What was your life like before all this started, before you went on your quest?

It was okay. I mean I was raised by a single parent, but she did a good job. She was a good mom, she did a really good job, I had a lot of support, uncles that were really close to me, good role models. I just wanted to go out and do my thing, period. So many years I blamed my mother, I blamed - oh, she made me do this because she didn't cater to everything I wanted. If I sit and try and really look at some of this stuff - the reasons I made up - they were just reasons. It's like a person wanting to commit suicide, and they need a reason to do it. You know, they're determined to do it anyway, but yet they need a reason. I had a good life as a kid, as a teenager growing up. I played football, went to school, had a job in the afternoon. I wasn't depressed, wasn't in the house with a bunch of rats and roaches and everything; I can't say that because I'd be lying. I had a really good family, but it was me. [laughs] It was something in me that, oh man, you just want to go out and go crazy. And that's how I really look at it: I wanted to go crazy. It's almost like the story of the prodigal son. He goes to his father, and he says, "Father, give me what's mine." And then he goes on his journey. I had a good life.

Do you think there's anything you could have done differently to avoid all that?

A lot. [laughs] A lot. While all my friends were getting ready to go to college and stuff, I wanted to go and be a marine. It was just the choices that I wanted to make. I thank God that they all worked out good. You know, now the end result is fine, but not everybody's end result turns out like mine. I believe that if I would have been more responsible - even with joining the service, that was running away - I didn't want to go to school anymore and I didn't want to be pressured by anybody, so I said, "Okay, I'll go fight in a war and do some of this stuff." I believe, being responsible - that's the biggest thing - this is what I tell my son now. You need to be responsible; if you lie, you need to say I lied. If you do something wrong, you admit you did it. But the main thing is be responsible. So that was my biggest problem; it took me a lot of years to learn to be responsible. So, yeah, if I had to go back I'd be more responsible.

When you were on the streets, did you ever wind up sleeping outside or going to shelters?

A few times, sure, oh sure. As a matter of fact, I preferred rescue missions. And I had no idea why. You know what I mean? I never knew the reason; now I do. I preferred going to the rescue mission to get a good meal, good bed, and you get to hear some preaching. And you would be surprised how many like that, except sometimes it's so hard for us to really become connected with it. It's still something you know that there's that desire to be a part of it and to hear it, but yet you still can't make the connection. But my favorite - I didn't like Salvation Armies, didn't like Coalitions - I liked rescue missions, I'd go there. There was a few times I had to sleep out. That was terrible; I didn't like that.

You had to sleep out?

Yeah, I'm trying to remember where I slept out. Each time I slept out, I think I can count the times. I slept out a few times, but not like some of the guys I know that sleep out every night; I didn't like that. I slept out a few nights in San Francisco, twice in New Orleans - one place I shouldn't have slept out at all - never had to, too much family and friends, just rebellion. That's about it. Mostly San Francisco, that was a hard place for me. The one problem I had in San Francisco, that was one of the places I used to play when I was selling drugs, and me and my girls, we would go to San Francisco and party a lot, live there. That was a hard place for me because I was trying not to get involved in that.

You used to go there and party?

Yeah, party and business. We used to do a lot of connections in San Francisco, and when I went back that last time, that was terrible. Like I say, man, part of that was because of the spiritual side that had been tapped into. The life was no longer exactly the same as it was before, and I caught myself really struggling hard there not to do wrong, you know. There was a few times I sold a little pot, I did a little of this and that, but nothing serious. But yet the struggle to not do wrong there, I mean really trying to stay above that; San Francisco is probably a very - I'm trying to think, and I have to use the Bible when I express it - very Corinthian city. Especially when you know where everything is; it's hard to be there and not be involved in some of it, because there's a lot of lasciviousness, a lot of evil, and I really had a hard time there. There were a few nights there that I slept out just to keep from being involved with different people there. Because if you go to their house, they're going to be doing this and doing that. So that was a hard place for me.

Did you always have enough food and clothing?

Yeah, it had gotten so bad, the one thing that's done a lot on the streets, and people don't realize, is I think sometimes we wind up leaving more clothes. You can always get clothes, especially if you're sharp; you can always get them. I think the sharper a person is that lives on the streets, the better he functions. It's sort of the ones who get on the streets and they become deadbeats: "Just, well, it doesn't matter, I'm not going to do anything. Why should I even attempt to do anything when you're going to do everything I need you to do?"

But if a guy or a woman is really sharp, they can really do quite well, quite well. There were some times, man, when I had to travel quick; I'd just leave everything. [laughs] You come along and you say, "I'm going to Denver." I'd say: "Great, let's go." And just not worry about, and when Denver comes, then we'll worry about those things then. It's funny in a sense, because there's the side that people don't talk about. Oh, we make it seem so bleak all the time, and real terrible. It is, but it's not. Part of it is chosen, and then the other part if forced, so we have to look at all of it.

Did the police ever bother you?

A few places; I believe after the first stop in Miami, I began to avoid arrest more, avoid police more. I went to jail more in New York than anywhere else. Once in Miami, a few times in New Orleans - a lot of times in New Orleans - they got me for prostitution - always prostitution and drugs. That was all I did. But the police never hassled me when I was just out there; never got hassled, but it's part of how you carry yourself, you know, where you hang, what kind of crowd you're with, it just all depends.

You mentioned prostitution. Were you working with women?
Yeah, not myself.

Do you think being on the streets is harder for a black guy than a white guy?
Yeah, that's just a reality anyway; it's harder to be in America living if you're a black guy. Some things, it's just the way they are, and you have to accept that. It's harder because they are singled out more; the least little thing, they'll pick them up, sure. Plus another thing is you don't live on the streets with identification. You've got to make the cops work for it. [laughs] If they catch you, you make them work for it. That's why, half the people you meet, they have no identification, and they are harassed a lot, a lot. I think it's harder on the streets for the black woman than anyone else, especially black women. Black men are always harassed, but you'll see more. It's the women; they have a harder time.

Why?
It's pretty bad, because most of the women, they have to survive basically around the dope houses, or the dope dealers, or whatever, if they're going to try to make it at all. And the others who are on the streets, you never see them. They have their own spots where they go, and they hide, they have to literally hide, because they get raped a lot, everything, it's bad, it's really bad.

How did other people - the people who weren't street people - treat you?
It all depends, it really does. And that goes back again to how you're carrying yourself on the streets. It's important to be on the streets and not let people know that you are. You know what I mean? You can function normally. Sometimes it's when you tell them that you live on the streets, and then there were times when people would say, "Where do you live?" You know, you're working with somebody, they say, "Where do you live?" You say, "At the mission." They say, "Why do you stay there with all the bums?" And then you tell them, you explain that the bum might be your uncle, or somebody you know, so don't stereotype people. But actually a lot of the people are not really that bad. You'd be surprised. People are concerned; they really are. I believe that we turn our heads when we see *certain* people on the streets, you know, there are certain ones we don't want to see, we really don't, and then that's when we have to be very careful, because all of us can fall in that category. So, for the most part, people treat you okay. I found a lot of people would try to help me because they knew that I was - San Francisco, bad, but yet - people tried to help because they saw me really struggling not to get involved. When they really see you're trying to make it, they'll try to help you. So we have to give folks credit. I believe more people are concerned than the system is

concerned, than some of the agencies that we've created. We're less concerned sometimes than the regular person on the street, we're less concerned.

Did you ever have to get food stamps?

Yeah, a couple of times: Portland. Let's see, I think Portland was the only place I got food stamps. San Francisco. [laughs] Portland and San Francisco, that was it.

How were you treated when you went to apply?

Terrible, they put you through the hoops, man. You've got to have everything. They want to know *everything* about you, your life history. "Where did you eat last month?" "How many meals did you have then?" "Did anybody give you a dollar?" "Do you remember anything?" You know, they want to know everything, and actually [laughs] it's crazy, it's really crazy dealing with them, they're crazy. That's one thing I really don't like; I was very funny about that. I only took food stamps when I really needed them. I believe there's too many families and kids, you know - a single man or a single woman can make it without. Because what's so bad, they'll give a guy on the street food stamps, but yet, you and your family need food stamps, they won't give them to you.

What did you do for medical care?

You just go to a clinic, go to a hospital, and you don't worry about it. If they bill you, so what? [laughs] I'm being honest. You know, what can you do? A lot of times there's certain places will treat you, and then there's the ones that won't treat you. So that's something - you really have to pray. You just pray and hope that God sent you to the right place to get help. A lot of your good cities have clinics just for the street people. That's one thing we need here in Orlando, is a clinic for people living on the streets. We don't have adequate medical care, and it's needed.

Some politicians think we need more programs to help homeless people and others say we're doing enough. What do you think?

A lot can be done, but first we need to stop pretending that we're doing so much when we're really not. All the money that's out there for homeless people is never getting to them. It's going to each agency; everybody's getting a little bit of the money. That's part of the reason I enjoy working for this kind of agency, because we're not getting the government funds and the grants and all this stuff. And the little money we do get, it comes straight from the churches and it goes back out, but some of your big agencies that get the big bucks, the money never touches the folks that are out here, never. There's a lot that can be done. We want to put people to work, educate them, get them the help they really need instead of making the problem worse. If we know that 40 percent of the people on the streets who are homeless are addicts, let's get them some help. They can't afford to go to treatment unless somebody helps send them, and if we don't have inexpensive treatment, where do they go? So it's still a Catch-22. We can open new facilities to help the people who can't afford to pay a lot of money. We can make affordable housing. But let people work for it. You'd be surprised how many people on the streets really want to do something for themselves, they really do. At the same time, what scares me, is that we're not doing it. We are making the homeless situation a situation, and it's constantly rising, and there is really no need for it. You know what I mean? I believe we could do something, and I don't see us doing a lot. Every week there's a new agency open, every week. So here comes the money, and it's coming from uphill, and it stops at 500 agencies, and then when it gets down to the man or the woman on the streets, they don't get anything. It's terrible, it's terrible.

Do you think there's more homeless now than there was six months ago?
Here in Orlando?
Yeah.
Yeah, but there's a reason. This is virgin territory for homelessness. When you've got cities like Atlanta and Miami, and Orlando is here in the middle, and these other cities have been hit so hard already, so now here is a nice place like Orlando, let's go there. Now Tampa has always been a stop for carnies. Now folks don't consider carnies to be homeless, but they are. They fall in the same category as the regular person on the street that's homeless, except they work, what, six months out of the year? And then they all go back to Tampa. After awhile we'll be just like the rest of the cities; you'll get the ones who want to stay here, and that's it. Now you actually have people who truly come here looking for work. I believe that they've been misinformed as to, well, what kind of work is here now. I remember when I first came, there was all kinds of work. Now the construction is almost over with - more technical and professional. So now what happens to the guy who came down to do the construction? He can't do the other jobs, so now he's just stuck here, and half the time what will happen, they may work him two or three days, and then he won't work for two weeks. So we create this thing; it's terrible. There's so much to it, so many sides of it. I wonder if we really take it all into consideration, because, like I say, once a person get out here, then we have to worry about drug addiction, poor psychosocial behavior, various other addictions that go with living out, because, first of all, if I don't have anything, then here comes somebody pushing drugs, and I can kind of drown the problem for a few hours, and then after a few months of this, the person's an addict.

Chris Trego, 27, is a native of Ontario, Canada, but grew up in upstate New York. She was interviewed in Jacksonville at the New Life Inn, a family shelter run by the City Rescue Mission, where she was a staff member. She has three children: Robert, 6; David, 4; and Jennifer, 1, who live with her.

What brought you to Jacksonville?
My husband was in construction, and he moved down here for his work and that's how I ended up here.
So you came with your husband. Are you still married?
Yeah, I'm still legally married.
How did you wind up coming here to the shelter?
Well, in 1989 I got pregnant, and two weeks before Christmas I got fired because they found out I was pregnant. And when I lost my job - and he was already unemployed for the last two months, from construction work - he got addicted to crack cocaine and gambling. And we ended up startin' to lose everything, and somewhere in March he got arrested for a previous probation violation, and he was put in jail and then extradited to Texas. And then I moved in with a neighbor because I got a 24-hour eviction notice from my landlord. And I was seven months pregnant at that time. I moved in with them. After livin' with them for about four months - they were real heavy alcoholics - and I paid my rent and my share of the electric both to them, and then they spent it before they were supposed to pay the rent. And then they came to me and told me they wanted me to pay their full rent and their full electric, and I said, "Well, I don't have that kind of money." And they said, "Well, then get your church people to do it." Because I was a Christian and they weren't, and they knew. And I said, "Well no, I'm not gonna ask something like that of them." By this time it's the end of July, so they said, "Well, if you're not gonna pay, then get out." So at that time we were living in the middle of nowhere, like seven miles to the nearest grocery store, and I had nowhere to go, so me and my three kids were walkin' down the streets with just what we had on, wonderin' what to do. I made a phone call and got a hold of my pastor's wife, and she called this place, and they gave me a place to stay for that night, and then a friend of mine brought me here the next day. It was definitely the finest shelter I'd ever seen in my life, ever. And I've been in several before in my life; I'd been in a Salvation Army once in Texas and a United Way shelter for the homeless in Knoxville, Tennessee, and United Way, you can't spank your kids, you can't discipline them, and they have some really awful rules [laughs]. And they don't help people, they just provide shelter and food, but that's it. They don't tell people what to do or

how to get out of the situation, which is the one major thing we do do here is we show people a plan of action, how to get out of the situation you're in. We don't just provide shelter; we provide a way out of homelessness.

I was here for three days, and the third day I was here there was an argument between two of the girls that were programmers, and they got real loud and started gettin' violent and stuff, and I stepped in the middle of the them and I said, "You're not gonna do that. This place was made by and for the Lord Jesus Christ, and you're not gonna do that here." And they both just kinda like shut up instantly, and the supervisor came out of her office just kinda like stunned, and they both just walked away. That afternoon the staff person that came in at 3:30 called me in the office and asked me if I would be the resident supervisor's assistant. I said, "Sure." She said, "That will probably pay for your stay here." And I was elated because I didn't know what I was gonna do; with three kids I couldn't go back to work, the baby was only six weeks old, you know, I was gettin' AFDC but I couldn't get it because the people that I was livin' with took my mail, and it takes like six to eight weeks to get a replacement check. I couldn't get a job because the baby was too young for day care, because they don't take children when they're that young at most day cares, and I didn't have the money for day care, regular day care.

So that paid for my stay here, and then on the eighth day that I was here the girl that was the resident supervisor left. The girl that was part-time in the afternoon called me in the office again and said, "How would you like to be the resident supervisor?" And I said, "Okay." [laughs] And I've been doing that. I did that as a program status, which meant in exchange for my room and board at that time, until August twenty-something, and then Reverend Ellison (the mission's executive director) called me in the office and asked me if I'd like to be put on staff because he liked the way I changed things, 'cause previously here they didn't help people really with different agencies - telling them where to go or anything like that. And when I came here I realized that's the major need. And since I'd been through the system myself, and worked my way off the system, I can show them how to do it. And I got in contact with all the different help agencies and found out what they did, wrote it down on a piece of paper, you know, got a good map set up of the town showing where everything is that helps people, got it all put together, and got it printed up so that people knew what to do, and then I counseled the women each step of the way on how to get things accomplished, how to go about working the different agencies to get it to your best advantage. And that brings you kind of up to date. [laughs]

You mentioned that you had stayed in some other shelters. How did you wind up going to them?

Both times it was because my husband was on drugs, both times. And then he got off of them and then we were fine, we were just fine; then we weren't just fine. [laughs] We weren't just fine at all. But it was never because of something that I had a lack in, because I've worked - except for the last three or four months of my pregnancy, and the first three or four months after the baby was born - I've worked since I was 11 years old, so that was never a problem. It was just, when you've got a spouse that's addicted to drugs or alcohol, especially when it's a husband, where the wife is obligated, while he's the head of the house, he's going to be taking, you know, he's not going to allow you to have money. It's almost as if it's an abuse situation of sorts, you know, it's kind of a psychological type thing where they, "I'm the head of the house, that's what the Bible says." And you're instantly turned into this meek wimp. [laughs] And you just do as you're told because you're in a type of fear, not necessarily fear of being hurt, but you've been convinced that you can't do it on your own even though you really can. It's kind of hard to explain. [laughs]

You mentioned you were fired from a job for being pregnant.

Uh-huh.

They told you you were being fired for that reason?

No, they told me I was being fired because I was inadequate at my job, but they told me that the day after I told them I was pregnant. [laughs] But I won. [laughs] I won. Now the records don't show that I was fired. The records show that I left, and that I was an excellent employee. That was all I cared about, 'cause I've never been fired in my life, never, and that meant a lot to me. The only reason I ever left a job was either to move to a better job or to move 'cause I had to move out of the area. That was always important to me, 'cause I've always had an excellent work record. There's a lot of women out there that have always worked really faithfully, and it was just circumstances that they lost their job, and not their personal flaw, or whatever, that caused it. Even women, drugs and alcohol, doesn't necessarily mean that they're not good at their jobs; it just means that they had a problem that they didn't know how to overcome, or weren't able to overcome. They wanna look at it as a disease, and they wanna look at it as this way or that way, but it's just a problem that they don't know how to deal with. There's only one way out of it in my opinion.

Which is?

Jesus. Jesus, because years and years and years ago, I was on drugs real bad, and I was in the world; I wasn't always a Christian. And I had like a $2,000 a week drug and alcohol habit. I could drink two-and-a-half, three quarts of vodka a day, with no problem. And as much dope as you could put in front of me, I could do.

What kind of drugs were you taking?

Methamphetamines, cocaine, crack, ice, marijuana, acid - well I quit doing that when I was in high school 'cause I had too many bad trips - opium, whatever, whatever was available. And the second midnight hit, January 1st, the very first second, 1984, I received Christ as my savior, and instantly [snaps her fingers] was delivered from all of it. I never desired or wanted it again, never again. Pretty awesome, huh? [laughs]

Did you pray for that or did it just happen?

I said, "God, I can't handle this anymore." And I said, "Lord, I know that you're the right way, but you need to prove to me that you love me. I need to know that I'm really loved, and that you really care about me and that you want to take care of me." And instantly I was delivered. And the next morning I went to church, and this girl I never met before asked me to go to lunch. The reason I never went to church before was because I did not have [switches to a tone of exaggerated pompousness] the proper attire, and had been accustomed to church people looking down their noses at me, and that's what kept me away from the church for so long. This girl asked me to lunch, and I said, "Okay, but I don't have any money." She says, "No, I mean lunch at my house," and I said, "Okay." We went over there, and we had a long talk while we were there, and I explained to her why I had always had a problem with church people, and that I'd asked the Lord to take care of my life the night before and all that. She says, "I just knew there was a reason God told me to have you come to lunch with me." Then we were fixin' to leave, and I was at the front door. She says, "Wait a minute." She walked back to her bedroom and she took everything that was on a hanger out of her closet in one big arm load, and she put in my lap and said, "The Lord told me to do this." And from that point on I've never had to worry about a thing to wear since. The Lord has always provided everything, every time [laughs], every time. I've got a lot of miracles in my life, a lot of them, and it's always 'cause of the Lord.

How were you treated when you were dealing with social service agencies, applying for AFDC and so on?

Like a dog. I've only met one caseworker - with food stamps, not AFDC - that was half-way decent in my entire experiences with them. That not only includes my own case, but everyone else's cases that I deal with. I've met one that did not treat people like they're dogs, like they're not takin' out of their own pockets. What they don't realize is that that's why we pay taxes, not just to support our government system and our police and everything else. It's almost like an insurance, because the United States is supposed to be the kind of nation that takes care of their own. But they do it begrudgingly, with a bad attitude, 90 percent of them; there's a great deal to do with the racial ratio in the local HRS, because you have to take a test to get a job like that. Certain races get 20 percent instantly added to their score for being a minority, and then other minorities get 10 percent automatically fixed on their score for bein' a minority. And they for some reason have a bad attitude. They're lower skilled, but they get a higher test grade, and they have a bad attitude, real bad attitude, which is really wrong. If you don't like working with people, don't work with people.

But they've got a real bad attitude. They're slow, they don't care about whatever situation you're in, they don't refer you to any agency unless it's just to get you off their back. HRS is very bad here, and I'm sure that it's very similar in a lot of other states. There's other agencies in town here that are pretty nasty to you also, even publicly funded, federally funded, and otherwise funded agencies in the area that, instead of saying, "We're out of funds," they'll say, "We ain't gonna help you." But in reality, they're just out of funds. But instead of saying that, they'll say, "We ain't gonna help you." That makes you think: Well what did I do? [laughs] And it really makes it so hard on homeless people, it really does. They're just like taken aback, they're insulted; here they are, they're tryin' to swallow their pride in the first place 'cause they have to ask for help, and then these people are making it worse by pounding them down into the ground. So it's easy for someone to get the mind concept that, well they're saying I'm dirt, so I must be dirt. When you get it repetitively that you're nothing, you're dirt, you're not good enough, you're asking for something you don't deserve - after awhile they get that concept in their mind 'cause they don't have anyone to tell them otherwise. That's why I'm glad to be there to say, "You are important; they're just not doin' their job right." Because it's very discouraging.

I've had more than one mother come crying, "They yelled at me, they said they wouldn't help, they wouldn't tell me what to do." And they don't know what to do. I have to sit down with them and explain what is possible for them, what other avenues they can take. There's very few agencies that are happy and willing to help. The housing and urban development on the state level has the same attitude as HRS. It's as if you were trying to move into their neighborhood. [laughs] Please. I've had so many women I've sent over there to pick up forms that are free, and they won't give 'em to 'em because they don't feel like it. And all they'd have to do is open a drawer and hand it to them, and they just don't wanna do it. Not because they don't have the forms, and it is their responsibility to give 'em out.

They're just too lazy to turn around, and too lazy to do it. So people end up staying homeless just because of their ignorance and laziness.

What was the worst part about becoming homeless for you?

The worst part about it for me was walking down the street with a six-week old baby in my arms, a three-year-old in one hand, a five-year-old taggin' along behind us, and seein' their faces, and thinking: I don't have any place to sleep tonight. That's the hard part, when you've got kids and you know that you've done everything that you can possibly do, and you're still homeless. Because I'm an intelligent person, I didn't go to college and all that stuff, but I have common sense, I have book knowledge, I've got what it takes to make it. But because of circumstances that hit me, that were of no fault of my own, I was put in that position, and I had to look at my kids's faces and say, "We don't have any place to go." That's the hardest part; it really is. When I was alone and on the streets, it was not a big deal about bein' homeless. So what? I could find a bridge, they've got the little ledges up there, so the pigeons have been there, take a newspaper and sweep it off. But when you got children, you look at their little faces, and you say, "We don't have any place to go." They don't understand. They don't understand. They're like, "Well, what did we do wrong?" Because children, no matter how young they are, they still feel responsible, like they should be able to do something. But they're helpless, and they can't do anything. And to look in their faces is really kind of horrifying, 'cause I've seen the same look in my kids' faces back then as I see today's little kids that come in now. Even little two and three-year-old kids, the look in their eyes when they first come in is just horrifying, 'cause there's so much fear and frustration and anger - sometimes at their own parents - because they don't know why. Heck, all they know is they don't like it. They shouldn't have to do it. Children should not have to be homeless. Society in America ought to care a little more about children. And they don't, not unless it's their own child. They don't even think about it unless it's their own kid. There's so few people that even think enough, when compared to how many people there are in Jacksonville, to how many people there are in Jacksonville that help the Rescue Mission or homeless people in general, it's such a small minority. It really is. We have a lot of people that really love and care about the homeless people, and they'll send in money, but to come personally and hand a homeless person a diaper when their baby needs one, a lot of people couldn't do that. They couldn't do it.

What do you think about the controversy about programs to help homeless people? Some people think we should be doing more, and others say we're already doing enough.

No, they're not doing anything. They're not doing anything. I don't see anything that the federal government, state government or the city government is doing to help, except maybe the Private Industry Council, and then all they do is get people jobs that pay so low that they can't get a place to live. And they create a repetitive poverty. What they're doing is they're creating a high class and low class, and nothing in between. You work at Burger King for $4 an hour. Maybe one day you'll make five bucks an hour and be a manager at the same time, a manager making five bucks an hour. Isn't that wonderful? [laughs]

And then you've got the high class, which are the people that can afford education, afford the college. And I'll bet you if you polled all the universities, colleges, etcetera, the majority of them, their parents are putting them through school. There's the few that are on scholarships and have really earned through trying hard all their lives, through high school and everything, to get their scholarships to go through. But how many people are there that are actually working their way through college that didn't have any support from their parents? It's probably not that big. I would have loved to have gone to college, but my parents couldn't afford it. I couldn't get enough grants or student loans to cover for it. I would have been working for 20 years after I got out in order to pay for it. It's not as easy as people think, especially nowadays. Ten years ago it was possible. It's easy to see why kids say, "Well, why finish high school, when at 16 years old I can get a GED and get a McDonald's job, where if I finish high school I still gotta work at McDonald's anyway?" There's no difference. What the Private Industry Council does is that they get federal grants, and they pay 50 percent of the person's paycheck to the employer for the first so-many days, and therefore they're more apt to hire people that go through PIC, which is good, but they're still lower-paying jobs, and they never get higher. It's sad. But that's the only thing I see the federal government doing. They give FEMA (Federal Emergency Management Agency) grants, but that's so piddily, there ain't much to it, because most of the time it doesn't even cover one half of the people who their electric gets shut off, or they get eviction notice, they can't pay their water bill, or they have an outrageous problem one way or another. It doesn't even come near. Sure they have Title 20 child care, which is a federally subsidized child care, but the child care facilities that they make you go to are disgusting; they ought to have their doors shut down. They leave babies, newborn all the way up to two years old, stuck in their car seats, cribs, and height chairs, and they're not allowed to get out anywhere else, they're not allowed to walk or crawl. My child was in the Title 20 child care for six months. She was walking in December; she quit walking, did not walk again, until I removed her from the child care five months later. That's the type of child care the federal government is providing. Where if you go to the regular companies that do not accept Title 20 funds, they're exceptional. And I see that from my experience, and it angers me that the federal government has such low standards, very, very low standards. They don't really care. They gave themselves a raise. They gave themselves a what percentage raise was it? Do you remember?

No.

But they gave the food stamp and AFDC people a five percent raise. That's a total of $9 for most people, and a four-person income for a month, a $5 food stamp raise. [laughs] "We can get five more cans of tuna fish this month, hon." You know? A single person can get like $91 in food stamps a month. Most people I know eat that much in a week-and-a-half, maybe two weeks, unless they're gonna eat rice and beans every day for a month, and then by the time they eat rice and beans for a month, they're gonna end up in University Hospital for the next month. It's not right. You cannot make it on $400 a month AFDC and two hundred and some dollars a month in food stamps when you've got three children and you're a single parent. You cannot make it. You live in substandard housing, even the city projects, well they're lower than substandard because they're always in the middle of the worst crack neighborhood there is. And the government is not controlling crack cocaine. They're not controlling any of the drugs in the United States because if they did, they'd have to lay off all the police officers and the DEA, they'd have to lay off half the FBI, gosh, the nation would go broke. They were already offered to buy out the entire Columbian stock in cocaine, and it would have cost them a lot less than what it costs to prevent it from coming into the country for one year, and they didn't do it, so it kinda tells you where their priorities are. [laughs] I don't really think the federal government cares about much. It's not real to them; it's not real. They don't come here to see it. Jimmy Carter was the last one to go learn and find out what people really cared about. Sure, Carter wasn't one of the most noted presidents in the world, but he really did care. I mean at least he went and looked, and he was the one that decided that homeless people had a right to food stamps, too, 'cause if it weren't for him all these homeless people would never be allowed to have food stamps, 'cause they don't have an established address and they don't have an established kitchen, that means that you can make them starve. That was their mind set. And there's still a lot of people that don't know that you don't have to have cooking facilities to get food stamps, you don't have to have a permanent residence to get food stamps. He cared, but you can only do so much when you've got Congress to check you, I guess.

Their priorities are not where they should be. If you can't take care of your own at home, don't start tryin' to take care of someone else's somewhere else, that's the way I feel about it. If I can't control my own children I'm not about to go tell someone else how to take care of theirs. And the United States isn't doin' it. They've created their own poverty, they really have. You know, their lax system, they're allowing so much garbage to happen, and they just haven't really cared. The same goes for medical. I just broke a tooth today and tried to find a dentist that would work with me. Unless I got $500 cash, they don't wanna talk to me. I haven't got that kind of money. [laughs] I mean, I put my little $5 a week in my savings account, and I'm thrilled to death. [laughs] Medical and dental and optical, the homeless don't get 'em, and if they do, it's not quality. I've had people that I considered a life and death situation have to sit at University Hospital for 18 hours.

Do you find that outsiders are responsive to the whole problem of homelessness?

When they see it, yes, when they see it. When they don't see it, no. You know, if they've not been in touch with it, they have no concept of it. It's like watching the whole thing on TV about the poor kids in Uganda that have no shoes and are wearing practically no clothes and stuff like that. It's not real. It's on TV, it can be in the newspaper, it can be on the radio, but it's not real until they see it with their own eyes in flesh and blood, right in front of them, staring them in the face. That's what it takes to get people to realize that it's real. There's so many people that see guys standing on the freeway saying, "Will work for food." They'll give that guy 10 bucks. But there'll be a mom with four kids sittin' here, and she can't even go out and make a phone call because she doesn't have a quarter. And they won't help her. But they'll help that guy on the road that's doing a scam, 'cause he's just taking the money to go do crack cocaine, 'cause if you offered him a job he ain't gonna take it, I guarantee ya. I've known too many people that do that. It's just a big scam, just a big scam. I knew a guy who used to make $5,000 a week doin' that. [laughs] It's just a scam. And that's really ruined it for the people who are really in need. But when they see it, they're willing to help, but if they don't see it, they don't think about it, out of sight, out of mind. Basically, that's where it's at. I'd love to see the mayor walk in this place and tour our second floor. I'd love for someone in the state Congress or the federal Congress to come in and check it out. This is what's really happening. It would be nice. They'd see that it's real. The amount of homeless people has doubled, if not tripled, in the last two or three years. It blows my mind.

Have you found that homeless people are pretty good about taking care of each other, watching out for each other?

Oh yeah, they're great about it. It's like a bond, you know. I've seen it in the guys as well as the women. I really have. The moms help each other out. A single woman, while she's gotta go places, she'll give up her free time to go with a mom and kids to help her out with the kids. Or two moms will work together; one mom will take all the kids to the park while the other mom gets stuff done, and the next day vice versa. They really bond together and they really help each other out. If one person finds out this agency is doing this, they'll tell everybody else. They work together for it. The easiest way to find out where our Mission is is go to the place where all the bums hang out, 'cause churches usually don't know, they have to look it up in the Yellow Pages or call First Call for Help or somethin'. Go to the park. Ask them, "Who helps you with food? Who helps you with clothing? Who helps you with shelter?" They'll know. They work together. It's like a bond, it really is, it's amazing. I can go anywhere in this city now, and people know me from all over. [laughs] There's a bond, and homeless people, they don't forget. They never forget where they came from. Even when they get out of it, they don't forget where they came from, which is amazing. Even with or without God, they don't forget. [laughs] But there is a major bond there.

Index

About the Author

PHILIP MICHAEL BULMAN is a freelance journalist. He has been a reporter for *The Denver Post* and the Fort Lauderdale *Sun-Sentinel*, and his articles have appeared in numerous magazines and newspapers, ranging from *Sierra* magazine to *The Washington Post*.